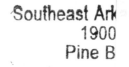

A Walk Atop America

FIFTY STATE SUMMITS
and a Dream to Reach Them All

DOUGLAS BUTLER

2007

Parkway Publishers, Inc.

Available from:
Parkway Publishers, Inc.
P. O. Box 3678, Boone, North Carolina 28607
Telephone/Facsimile: (828) 265-3993
www.parkwaypublishers.com

Library of Congress Cataloging-in-Publication Data

Butler, Douglas, 1954-
  A walk atop America : fifty state summits and a dream to reach
them all / by Douglas Butler.
      p. cm.
  ISBN 978-1-933251-44-8
  1. Mountaineering--United States--States. 2. Butler, Douglas,
1954---Travel--United States. 3. United States--Description and
travel. I. Title.
  GV199.4.B88 2007
  796.52'20973--dc22

2006102688

Book Edited by: Patty Wheeler
Book Design by: Aaron Burleson, Spokesmedia

In Memory of Dad
Father, Mentor, Friend

Climbing also challenges
those who wait at home.

To Mother and Sheryl
with love and thanks

Disclaimer

Activities described in this book are inherently risky. Accidents may result in severe injury or death; life-threatening medical symptoms may develop suddenly, and chronic conditions frequently worsen at higher altitudes.

This is not a training manual or guidebook. Always hike and climb within your ability, learn the proper use of equipment, train and climb with experienced mountaineers or qualified guides, and take all necessary safety precautions.

Enjoy the outdoors...and leave no trace.

This book relates the author's experience and observations. Names and identifying characteristics of some individuals have been changed to protect their privacy.

COVER PHOTOGRAPHY

COVER (BACKGROUND)
VIEW FROM ATOP MT. MCKINLEY (DENALI), ALASKA

FRONT COVER (INSET)
MT. WHITNEY, CALIFORNIA

BACK COVER (UPPER)
MT. RAINIER, WASHINGTON

BACK COVER (LOWER)
THE AUTHOR ON GRANITE PEAK, MONTANA
PHOTO BY TOM TORKELSON

ACKNOWLEDGEMENTS

Many people contributed to my enjoyment as I sought America's highest summits: Skilled guides who taught me climbing skills then guided me on the most challenging peaks; mountaineering companies that helped surmount logistical difficulties; climbing companions who made these ascents safe and enjoyable; park rangers and Forest Service employees who advised about routes and conditions and frequently went the "extra mile" to make my visits successful and pleasurable; and the hundreds of people—on and off the mountains—whose kindnesses, large and small, made this such an incredible journey. To each, a heartfelt thank you.

As with climbing, writing a book requires the assistance and encouragement of many individuals. I wish to thank Natalie Beardslee for reviewing this manuscript; Sandy Pinto for her critique and proofreading; the Blue Ridge Writers Group for patiently listening to many chapters and providing insight and encouragement; the Ashe County Public Library's staff for assistance with research and word processing; the American Alpine Club's Henry S. Hall Library for obtaining out-of-print titles and original articles; and Patty Wheeler for her advice and fine editing.

And finally a special thank you to my mother and Sheryl, who each endured long absences and apprehensive waits while I scaled remote summits. Then as I prepared this manuscript, each read and reread its many incarnations, eventually knowing these words nearly as well as I, and providing invaluable advice as to form and content.

STATE HIGH POINTS

State	Highpoint	Altitude in feet	Chapter
Alabama	Cheaha Mountain	2,405	5
Alaska	Mt. McKinley (Denali)	20,320	23
Arizona	Humphreys Peak	12,633	12
Arkansas	Magazine Mountain	2,753	7
California	Mt. Whitney	14,494	13, 21
Colorado	Mt. Elbert	14,433	11
Connecticut	Mt. Frissell (South Slope)	2,380	8
Delaware	Ebright Azimuth	448	22
Florida	Britton Hill (Lakewood Park)	345	5
Georgia	Brasstown Bald	4,784	4
Hawaii	Mauna Kea	13,796	7
Idaho	Borah Peak	12,662	11, 20
Illinois	Charles Mound	1,235	3, 9
Indiana	Hoosier High Point	1,257	18
Iowa	Hawkeye Point	1,670	3
Kansas	Mt. Sunflower	4,039	15
Kentucky	Black Mountain	4,139	6
Louisiana	Driskill Mountain	535	7
Maine	Mt. Katahdin	5,267	17
Maryland	Backbone Mountain	3,360	6, 17
Massachusetts	Mt. Greylock	3,487	8
Michigan	Mt. Arvon	1,979	9
Minnesota	Eagle Mountain	2,301	9
Mississippi	Woodall Mountain	806	5
Missouri	Taum Sauk Mountain	1,772	7

STATE HIGH POINTS

State	Highpoint	Altitude in feet	Chapter
Montana	Granite Peak	12,799	10, 19
Nebraska	Panorama Point	5,424	15
Nevada	Boundary Peak	13,140	13
New Hampshire	Mt. Washington	6,288	17
New Jersey	High Point	1,803	8
New Mexico	Wheeler Peak	13,161	12
New York	Mt. Marcy	5,344	17
North Carolina	Mt. Mitchell	6,684	4
North Dakota	White Butte	3,506	14
Ohio	Campbell Hill	1,549	18
Oklahoma	Black Mesa	4,973	15
Oregon	Mt. Hood	11,239	16
Pennsylvania	Mt. Davis	3,213	6
Rhode Island	Jerimoth Hill	812	17
South Carolina	Sassafras Mountain	3,560	4
South Dakota	Harney Peak	7,242	9, 14
Tennessee	Clingmans Dome	6,643	4
Texas	Guadalupe Peak	8,749	15
Utah	Kings Peak	13,528	20
Vermont	Mt. Mansfield	4,393	8
Virginia	Mt. Rogers	5,729	4
Washington	Mt. Rainier	14,410	2
West Virginia	Spruce Knob	4,861	6
Wisconsin	Timms Hill	1,951	9
Wyoming	Gannett Peak	13,804	10

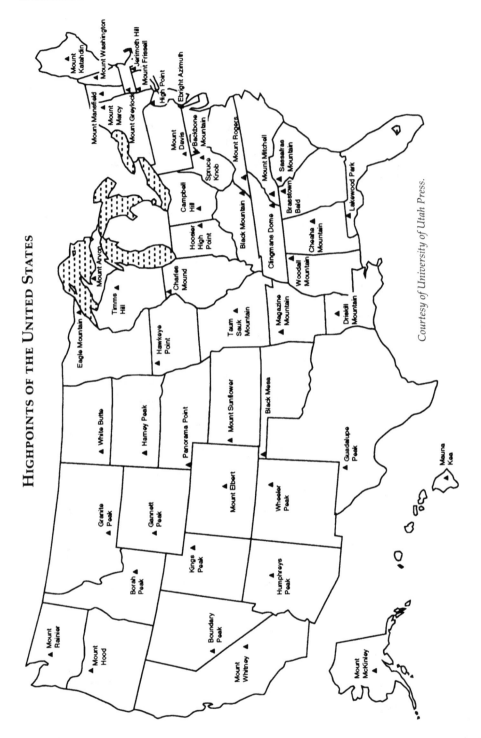

HIGHPOINTS OF THE UNITED STATES

Courtesy of University of Utah Press.

Mount Katahdin

Mount Washington

Jerimoth Hill

Mount Frissell

Mount Mansfield

Mount Marcy

Mount Greylock

High Point

Ebright Azimuth

Mount Davis

Backbone Mountain

Mount Rogers

Mount Mitchell

Sassafras Mountain

Lakewood Park

Campbell Hill

Spruce Knob

Hoosier High Point

Black Mountain

Clingmans Dome

Brasstown Bald

Cheaha Mountain

Woodall Mountain

Eagle Mountain

Mount Arvon

Timms Hill

Charles Mound

Taum Sauk Mountain

Magazine Mountain

Driskill Mountain

Hawkeye Point

White Butte

Harney Peak

Panorama Point

Mount Sunflower

Black Mesa

Guadalupe Peak

Granite Peak

Gannett Peak

Mount Elbert

Wheeler Peak

Mauna Kea

Kings Peak

Humphreys Peak

Borah Peak

Mount Rainier

Mount Hood

Boundary Peak

Mount Whitney

Mount McKinley

x

FOREWORD

State Highpointing. What an unusual hobby. The highpoints vary from a highway intersection to a world class mountain. However, each has a charm all its own. Many are popular peaks, and people often reach one of these well-known summits without realizing that it is also a state highpoint. Somewhere along the line, one discovers that there is a list and a club which promotes visiting all fifty. At that point, addiction usually sets in and there is no turning back. It becomes an obsession, in fact, a quest.

"The Dream" of Dr. Douglas Butler is his quest. For years, Dr. Butler kept "The Dream" alive. When the opportunity finally presented itself, he set out to reach the highest point of every state. In this book, he captures both the thrill of pursuing that goal and the disappointment when events defeat summit attempts. But along the way, there are unexpected adventures.

As someone once said, "The state highpoints are all over the country." That is the beauty of this passion. One visits places that might otherwise never be considered as destinations. Dr. Butler eloquently describes these places and the folks he met, capturing the unique charm of every highpoint. Even the "lowliest" has something interesting to offer.

It is not necessary to reach all fifty state summits to enjoy this interest. It is the sense of achievement and self satisfaction of doing something that no one can do for you that brings the most enjoyment. Dr. Butler relates this pleasure in every chapter. Surely *A Walk Atop America* will inspire some of you to begin the pursuit of "Your Dream," whether it be state highpointing or some other long-thought-of adventure. Enjoy.

— Don W. Holmes
Author of *Highpoints of the United States —*
A Guide to the Fifty State Summits

TABLE OF CONTENTS

CHAPTER 1

THE DREAM

I pushed the heavy, gunmetal-gray door open and stepped from the emergency department into the sticky, southern night air. Twelve hours earlier I had entered this hospital as I had for seven years—emergency physician and department director, a middle-aged doctor at the peak of his career. Now I was leaving, not only this shift but this hospital and for much of the next year, my profession of more than two decades.

The aging door closed with a dull thud as sorrow and anxiety mixed with relief and anticipation. For I was embarking on a journey long considered, so long in fact that I now simply referred to it as The Dream.

Conceived in the early 1970s, this idea was at first an adolescent yearning typical of that era—touring the nation for months, living in a converted van, seeing new sights, and meeting interesting people. Reality intervened as I advanced from college to medical school, residency to private practice, and finally to farm and family. There never seemed time for such fantasy.

But The Dream refused to die.

In my thirties I traveled to exotic locales—West Africa, Patagonia, the Arctic and Amazon. Then I began mountaineering, thriving on the challenges and excitement, yet also savoring the environments and cultures encountered en route.

Periodically The Dream forged into my consciousness: when I closed my solo office practice seven years earlier to return to emergency medicine; when contract changes decimated the emergency department's physician staff; and each of several occasions when this rural North Carolina hospital I was now leaving had teetered on the brink of bankruptcy. Each time I considered the plan but delayed its start as new professional opportunities emerged.

But I refined my ideas during this turbulent period, breaking the itinerary from a single long trip into a series of shorter excursions. I sought more than a yearlong collection of self-indulgent diversions or a series of unrelated adventure travel trips, packaged tours that often rush past native cultures and spectacular scenery while scurrying to the "destination." Instead I envisioned an unhurried journey of discovery, learning, and personal growth—seeing our vast land and meeting its people while learning of our history and many cultures.

And it was during this time that I added another goal to The Dream: to stand atop the highest point in each of the fifty United States.

"Highpointing"—reaching a state's highest geographical point—was not new to me. I first heard of this idea in 1970 when my high school math teacher, an accomplished climber and early "highpointer," told of his quest to touch each state's loftiest point, a desire that to a teenager seemed odd but curiously intriguing. Yet thirty years later, fewer than 100 individuals had touched all fifty state summits. Maps and guidebooks showed why: Many of these points were difficult to reach; some could be climbed only two months out of the year; fourteen were located on private property, often with restricted access; a dozen rose more than 10,000 feet above sea level; and one required a climb that ranked among the planet's most challenging ascents.

In the mid 1990s I had reached a handful of these summits; over the past two years, I had succeeded on a dozen more. But with the exception of Washington's Mt. Rainier, all had been easy hikes. Now within twelve months I hoped to reach the others.

Yet as I drove home, doubt and anxiety filled my mind. Doctors rarely take a two-week vacation, much less a yearlong professional leave. I knew of no other physician who had taken such a lengthy break, found no accounts of such an endeavor, and remained cognizant of the threat this employment gap would pose to my career.

I had decided against seeking corporate sponsorships or applying for grants. Instead I economized and simplified my life, knowing that expenses would continue while income would not. Suddenly, however, this long-anticipated opportunity seemed scary in its emptiness and frightening in its lack of security. No amount of planning, rationalizing, or research can fully prepare one for the freedom—and fear—of leaving employment to begin such a quest.

Tomorrow there would be no job.

I awoke the next morning, no longer emergency department director nor practicing physician. Since kindergarten I had been a student, part-time employee, or working doctor—and sometimes a combination of these. Today, for the first time in forty years, I was none of them. Although I no longer held an exalted place in the pantheon of jobs and felt strangely out of place, I did not feel unemployed. I had places to go, things to do, and dreams to follow.

Later that morning, I waited in a slow line at the post office. Yesterday people had waited to see me. They, or their insurance companies, were billed a princely sum for a few moments of my time. Today that time was less pricey, and the only line was the one in which I stood.

"When are you climbing again, Doc?"

Startled, I turned and recognized a former patient. "Hmm, in a few days. Taking care of last minute details," I stammered.

Carl, dressed in lightly faded bib overalls, was an affable farmer and retired saw miller who had an insatiable curiosity—and a penchant for direct questioning that rivaled a seasoned reporter's.

"Where ya' goin' this time?" he inquired, loudly enough to turn a few heads.

"Out west," I softly responded, hoping to divert the conversation.

"Gee. How long ya' goin' be gone?" he demanded.

"Don't know for sure. There are a lot of peaks out there to climb. See how the weather holds."

My nonchalance caught him off guard. He pushed a wad of chewing tobacco into his cheek as he formulated his next question. But the clerk motioned me toward the counter, ending the discussion.

Finished with my business, I nodded politely as I passed Carl. "Must be nice to be free to take off like that," I heard him grumble as the door closed softly behind me.

Then, the realization hit. Yes, I am free. Free to observe the world closely, free to think deeply, and free to experience the full beauty and joy of life.

I never again questioned the decision to take a year off. I would embrace my choice fully, enjoy it fully, and live it fully.

The Dream had begun.

CHAPTER 2

FIRE AND ICE

Mt. Rainier

Before I became a dedicated state highpointer, I had been a mountain climber. However, I became a mountaineer somewhat unintentionally.

Six state highpoints require technical climbing skills—the need to rope up, ascend vertical rock faces, traverse steeply angled snow and ice, or rappel sheer cliffs. A decade before leaving the emergency department to begin my yearlong highpointing odyssey, my goal was not technical climbing or state summits, but an ascent of Mt. Kilimanjaro, the legendary volcano that towers three miles above the east African savannah.

To prepare for this six-day trek—a rugged walk during which porters and animals carry most gear—I began jogging, lost twenty-five pounds, and hiked nearby trails carrying a pack weighted with water bottles, books, and sand bags. Despite intense conditioning, however, I felt it necessary to test myself at altitude before attempting such a lofty and remote peak.

Altitude illness—ranging from mild headaches and nausea to life-threatening fluid accumulation in the brain and lungs— is the greatest risk confronting mountaineers. It is impossible to predict who will suffer or how severely. Symptoms may occur at 8,500 feet above sea level, but both the likelihood and severity of problems increase with altitude. Highly conditioned individuals such as runners and triathletes seem most susceptible; men have more problems than women; and younger adults are more prone to this condition than middle-aged climbers.

To experience the effects of altitude and determine how my body would adjust to low oxygen levels, I enrolled in a five-day mountaineering course offered by Rainier Mountaineering, Inc., hoping to learn basic camping skills and introductory climbing techniques in a high altitude environment. The printed itinerary didn't sound difficult—four days of "skills" followed by an ascent of Mt. Rainier (14,410 feet).

But only later did I learn that Rainier Mountaineering, Inc., known also as RMI, is the premier training organization for aspiring Himalayan climbers. Founded in 1969 by Lou Whittaker, an accomplished alpinist and twin brother of Jim, the first American to summit Mt. Everest, 34 RMI guides have reached the planet's tallest summit.

When the equipment list arrived I was stunned. I read the page-long list: two fleece or wool sweaters; two pairs of fleece or wool pants; two capilene shirts; two pairs of long capilene pants; waterproof, but "breathable" jacket and similarly designed pants; three pairs of wool socks; three pairs polypro sock liners; heavy, warm, waterproof gloves; thin, lightweight gloves; wool hat; balaclava; glacier glasses; leather hiking boots; plastic, double-shell mountaineering boots; crampons, ice ax, climbing harness, carabiners and belay device; winter-rated sleeping bag; sunscreen—and a backpack roomy enough to carry all these items.

My local outfitting store helped. The knowledgeable associates located each item and, when necessary, demonstrated its proper use. I borrowed what I could, used what I had, and bought the rest.

I paid more for one set of fleece clothing than for a business suit. Rain gear cost more than a cross-country plane ticket. Capilene underwear, a quick-drying, high-tech fabric that wicks perspiration and moisture from the skin, retailed for $100—a huge increase in price and technology from the cotton "long-johns" of my youthful summer camp days. Then the salesperson told me that I needed "stuff sacks" to organize, compress, and protect these items. In all, the bill exceeded $1,000.

At home I spread it out. The clothing and gear I was expected to carry up Mt. Rainier nearly covered the living room floor. I looked at the aging external-frame Kelty backpack I had borrowed and wondered how all these items, plus five days of food and a "small amount of assigned group gear," would fit into this small green canvas sack.

After a few feeble attempts to fit everything into the pack

and with little time before departure, I gave up, instead placing it all into a suitcase and large duffel and hoping it would somehow fit when I arrived at the mountain.

On the southern flank of Mt. Rainier, nineteen clients and seven guides met at a place called Paradise, an aptly named location 5,420 feet above sea level. Inside a small chalet, each climber spread their gear onto the floor. Prompted by a checklist, a guide reviewed each piece. My gear passed inspection; I did not. I was wearing blue jeans, flannel, and t-shirts—all cotton garments. Cotton, the guide chided, was a dangerous fabric, one that quickly becomes wet from perspiration or rain. When damp, this natural fabric loses all insulating ability, potentially allowing hypothermia.

Chastised, I retreated to change. As I stepped into my capilene, I realized that at least this was one less set of clothes to fit into the backpack. When I returned, a bulging Ziploc bag filled with candy, nuts, meats, and cheese—lunches and snacks for five days—topped my pile. Meanwhile other climbers were loading their packs easily and efficiently. I began tentatively, placing items into each of the pack's compartments, filling these pouches until zippers strained and the thin fabric stretched. But after all compartments were full, many items remained on the floor. Then I hung climbing gear and water bottles from the pack frame, draped assorted clothing over the top, and tied two sweaters around my waist.

As I tried to heft this hopeless mess onto my back, we were instructed to come forward and receive our share of "group gear"—cooking pots, lightweight gas stoves, climbing anchors, ropes, and more food. Nineteen roughly equal allotments were stacked atop two tables. Each climber was expected to carry one of these piles in addition to their own gear and food. I was last in line. As I stepped forward, I faced an unwieldy collection of oddly shaped items, topped by a loaf of bread. A stern-faced guide stood behind the table.

I looked at the bread, then at the guide. He looked at my bulging backpack, then at the bread. Thankfully, he carried the entire pile.

I hoped that enthusiasm and fitness would overcome my inexperience. Starting near the head of the line, I kept pace easily. As we ascended the well-maintained Skyline Trail from Paradise, we remained unroped, instructed to walk single file an arm's-length apart, maintaining a steady pace. If one needed to rest, adjust their pack or even take a picture, they were to step from the line. If other hikers approached, and many did this late August weekend, our group moved in unison to the side of the trail, allowing others to pass. Like a long snake, twenty-six climbers, each a yard apart, ascended the winding path.

But the scenery was spectacular, and marching singly-mindedly through such beauty seemed a sacrilege. I stepped from the line to snap a photo, then re-entered near the snake's belly. Twice more I stepped out to photograph the expansive view, eventually reaching the line's end. There, despite keeping up with the group, I was scolded by a junior guide to "quit taking pictures and just walk."

As we ascended, the altitude and physical exertion each took a toll, and by early afternoon the tightly regimented line had disintegrated. While the strongest climbers forged ahead, others lagged, panting and coughing, struggling from the lack of oxygen in the thin mountain air. Guides helped the slowest clients, taking backpacks and strapping them atop their own, one guide carrying 150 pounds up the steep slope.

I kept my pack—and maintained a steady pace. Conditioning had helped, at least this first day.

After supper, we crowded into the bunkhouse at Camp Muir 10,800 feet up the mountain, and each person told of their mountaineering experience and climbing goals. One couple had just returned from their honeymoon, a month-long trek in Nepal. An athletic-appearing young man had completed the "Colorado 14'ers," climbing all fifty-four of that state's mountains that stand more than 14,000 feet high. Most participants had rock and ice-climbing experience; one had ascended to the South Col, 26,000 feet high on Everest. When my turn came, I related that I was a hiker, adventure traveler, and photographer, here to learn mountaineering basics. Only one other climber had so little experience.

During the next three days I learned to use an ice ax, tie climbing knots, and walk on glaciers while roped with others. Sliding down icy slopes, our group practiced self-arrest, rolling

The Making of a Climber
The author practicing technical ice
climbing on Mt. Rainier.

and twisting our bodies to firmly implant long metal axes into the frozen surface, thereby stopping or arresting a fall. After learning crevasse rescue, a technique employing ropes and pulleys to lift a climber from an icy abyss, each participant was given the dubious opportunity, while double-roped for safety, to jump into a crevasse, experiencing the sensation and full force of a fall.

The course was fascinating. I found living and climbing in a glaciated mountain environment exhilarating. Rainier, however, is a dangerous peak, a mountain of many moods with weather that can change quickly and topography that can be unforgiving of even the slightest mistake. Eighty-four climbers have died on Mt. Rainier since 1887. A week before our seminar, two men fell to their deaths after an ice storm coated the upper mountain with two inches of clear, hard ice, rendering crampons and standard glacier travel methods nearly useless. Since then, no one had summited. As a course finale we would try, but were told we would probably turn back far short of our goal.

Hours before our summit attempt, the calm weather we had enjoyed began to change. Cirrus clouds thickened during the afternoon, and shortly after sunset the wind intensified. Strong gusts shook the sturdy bunkhouse throughout the night. Between the wind's roar and the anticipation of the upcoming summit attempt, sleep did not come easily.

At 1:30 a.m., a typical time for an alpine start, we awoke. Snow and ice-climbing is safest during cold, nighttime conditions; sun and daytime warmth allow melting, markedly increasing the risk of ice and rock falls. Ideally most of an ascent is completed before daybreak, sunrise enjoyed from the summit, and the descent completed by noon.

On this cloudy night, our only light was from individual headlamps, small battery-powered units worn by each climber. We dressed, ate, and packed, then tied ourselves to the climbing rope—all by these small cones of illumination.

By 3:30 a.m. everyone was outside, roped up and ready, a rapid preparation for a large group. However, the wind raged unabated. Low dense clouds obscured all light save for the thin headlamp beams that pierced the murky darkness a mere twenty feet. The wind-driven cold bit deeply despite many layers of clothing.

Then we began to move. One climber at a time; one rope-team at a time. Waiting until the rope in front was nearly taut, each climber would step out, walking at the same pace as his forward teammates, leaving minimal slack. As one team of six climbers moved away, evenly spaced along a 160-foot-long rope, another team stepped up and repeated the process, leaving one climber at a time and walking with a uniform and steady pace.

Minutes after leaving Camp Muir, we crossed a small ridge and into the wind's full force. The gusts that had shaken the bunkhouse all night had been attenuated, partially deflected by the mountain's topography. I was stunned by the storm's fury. Spoken commands could not be heard over the wind; communication was by tension and tugs on the rope as we ascended a thin path packed deeply into firm snow. In the dense darkness there was no sense of location or direction, only the feeling of steadily climbing—sometimes gradually, sometimes steeply—always buffeted by the gale.

Darkness yielded to faint morning light as we suddenly climbed above the clouds, a layer of overcast that hugged the mountain's flanks and extended to the horizon. Valleys and hills were obscured by this foreboding gray layer, but at 11,000 feet the area's two tallest peaks, Rainier and Little Tahoma, jutted ice-streaked rocky heads above this vast gray sea.

Despite the clear sky, the wind raged. The intensifying orange band of pre-dawn light, although beautiful, offered no warmth. Bent low with only faces exposed, our cheeks felt the constant sting of wind-driven ice granules stripped from the glacier's surface. One petite climber was lifted off her feet and blown to the ice, the rope held by others stopping her fall. Another gust ripped glasses from a near-sighted climber's face; the following team found the eyewear despite the darkness. Still we advanced.

At Ingraham Flats we stopped to weigh our options. Weak climbers often turn back here, groups rest and occasionally wait out storms here, and some alpinists even camp here. It is one of the most protected places on the mountain.

It is also the site of the worst tragedy in American mountaineering history. In 1981, twenty-five climbers paused at this level expanse. Although generally a safe location, a huge mass of snow and ice slid down the mountain that day, the avalanche sweeping eleven people to their deaths. A photograph developed from the film found in one victim's camera hangs as the centerpiece of a simple yet poignant memorial in the park's visitor center. I did not see the photo nor learn of the tragedy until after our climb. But the image is dramatic, showing the pyramidal summit of Little Tahoma jutting through a sea of clouds, a scene strikingly similar to the view now before us.

Discussion was difficult over the roar of the wind. Few words, however, were necessary. Even if the upper mountain hadn't been dangerously icy, this storm alone would have necessitated retreat. The discouraged looks on the guides' faces and the howl of the wind said enough. Our summit bid was over.

We turned and descended back into the clouds and reached camp without incident, despite the stormy conditions. Below Camp Muir the wind eased and we unroped, descending first the snowfield and then the winding trail. The first day's regimentation was forgotten; we walked down in small groups, chatting with new friends.

Although far from an accomplished mountaineer, I had become enamored of the high mountain environment, and during these five days had discovered that I could acclimate and perform well at altitude. Stories of great mountains in the Andes, Alaska Range, and Himalayas enthralled me. I indefinitely postponed trekking up Kilimanjaro; instead I would attempt other technical climbs.

Poor weather, however, plagued my efforts. In Mexico, I endured the biggest snowstorm in forty years. On Popocatepetl (17,887 feet), the climber's dormitory, normally a thousand feet below snowline, was closed—buried beneath six feet of fresh powder. Again we retreated without summiting. Three days later we attempted Pico de Orizaba (18,701 feet), Mexico's tallest mountain. Our luck was no better.

As we descended, Channing Hall, a friend I had met on Rainier asked, "Doug, where do we go next?" I was too discouraged to answer. In fact, I thought myself finished with mountaineering. After the first four days on Mt. Rainier, I had experienced little but wind, cold, snow, and failure on the mountains. Despite paying hefty fees for outstanding guides, purchasing the best equipment, and pursuing a vigorous conditioning program, I had yet to reach a summit. I thought of many places to visit and other activities to enjoy, pursuits that seemed far more enjoyable than freezing in a tent pummeled by snow and wind.

Channing's persistence is the reason I continued climbing. An unstoppable optimist, he organized another northwestern excursion, this time to both Mts. Baker and Rainier. All I needed was to buy a plane ticket and food, pay guide fees, and show up with gear, ready to climb. Sheryl, my friend and confidante, urged me to accept the offer. So encouraged by others—and wanting to reach at least one summit during my mountaineering "career"—I gave climbing one more try.

In August, a high-pressure system brought blue skies and light breezes to the Pacific Northwest. We first summited Mt. Baker (10,775 feet), a snow-covered volcano deep in the rugged North Cascade Mountains. Our guide was prophetic when, after congratulating me atop the mountain said, "May this be the first of many summits."

On Mt. Rainier, Channing had arranged for Jason Edwards, our course leader the previous year, to again guide us. This time Jason also invited Nawong Gombu, a colleague and Sherpa from Nepal to join our team.

Gombu, as he preferred to be called, had participated in many Himalayan climbs. At age sixteen, he had joined the 1953 British Everest Expedition as a high-altitude porter. On that historic climb his uncle, Tenzing Norgay, and New Zealand beekeeper Edmund Hillary summited Everest, the first documented ascent of the world's tallest mountain.[1] Ten years later Gombu returned to Everest and, with Jim Whittaker, reached the summit, placing the first American flag atop the peak.

---

[1] In 1924 George Mallory led a British team to Everest's north side. Famous for his quip about climbing mountains "because they are there," this was the veteran climber's third Everest try. Mallory and his partner, Andrew Irvine, were seen by teammates 1,000 feet below the summit. The men were ascending strongly, but clouds moved in and blocked further telescopic views. The two climbers never returned. In 1999 Mallory's body was discovered by an American expedition (led by a senior RMI guide), but Irvine's body—and Mallory's camera—have yet to be found, prolonging the debate as to whether either man reached Everest's summit before perishing.

At fifty-five, Gombu remained strong and trim. Barely five feet tall, he carried huge loads at high altitude yet moved easily across difficult terrain. Residing much of the year in the Himalayan foothills near Darjeeling, India, Gombu had spent many summers on Rainier. In fact, if successful, this climb would be his eightieth ascent of the mountain.

With experience I packed my recently purchased, internal frame backpack easily and efficiently. We reached Camp Muir in early afternoon, slept early then arose at 11:30 p.m. for the summit bid. With mild breezes beneath a star-filled sky, we crossed the Cowlitz Glacier past Ingraham Flats, where a year earlier we had turned back, to the base of Disappointment Cleaver, an appropriately named ridge that is the climb's most physically demanding portion. One of nine teams on the mountain that day, we ascended this long rocky spur along a poorly marked path then stepped again onto snow and ice which we followed to 14,000 feet and the crater rim.

Here, many climbers stop. RMI awards summit certificates for reaching this point. However, the true summit, Columbia Crest, barely a hundred feet higher, lies across the quarter-mile-wide crater. Crossing this high-altitude expanse is time-consuming and therefore risky. Last year the weather had changed quickly and deteriorated rapidly, and we knew any extra effort at this altitude weakens climbers for the descent.

Yet, I had never considered reaching any point short of the true summit. Thoughts of turning back stunned me.

A steady wind blew across the crater—not the howling gale of a year earlier but a wind strong enough to lift ice crystals and carry them in ever-changing white wisps half a foot above the frozen surface. It was midmorning, late to be still short of the summit. Six of the day's seven previous teams had "summited" here; only one had crossed the crater.

Jason and Gombu congratulated us then asked how we felt. We had been slow but felt strong and wanted to continue. Despite the wind, the sky was clear with no signs of approaching storms. In an oxygen-starved environment nearly three miles above the ocean, we pled our case.

The guides conferred, and our determination and persistence were rewarded with a qualified yes. Yes, but only if we maintained a steady pace across the crater floor. Slowing or delay would necessitate turning back.

We started across, taking one breath with each step. Progress was agonizingly slow, but we advanced steadily.

Geologists classify Mt. Rainier as an active volcano even though there is no molten lava flowing down its sides or great plumes of ash rising above it. Instead its crater is a shallow bowl—cold and windswept, buried year-round beneath snow and ice. A few rocks are exposed around the crater rim, some windswept free of their snowy mantle, others kept clear by warm gases escaping from volcanic vents.

At the base of Columbia Crest we briefly stopped. Here the ground was free of snow, the exposed rocks heavily weathered. Two small holes, openings little larger than a fingerbreadth in diameter, perforated the granular surface. The surrounding area was warm; wisps of steam rose intermittently from each vent. With each burst a faint sulfurous odor filled the air before the breeze dissipated the unpleasant smell.

I moved closer for a better look. Between wisps of gas these holes seemed unremarkable. In other regions and at lower altitudes they might have been formed by insects or small rodents. But here, looking into these holes, I stared down the gullet of an active volcano.

Mt. Rainier has not always been this docile. It is a young mountain, less than a million years old. During a geologically brief lifespan, this volcano has erupted many times, the last event 1,000 years ago. But today, and for much of the two centuries since British Captain George Vancouver first saw this peak and named it for his friend and colleague Rear Admiral Peter Rainier, the mountain has been quiet. Yet Native American lore tells of fire and molten rock high near the summit they call Tahoma, and geologists today warn that it is only a matter of time before another major eruption occurs.

Although intrigued by gas belching vents and amazed at standing on an ice-covered mountain born of hot magma, we could not linger. The summit stood directly above.

We began up the final crest. Step. Breath. Step. Breath.

Then we could climb no higher. To the south we looked down upon snow-covered Mt. Adams and the jagged silhouette of Mt. St. Helens, scarred from its 1980 eruption. Seattle, partially hidden by haze, lay to the west; Mt. Baker, the highest mountain in the North Cascades where we had stood four days earlier, was below us to the north.

We were on top, atop the most heavily glaciated peak in the "lower 48"—and the highest point in the state of Washington. Channing sported a beaming smile despite his fatigue. I was ecstatic. Reaching a summit made the process fun—a wonderful achievement following a challenging but enjoyable ascent. We took celebratory photos then images of the magnificent scenery below. I could have stayed for hours, savoring the accomplishment and enjoying the view.

But climbers are transient visitors to these lofty heights. Each step, each breath drains precious energy. One must descend before weakness, dehydration, or altitude illness begins. As we prepared to leave the summit, Jason reminded us that, "Guys, we are only halfway there." Then we retraced our steps down the summit crest, across the crater floor, down the Cleaver, and past Ingraham Flats, reaching Camp Muir thirteen hours after our nighttime departure.

There would be many more summits. I returned to Mexico and scaled Popocatepetl, Orizaba, and Iztaccihuatl, the three highest peaks in that country. I climbed Ecuador's Cotopaxi, the world's tallest volcano—two feet taller than Mt. Kilimanjaro (which I have yet to attempt)—and summited South America's Cerro Aconcagua (22,861 feet), the highest point in the western hemisphere.

However, climbing never became an exclusive pursuit. My interests in photography, kayaking, human culture and history never waned. As I traveled and climbed, I occasionally recalled my high school teacher's goal of reaching all fifty state highpoints. I even summited a few myself—if I was near them—in case I ever became "serious" about highpointing.

Chapter 3

Seeking Summits
Iowa

State highpointing has challenged climbers for decades. Arthur Marshall, after ascending a small hill near Richmond, Indiana, in 1936, became the first known "completer." Traveling by car and stage, passenger train and narrow gauge railroad, he spent portions of seventeen years finding and climbing each of the then forty-eight state summits, making early ascents of major western peaks including the third recorded ascent of Montana's Granite Peak. In 1930 he summited Hyndman Peak, then believed Idaho's loftiest mountain, but had to return the following year to climb Borah Peak after that Idaho summit was found to be taller. Other highpoints were yet to be officially determined. Uncertain which was higher, Marshall climbed two mountains in Arkansas, three hilltops in Delaware, and five in Indiana.

No one else completed the highpoints until 1950. However, three men did so that decade before Alaska and Hawaii achieved statehood.

John "Vin" Hoeman became the first "50 completer," ascending his final state summit, Minnesota's Eagle Mountain, in 1966. Fourteen years later Frances Carter became the first woman to climb all fifty. By 1990, eleven people had ascended each state highpoint; seventy-six more would do so during the next ten years.

Records were established. Todd Huston and Robert "Whit" Rambach sought to climb the highpoints as quickly as possible. In 1995 they spent just sixty-six days to ascend all fifty, a record that lasted a decade and a feat even more remarkable because

Todd is an amputee, having lost his leg in a childhood boating accident. After his final ascent Todd coauthored a book about his life and climbing experiences, while Whit continued climbing, becoming the first of only two people to summit each state twice.

Galen Johnston is the youngest completer—age twelve—and half of the only mother-son team to climb all fifty. He and his dad Dave, the only person to have summited each of the highpoints during winter, are one of only four father-son teams to have summited all fifty. Cal Dunwoody, on the other hand, was seventy-seven when he topped out on Florida's sandy Britton Hill in 1998, becoming the oldest completer. However Wayne Balcolm has climbed all the highpoints after age sixty-six, the only person to have summited all the states so late in life.

But I was not interested in a race. Nor, at age forty-five, was I near any record setting extreme. Instead I sought to enjoy the experience, unhurried by time and unencumbered by all but a few basic rules. As I planned The Dream they became guiding principles:

1) Safety must always be the highest priority.

2) This endeavor was to be fun. I had not boasted of my plans nor sought publicity. I was beholden to no sponsor. If at any time this quest became monotonous or stressful, if I became lonely or desired to return home or to the world of medicine, I could—and would—guilt-free.

3) Reach the true summit. The Highpointers Club, and guide services such as Rainier's RMI, occasionally accept locations other than a mountain's loftiest point due to access issues, perceived safety or speed. However, if I was expending the effort to climb a mountain, I wanted to touch its true summit. The only exception would be on large, flat highpoints without a clearly defined top. On these, I would touch the highest apparent point then walk across the summit plateau to the official marker, not fretting about which particle of soil or tuft of grass was highest on an otherwise featureless summit.

4) Reach the top in any style desired. I felt no obligation to walk beside a paved road to "hike" to the top. If I could drive to the summit, I often did. Conversely, if a challenging hike or more aesthetic climbing route was possible, I often chose that path instead of an easier "standard" ascent.

Finally, when I left the emergency department, I decided not to again climb the already completed highpoints, most done in the unhurried style in which I hoped to do the rest. I felt no need to touch these summits a second time to reach all within a 12-month period or single calendar year. Instead I would use the extra time to visit additional attractions near yet-to-be-climbed peaks.

In 1993, floods inundated Iowa. The Mississippi River and its tributaries were at record levels; low-lying areas were underwater and the rest of the state deep in mud. Amusement parks and tourist attractions were closed, and flood-swollen lakes were too dangerous to canoe. However, my then ten-year-old son, Jon, and his mother had just moved to the state; I needed something to interest him during my weeklong visit. As we scanned the atlas, seeking a high and hopefully dry site, I noted "highest point in Iowa," printed in small letters on the map.

"We could climb Iowa's highest point," I suggested half-jokingly, recalling his interest in my recent ascents of Mts. Baker, Rainier, and the Mexican volcanoes.

"Cool, Dad," was his enthusiastic and unexpected response.

Then I looked more closely. The map had no red dot, state park, or road to the site. Instead the highest point was labeled in an otherwise blank white area in rural northwestern Iowa.

I looked at Jon. He was excited, preparing to go "mountaineering." Again I looked at the atlas, wondering if we could even find the place. However, I voiced no doubts. A state highpoint I reasoned, even that of Iowa, shouldn't be too difficult to find.

An hour later we turned from the paved highway and entered the region denoted by the map's white void. Cornfields, fencerow to fencerow, extended for miles, the crop lush and green after weeks of soaking rain. Gravel roads bordered by shallow ditches cut through otherwise uniform fields, while muddy lanes led to distant farmhouses, whitewashed structures dwarfed by surrounding barns and silos.

I looked across the gently rolling terrain, hoping to see a prominent hill. There was none.

I had expected, or at least hoped, to find a sign directing me to the highest point. Again, there was none.

Instead we encountered a maze of unnamed and unnumbered roads, low visibility and a steady drizzle. There were no gas stations or convenience stores in which to ask directions. And each road looked the same—long dirt paths bordered by sharply demarcated fields.

Then I saw a middle-aged man clad in mud-splattered denim. He was bent low, struggling to clear a drainage ditch beside a deeply rutted driveway. I slowed to ask directions. But he never looked up.

I drove on wishing not to bother him. No, that was only an excuse. Really, I was afraid. Afraid of what he might think—of two strangers searching for an obscure geographical point. The highest point of *what*? In *these* conditions? Would *he* be scared? Might the police be called? And would the next day's local headline read, "Arrested North Carolina man claimed to be seeking 'High Point?'"

But as we drove on, I found no signs or indication of the state summit. I turned around, resolving to ask directions. Our quest was honorable; we were on public roads. If the highpoint was inaccessible, on restricted private property, or unreachable in these conditions, I needed to know. I had seen enough muddy roads.

The man was still there, now standing and looking at a shallow excavation, his knee-high boots ankle-deep in muck. He turned as we slowed and pulled alongside.

"Excuse me," I said, rolling down the window, as cool mist blew into the car. "My son and I are looking for the highest geographical point of Iowa. The map shows it near here."

"Well," he said slowly, obviating any need for a lengthy explanation. He seemed unfazed by my quest. "You need to go past Ray's place," he said after a moment of thought. "You know where he lives, don't you?"

"No, sir, I'm from North Carolina."

"Hmm," he muttered, as his weathered face expressed intense concentration. "It's the white house a little past the big cornfield up ahead. Take the dirt road to the right a ways—past two, maybe three crossroads. Then go left a mile or two...you can't miss it. It's on the left."

I tried but couldn't get clearer directions. Thanking him, I drove away in the direction indicated, past cornfield after cornfield, houses and side roads until we were totally lost.

Then I saw another man, struggling to free a tractor buried nearly axle-deep in the soft roadside shoulder. He was gracious and friendly—and not surprised by my request. He tried to help but gave similarly convoluted local directions. I simply didn't know Ray or Sam, Dave or Jackie, or where any of them lived.

We met others that damp afternoon, and asked about the highpoint so often that I wondered if we might again question someone queried earlier. But all were friendly and tried to be helpful; no one was taken aback or even mildly surprised by our quest. For an hour and a half we endured rain and drizzle, slippery roads, and earnest but fruitless discussions.

I knew I should give up. This search was accomplishing nothing. And what were we seeking—the highpoint of one of the flattest states in the nation? Jon, however, was having a great time, feeling like an adventurer traversing Iowa's vast fields of maize.

Somewhere, as we unknowingly passed Dave or Sam's place, this quest evolved into a challenge. The highpoint existed. No one had told us it was inaccessible, closed to the public, or even discouraged our search. We would find it—even if it took the rest of the day.

Again I slowed, approaching a man retrieving his mail. I asked my now well-rehearsed question.

His eyes lit up; his face showed confidence. "Why yes, the Sterlers. They live right around the corner. Go left there," he said pointing to a road barely a hundred yards away. "They live in the first house on the left. The highpoint is on their property. But ring the bell first. They like to meet highpointers."

We turned then pulled into a short driveway beside a well-maintained house. But no mountain—not even a hill—could be seen, just a barely perceptible incline in an otherwise flat landscape.

I rang the bell. A neatly dressed woman opened the door. "My son and I would like to visit Iowa's highpoint," I asked timidly. "Is that possible?"

"Why yes, of course," she answered, smiling. "It's at the end of the feed trough. But first, why don't you come in for a minute?"

She gave us literature detailing Iowa's agricultural products, a coloring book for Jon and a key chain commemorating the state highpoint. "It wasn't long ago that Ocheyedan Mound, ten miles from here, was considered Iowa's highest point," she said, before adding with considerable pride, "A recent survey showed this area higher. The state summit, we are told, is at the end of the feed trough. We've had visitors from nearly every state so please enjoy your visit, and don't forget to sign the register."

We thanked her then walked alongside a roofed metal bin toward a rusting license plate reading "HIGH PT" that had been nailed to the structure's far end. There I congratulated Jon on reaching his first summit. We undertook the mountaintop routine: celebratory photos, scanning the surrounding "lowlands," and perusing the summit register.

This spiral notebook's list of visitors, however, was lengthy—signed by climbers and highpointers from across the nation. One man had climbed Mt. Rainier days earlier, writing here of his relief at "the absence of headaches and altitude illness on this 'summit.'" Others wrote of completed highpoints, a number often totaling in the 20s or 30s. Despite this summer's inclement weather, dozens of visitors had journeyed to this remote location.

We signed our names, listed our hometowns, and inscribed our thanks to the Sterlers for their hospitality and highpoint access[2]. Soon, however, the drizzle intensified into a steady shower. It was time to leave.

Returning to the motel, Jon asked if we could do another highpoint. That evening, for the first time, I searched the atlas seeking state summits. But the highest geographical points of South Dakota and Nebraska were near their western borders, Minnesota's was in that state's extreme northeastern corner, and Missouri's highest peak was nearly 500 miles to the southeast. Illinois' Charles Mound was closest, but even that was 300 miles away.

Looking further afield I noted highpoints in remote, beautiful, and less developed regions. Five were in national parks, seventeen in national forests, and two in designated wilderness areas. Reaching all fifty would be a challenge, requiring mountaineering skills in the west, winter-camping and expeditionary abilities in Alaska, long hikes on many peaks, and a love of adventure on all. Then I recalled my youthful idea of touring the country and briefly considered how highpointing might be

---

[2] At the time of our visit, Iowa's highpoint was unnamed. However, in 1998, the Iowa legislature decreed that the state summit would be known as Hawkeye Point, a name chosen to honor all "Hawkeyes," a common nickname for the state's citizens.

A Sunnier Day
Fog and rain precluded quality summit photos in Iowa. This image, taken later atop South Dakota's Harney Peak, shows the author with his son Jon.

combined with such a journey.

But we would not reach any other state summits this trip. During the next four days Jon and I walked up Ocheyedan Mound, the chalky hill formerly recognized as Iowa's highest point, then visited a preserved remnant of the original tall grass prairie, a tiny parcel of the vast grassland that once covered the entire state. We followed a self-guided driving tour of glacial landscape features and hiked, picnicked, and played baseball between rainstorms.

Although we had enjoyed reaching Iowa's highest geographical point—and I had scanned the atlas seeking other state summits—highpointing had yet to become a priority for either of us. Three years would pass before we stood atop Illinois' Charles Mound, Jon's second state summit. During those years my state totals increased only slightly faster as I reached just a handful of summits, mostly drive-ups near my North Carolina home.

The leisurely pace enjoyed in Iowa, however, set a pattern I would follow at most state summits. And although these hilltops paled in comparison to the technical mountaineering and adventure travel that took me to five continents, reaching fifty summits remained an intriguing challenge—and an idea that wouldn't go away.

Mt. Mitchell, North Carolina
The highest mountain east of the Mississippi River. Dr. Elisha Mitchell, for
whom the mountain is named, is buried at the tower's base.

CHAPTER 4

A CHANGING LANDSCAPE

The Southern Appalachians

"**D**o you have any guidebooks for the state high-points, the highest geographical point of each of the fifty United States?" I inquired, responding to a mailing received shortly after returning from Iowa. The catalog from this small, independent book retailer specializing in adventure travel listed hundreds of titles—but none relating to state highpoints.

"Yes, we do," the bookseller answered, not sounding the least surprised by my request. "Actually, there are two in print, but we have only one in stock."[3]

Highpoints of the United States, a 238-page tome by Don Holmes thus became my backpack companion for many of the remaining highpoints. A now retired aeronautical engineer and "50 completer," Don writes with the precision and clarity expected of his profession. Directions to each highpoint are given from nearby towns; turns and landmarks en route are measured to the nearest tenth mile. Hiking routes, both standard and alternate, are described in detail and schematically shown with simple line maps.

---

[3] Four guidebooks are now available. *Fifty State Summits: Guide with maps to state highpoints* was written in 1988 by the late Paul Zumwalt, a surveyor and early highpointer. A hiker into his 90s, he lovingly recounted ascents and adventures on many highpoints—he did forty-four of them—often in the company of his late wife Lila. In 1999 Charlie Winger (another 50 completer) and wife Diane co-authored *Highpoint Adventures*. Modern graphics and web addresses are combined with interesting facts and trivia in this accurate guide that is produced in both full- and pocket-sized versions.

However, during the five years following my soggy ascent of Iowa's highest knoll, I remained in "highpointing denial." Although possessing a guidebook to the state summits, I prided myself on being a technical mountaineer, rock climbing in Yosemite, ice climbing in the Sierras, and ascending great Andean peaks in South America. Highpointing, especially through the south and southeast, seemed tame, something to do after my technical abilities waned, something for when I was "older."

Yet I seemed drawn to these hills, peaks so diminutive that locating them was sometimes a greater challenge than ascending them. Seven state summits, those of North Carolina, South Carolina, Georgia, Tennessee, Florida, Alabama, and Mississippi, can be reached by walking less than a mile—in total.

Unfortunately, this ease leads to a false sense of complacency in some beginning highpointers and a belittling of these summits by others. Here one can reach double-digit state totals before buying a pair of hiking boots. Conversely, climbers from other regions often rush through the south, "bagging" summits as quickly as possible by driving up, touching the top, photographing the summit marker then hurrying on to the next.

On a September weekend, as summer's green gave way to autumn's crimson and gold, Sheryl and I traveled to Virginia's Mt. Rogers (5,729 feet), the most challenging of the southeastern state summits and the only one requiring more than a half-mile walk. Located in the Mt. Rogers National Recreation Area, the largest such federally designated reserve in the southeast, Virginia's highest peak is an hour from my home. I had visited this sprawling park many times, cross-country skiing along logging roads and abandoned railroad grades in winter then watching the springtime production of maple syrup from the nation's most southerly growth of sugar maple forests.

Beneath blue skies and a Canadian high-pressure system, we followed the Appalachian Trail across hilltop meadows called "balds" and through dark rhododendron thickets, known locally as "ivy hells." These "hells," however, were beautiful—clumps of 20-foot-tall rhododendron, trunks and branches intertwined, each mass of densely packed vegetation covering up to several acres. Today the four-mile-long summit hike skirts many of these thickets and, with the use of modern machinery, has been cut through others. But to European explorers and early settlers these were impenetrable obstacles. Not a man, much less a horse, could navigate through this herbaceous gridlock.

We hiked steadily up moderate slopes; as we gained altitude, the air chilled noticeably. Near the top a short spur trail led to the summit, a densely wooded knob with none of the long-range views enjoyed during the ascent. An aging wooden sign lettered simply "Mt. Rogers—Elevation 5729 Feet—Highest Point in Virginia," marked the summit. We congratulated each other, snapped a few photos then walked a short distance to an overlook to rest, eat, and enjoy the view.

At times like these, with fair skies and ideal conditions, the tameness of highpointing seemed a welcomed change from the rigors of high-altitude mountaineering. Though not committed to highpointing all fifty, I increasingly planned vacations that "happened" to take us near state highpoints. These trips were loosely structured, and to avoid summer's stifling heat and humidity, all southern trips were made in the spring and fall.

On another trip we visited the most geographically compact group of highpoints in the nation. In the southern Appalachian Mountains, the state summits of Tennessee, Georgia, North and South Carolina lay within a 50-mile radius. These four peaks are among the sixteen state highpoints, nearly one-third of the national total, located in the Appalachian Mountains, an inland chain of interconnected hills and ridges extending from northern Alabama to Maine.

They are among the oldest mountains on earth. Formed by a complex series of geological events lasting 200 million years, the Appalachians rose to their full height long before dinosaurs walked upon the land. Today, after 350 million years of erosion, they are mostly rounded, heavily forested, and a fraction of their former height. Yet in places they remain tall and rugged. North Carolina's Mt. Mitchell (6,684 feet)—a mountain I had strolled up a decade earlier, unknowingly summiting my first state highpoint—is the highest peak east of the Mississippi River.

Few natural passes, locally called "gaps," bisect the steep escarpments found in the southern Appalachians. Deep valleys separate parallel ranges. Explorers and pioneers struggled to cross these mountains, and the few people who settled in this isolated region became self-sufficient, developing a unique mountain culture.

Today, modern highways cross these ranges and two remark-able routes, each constructed during the 1930s, travel length-wise along scenic ridgelines and over some of the tallest peaks. While hiking up Virginia's Mt. Rogers we had encountered one of these routes, the 2,100-mile-long Appalachian Trail, a foot-path extending from Georgia to Maine. We now drove south on the other, the Blue Ridge Parkway, a 469-mile-long roadway.

Regularly listed among the nation's most scenic auto routes, 20 million people annually travel portions of this two-lane road that runs from Virginia's Shenandoah National Park to the North Carolina entrance of the Great Smoky Mountains National Park. Constructed during the Depression to create jobs and foster tourism in this beautiful but economically disadvan-taged region, the parkway is now the National Park Service's most-visited attraction. However, there have been persistent, but never officially confirmed, reports of another, more somber rea-son for this road. Combined with the Skyline Drive, a 105-mile extension northward to Front Royal, Virginia, near Washington, D.C., it provides quick access from our nation's capital into some of the most rugged terrain east of the Rockies. Intended or not, it could have served as a military highway during the Second World War—or a route of evacuation today in the event of an attack on our nation's capital.

The light greens of early spring were beginning to cover winter's bare tree branches as we followed the parkway around mountains and along high ridgelines. Driving this winding roadway is like traveling in a different era, crossing bridges of hand-hewn stone and passing through narrow tunnels blasted from steep hillsides. The trees which line much of the route, although often only a thin corridor through this increasingly developed region, provide a peaceful sense of isolation.

South of Asheville, North Carolina, we left the bucolic splendor of the parkway and followed busy roads past a bizarre mix of cheap tourist attractions, commercial development, and pricey gated communities of second homes and retirement con-dos that increasingly dominate this region. Golf courses cover the valleys and hillsides where mountain inhabitants eked out a living raising corn and tobacco just a decade ago; strip malls and convenience chains now replace once-ubiquitous country stores. Five national forests are located in this region; however this level of protection slows, but doesn't stop, the accelerating development.

Brasstown Bald (4,784 feet), Georgia's highest point, is surrounded by one of these forests, the Chattahoochee. However, Georgia has chosen to "celebrate" and "honor" its highpoint by developing it. Brasstown Valley Resort, a 503-acre state-owned lodge and conference center, is located on the mountain's south side. The structures are modern, upscale, and tastefully designed but nevertheless shockingly out of place.

The Bald was crowded when we visited on a beautiful spring day. Cars filled the large parking lot, while Sheryl and I shared the quarter-mile-long paved summit trail with dozens of others as we strolled up the gently sloping path toward the observation platform, a tower of concrete and stone built in 1965.

Atop Georgia the air was clear, the industrial pollution from the Tennessee Valley that often blankets this region kept at bay by a brisk northerly breeze. Views were expansive; forested hills rolled away in all directions. Save for the resort, surprisingly little evidence of human impact or development was seen.

We relaxed, enjoying the view. Warmed by the springtime sun, I scanned the surrounding landscape, searching the eastern horizon for Sassafras Mountain (3,560 feet), South Carolina's state summit and a peak we would ascend on a later excursion. Then I turned and looked to the southwest, trying to locate Springer Mountain, the southern terminus of that other mountainous path, the Appalachian Trail.

Popularly known as the AT, this footpath extends nearly the length of the Appalachians, from Georgia's Springer Mountain to Maine's Mt. Katahdin. Completed in 1934 and marked by simple white blazes, it passes through fourteen states and traverses six state highpoints. But although the trail begins less than thirty miles from Georgia's highest point, Springer Mountain was unmarked and I saw no evidence of the route beneath the tree canopy.

A year later, not far from Brasstown Bald, we again encountered the AT, this time at Clingmans Dome. At 6,643 feet, this mountain is Tennessee's, and the Trail's, highest point—and the nation's most visited state summit. Located in the Great Smoky Mountains National Park, a wilderness area straddling the Tennessee-North Carolina border, the Dome is visited by an estimated 40 percent of the ten million people who tour the park each year.

For the highpointer, it is an easy walk-up. A curving concrete ramp leads from a paved parking lot to the large observation deck atop the summit. Most visitors, however, don't know, or don't care, that Clingmans Dome is Tennessee's highest point. Instead they come to see the Smokies—range after parallel range—and the soft haze for which these mountains were named.

On a chilly spring day, we joined hundreds of tourists crowded onto the open observation deck. But low clouds and dense fog blanketed ridgelines and filled the valleys, obscuring the view. Here in one of the wettest regions of the country—where eighty inches of precipitation fall annually, the highest total east of the Rockies—mosses and ferns flourish in cool seeps, and more species of amphibians exist than anywhere else on the planet.

We didn't stay atop Tennessee long but descended a short distance to the Appalachian Trail where we met two young men, resting beside heavily loaded packs. They were "thru-hikers", attempting to walk the entire length of the Appalachian Trail—all 2,172 miles of it—in a single hiking season. Appearing strong and obviously enjoying the experience, they laughed as they shared tales of rain, seemingly endless series of steep hills, and even a late-season snowstorm they had endured after leaving Georgia.

Not everyone attempting a thru-hike experiences such joy. Each spring, more than 2,000 backpackers start north from Springer Mountain, hoping to reach Mt. Katahdin before winter's early snows. Only about 400 will succeed, taking the five million steps required to complete the journey. Clingmans Dome, 230 miles north of Springer Mountain, is barely a tenth of the way there. Yet by this point, fully one-third of the hikers give up.

We met others that foggy day. A disheveled-appearing middle-aged man hiked alone; his matted, sandy-colored hair fell below a knotted bandana. He walked strongly but stared blankly ahead, never diverting his gaze to notice the environment through which he passed. When asked if he was a thru-hiker, he nodded affirmatively but never spoke or changed expression as he plodded on.

Another couple followed, trudging up the steep trail toward Clingmans' summit. Husband and wife—at least for now—they walked silently, heads down, 100 yards apart.

"My wife is struggling," the man told me as he leaned heavily on his walking stick, waiting for her to catch up.

His wife looked defeated, knees and shins abraded, the crusted scabs caked with mud. "We've had rain every day for two weeks," is all she uttered as we passed.

It seemed unusual to be a spectator, watching others attempt great feats. As the late morning sun thinned the lingering fog, I recalled previous climbs and my reaction to success—and failure.

After summiting Argentina's Aconcagua, I walked twenty-five miles from basecamp to the nearest roadway in a single day. Near the park entrance a local tourist approached, asking if I was a climber.

"Sí," I responded.

"To the top?" he asked in Spanish, raising his eyebrows as he looked toward the distant peak.

"Sí. Hasta la cumbre," I said proudly, smiling and pointing toward the mountaintop. My white teeth contrasted sharply with my sun and wind burned face, covered with three weeks of dirt and grime.

"Wait," he said in English, holding his hand up as if to stop traffic. "Photo please." The excited man waved his family forward, quickly posing them around me. He shot the image with the mountain a spectacular backdrop then shook my hand, congratulating and thanking me profusely as if I were a returning hero.

Even when the results aren't as triumphal, however, a climber is often seen as a bold adventurer. In Mexico, as our discouraged group retreated from the snow-closed climbing lodge at Popocatepetl's base, we met some of the thousands of Mexicans who had driven into the mountains to enjoy the rare snowfall. To them the snow was a beautiful novelty; to us a reminder of the winter we tried to leave behind—and the cause for failure on this mountain.

Many in our group were grumpy, a few downright surly. I walked quietly trying to find solace in the beautiful scenery, looking up at the white summits of Popocatepetl and Iztaccihuatl soaring above the snow-dappled conifers.

A mile from the van a group of smiling young Mexicans approached tentatively. "Alpinista, señor?" one asked.

"Sí," I responded flatly, not feeling like much of a climber. Retreating from yet another summit in failure, it seemed that only my attire and technical gear qualified me as a mountaineer.

But the youthful Mexicans were excited, asking for a photo with a "real alpinista." I posed with each then chatted in a mix of basic English and elementary Spanish as we continued down. Linguistic challenges prevented deep discussions, but their excitement and friendliness lightened my mood and eased the disappointment as I trudged the final mile. Meeting these people was the highlight of the climb—and an early hint that, for me, climbing would entail more than simply reaching summits.

CHAPTER 5

SPEAKIN' MISSISSIPPI

The Deep South

"Only Positive Mississippi Spoken Here," read the sign welcoming us to the state. Home of William Faulkner and John Grisham, Elvis and Jimmy Buffet, the state has been ridiculed and vilified by the press, especially after some of the most egregious civil rights-era incidents occurred here. Mississippi tries hard to improve its image, but even today ranks at or near the bottom of the nation in many socio-economic measures.

Yet I had come with an open mind. I had "visited" Mississippi only once before, driving through its narrowest portion, the Gulf Coast, but never stopping. Now I hoped to tour much of the state, especially its more rural northern and central regions.

Woodall Mountain, Mississippi's highest point at just 806 feet above sea level, is located in the state's northeastern corner. Seven miles after crossing the state line, Sheryl and I turned from a paved highway onto a deeply rutted gravel road that led steadily uphill to an isolated clearing dominated by a rusting radio tower. I wanted to think "positive Mississippi," but Woodall Mountain's litter-strewn summit was a mess. Spindly grass grew from bleached, rocky soil. Scrubby pinewoods surrounded the clearing, blocking distant views. There was no monument or register, and except for still shiny beer cans and glistening shards of recently broken brown glass, it seemed no one had visited here for months.

A USGS benchmark[4] identifying this as Woodall Mountain was slightly below the knoll's loftiest point. We touched this marker then strolled across the clearing's highest apparent elevation. But the summit was a lonely, uninviting place; we stayed just minutes before descending, still seeking "positive Mississippi."

Along the nearby Natchez Trace, however, I discovered a more scenic area. Once little more than a series of loosely connected Indian trails, the Trace extends from Natchez, Mississippi, to Nashville, Tennessee, passing within ten miles of Woodall Mountain. By 1810 this footpath had become the southern frontier's most heavily trafficked route with taverns and inns lining its path. Yet nearly everyone walked in the same direction: north.

This movement, however, was neither mass migration nor exodus but part of an annual trade route. Each autumn thousands of Ohio Valley farmers floated crop-laden flatboats down the Ohio and Mississippi Rivers to Natchez and New Orleans. There they sold everything: crops, supplies, even the lumber used to build their boats. Then they walked home along the Natchez Trace, their footsteps eroding and compressing the trail.

The Trace's glory years, however, lasted barely two decades. Like many frontier achievements, this route was soon replaced by further technological advances. Steamboats began plying America's great inland waterways. Travel on these vessels was faster, easier, and safer, and by 1830 use of the Trace had declined dramatically. Yet the thousands of sojourners had left an indelible mark on the land, for the path, although covered by vegetation, can still be discerned.

---

[4] These embedded disks generally list a peak's name, altitude, coordinates, and survey date. Most have been placed by the United States Geological Survey (USGS), part of the Interior Department. However, some mountains are marked with similar disks of the United States Coast and Geodetic Survey (USCGS), the nation's first civilian scientific agency, and today a division of the Commerce Department. Other altitudes have been marked by state groups. A few peaks, including California's Mt. Whitney, have benchmarks from multiple surveys, which differ slightly in recorded altitude.

The Natchez Trace Parkway, a modern 442-mile-long road-way administered by the National Park Service, now parallels the old route. Near Tupelo, not far from Woodall Mountain, we parked beside the pavement then walked a short distance to a cleared segment of the original footpath. Earthen banks six feet high rose to the level of the surrounding terrain, the deeply-worn route testimony to the erosive power of millions of human footsteps. Stately hardwoods—tupelo and oak, sycamore and maple—arched over embankments and trail, filtering the bright sunlight through branches beginning to leaf out. Rotting leaves covered the trail, the soft mat of decaying vegetation silencing our footsteps. Birds sang loudly in the forest canopy. The late morning air was comfortably warm and held the crisp smell of spring.

I walked slowly, enjoying each quiet step and savoring the moment. The trail rose gently then curved left and leveled off. Thirteen neatly aligned headstones filled a small clearing beside the path, each marking the grave of a Confederate soldier. None of the deceased were individually identified; the battle in which they perished was not named. Probably they died in a "skirmish," one of countless Civil War engagements defending bridges, destroying supplies, or repelling small attacks. Thousands of soldiers from each side perished in such nameless and largely forgotten firefights, most without the honor of such neatly maintained graves.

The sunken path continued north but was uncleared beyond the cemetery. We retraced our steps, then early the next morning, as wisps of fog hovered over freshly planted fields, journeyed to Brices Cross Roads National Battlefield, site of a much larger and more widely known Civil War engagement twenty-five miles southwest of Mississippi's highest point. Here Union General William Tecumseh Sherman engaged the brilliant Confederate cavalry commander Nathan Bedford Forrest, vowing to "catch that devil Forrest if it takes all winter and bankrupts the national treasury." Sherman, however, accomplished neither, instead suffering a tactical defeat at Brices Cross Roads.

Although the battlefield is managed by the National Park Service, there was no visitor center, few interpretative signs, and only a tiny pocket map to guide us through this isolated area. Parking beside a historical marker, we walked a short distance down the road to photograph an aging barn located on the battlefield. Then we strolled another quarter-mile down this rural lane enjoying the cool, humid morning.

Returning I was startled to see three pickup trucks parked near our car. Five men stood outside, leaning against the trucks. It was obvious they weren't leaving any time soon.

I walked slowly, trying to appear calm, but stereotypes of "negative Mississippi" raced through my mind. Some of the most notorious murders of the civil rights era—Medgar Evers, Emmett Till, and the 1963 killings of three northern white freedom riders occurred here, as did more lynchings than in any other state.

"Howdy," I said, approaching my car and the group, camera clearly visible, hoping to show myself as the curious tourist I was.

"Morning," drawled one of the men at length. He spoke the word dryly.

Conversation generally follows an informally ritualized protocol in many regions of the south. Parties know the questions they want answered, but direct questioning is considered impolite.

"Nice morning," I volunteered, trying to study the men's facial expressions without making prolonged direct eye contact. They ranged in age from about thirty to near seventy; all had tanned, weathered features; none smiled.

"Yep, spring is here," another responded.

An uneasy silence followed. I decided to indirectly answer the yet unasked question. "So this whole area is part of the battlefield?"

"Yes," replied the oldest, a stately appearing man who had previously been silent. His neatly trimmed white hair protruded a short distance below the sides of a cap advertising a local feed mill. "The battle was all around here. Five, even ten miles away."

"Hmm," I acknowledged, briefly scanning the surrounding fields.

"You interested in the War Between the States?" inquired another older man, using the preferred southern terminology for the Civil War.

"Yes," I responded, before adding, "we're from North Carolina, vacationing and touring here in Mississippi." I did not elaborate nor mention highpointing, still feeling it a strange quest and difficult to explain, especially in a region where state summits are drive-ups.

"This was a big victory for Nathan Bedford Forrest, wasn't it?" I inquired, already knowing the answer. With the mention of the Confederate general's name, the men seemed to relax. As in most of the south, memories of this war run deep and here, a century and a third later, Forrest is still considered a hero.

Led by the older gentleman, the group described the battle, troop movements, and strategies as if they had just occurred, then told of unmarked battle sites and still-standing houses used as field headquarters and hospitals. For twenty minutes they shared memories, fact, and opinion. Their knowledge of the battle amazed me, but the depth of their emotions yet today about the Civil War was even more shocking.

The atmosphere had thawed. I thanked them, shook hands, and Sheryl and I drove away, following the back roads described, roads not shown on my little map, and visiting sites vividly detailed. An hour earlier, these historical locations, most unmarked by the Park Service, would have seemed little more than freshly planted fields of corn and cotton. Although I never fully understood all the troop movements the men described, nor each individual engagement during the two-day battle, I left the area, and Mississippi, with feelings of "positive Mississippi"—and a better realization of the underlying emotions here, emotions about the Civil War and related history that seemed deeper than in many other regions of the south.

The civil rights movement of the 1950s and 60s, another facet of the struggle for freedom and equality, is this region's second great defining event. On another southern excursion—en route to Florida's Britton Hill, the nation's lowest state highpoint—Sheryl and I traveled through central Alabama, arguably the heart of that twentieth century struggle.

Selma, a quiet town of 23,000 inhabitants sixty miles west of the state capital Montgomery, was the scene of perhaps the most graphic images of the civil rights movement. On March 7, 1965, a day now called "Bloody Sunday," 600 marchers crossed the Edmund Pettus Bridge, attempting to march to Montgomery, seeking the right to vote. As they descended from the elevated span over the Alabama River, horse-mounted deputies and

Alabama state patrolmen charged the marchers, lobbing tear gas into the crowd and beating unarmed people with nightsticks. Television cameras recorded the event; national networks interrupted regularly scheduled programming to air brutal images that shocked and outraged a nation.

But I found no mention of this bridge, or of the voting rights march, in any travel brochure or guidebook. I needed to inquire locally before learning that the bridge still exists, its location, and that it remains Selma's principal route across the Alabama River.

A remarkably scenic span, this bridge gracefully arches high over the water. Its painted metal beams glowed a soft burnt orange in the late afternoon light on this clear, spring day. Large black letters on the crosspiece between the parallel arches read "Edmund Pettus Bridge." It was as if time had stood still; the backdrop seemed unchanged from those grainy television images thirty-five years earlier.

A few cars crossed the four-lane span; an unobtrusive National Park Service kiosk was located nearby. We followed the same narrow sidewalk taken by the marchers that fateful spring day, ascending steadily to mid-river then descending steeply to the far bank where the confrontation had occurred, trapping the forward marchers at the bridge's base.

Cars passed, our presence evoking no apparent response. Then I knelt to photograph the scene. After just one photo, a car full of white teens slowed. With fists waving, fingers pointing, and horn honking, the adolescents jeered at us through open car windows as they passed, ever so slowly. Here too, it seemed, history had not been forgotten.

Two weeks after Bloody Sunday, marchers again crossed the Edmund Pettus Bridge toward Montgomery, this time accompanied by troops of the 82nd Airborne Division. Ordered to Alabama by President Lyndon Johnson, these federal soldiers scouted the route for snipers and guarded nighttime campsites while helicopters patrolled from above during the five-day march.

We followed that same route, U.S. Highway 80, today an aging roadway passing through quiet countryside. An uncomfortably hot April sun beat down on the scrubby trees and brush that are quickly reclaiming abandoned farms. Plowed soil looked dull and lifeless, depleted of nutrients taken decades earlier by

The Edmund Pettus Bridge, Selma, Alabama.

the annual cultivation of "King Cotton." Aging houses, small and outnumbered by trailers, were scattered widely across the landscape. Save for highway traffic, nothing moved.

Protected by federal forces, the marchers reached Montgomery without incident. There on the steps of the state capitol, below the portico where a century earlier Jefferson Davis had been inaugurated president of the Confederate States of America, the marchers rallied, demanding the right to vote.

Montgomery remains a city of history, irony, and contradiction. Standing beside the bronze star commemorating the exact location where Davis took the oath of office, I looked west, past the steps where the marchers had rallied, to a small brick building one block away. Dwarfed by modern state office buildings, this modest structure is Dexter Avenue Baptist Church where a young minister, Martin Luther King, Jr., rose to national prominence during the 1955 Montgomery bus boycott.

Three blocks further west, still within view of the capitol, is the Winter's Building. From here, in 1861, a telegram was dispatched ordering the shelling of Fort Sumter, the military action that started the Civil War. But immediately across the street is the bus stop from which Rosa Parks boarded a city bus one afternoon in 1955. When she refused to move from a seat designated for whites only, she was arrested, leading to the bus boycott—and the beginning of the modern civil rights movement.

Alabama, like much of today's south, is a contrast of affluent suburbs and struggling rural regions. A year earlier we had toured the northern half of the state and ascended Cheaha Mountain (2,405 feet), Alabama's loftiest peak—and the southernmost of the Appalachian state summits. Now en route from Montgomery to Florida's panhandle and Britton Hill, we passed through Sprague and Strata, Luverne, Brantley, and Opp—rural hamlets that once served a farm economy but today sport little more than boarded-up buildings and a few struggling businesses.

At the Florida state line we reached Florala, an aging town trying to maintain a well-kept appearance. But on this already-hot spring morning, no one was seen and nothing stirred along the town's wide main street. A small brick building, a remodeled gas station, occupied a prominent corner; hand-cranked gas pumps topped with clear glass cylinders stood in front. We stopped to photograph this well-preserved but now inoperable equipment, marveling at the town's eerie silence and feeling as though we were visiting an abandoned movie set.

Two miles southwest of Florala, a rectangular polished granite monument in Lakewood Park marks Florida's highest point, a sandy knoll barely a hundred yards above sea level. Picnic tables and comfort facilities grace the "summit plateau," and a short nature trail circles through the surrounding forested "wilderness," where some claim the highest mound of sand is located.

But summiting Britton Hill, all 345 feet of it, is fun. Like Iowa, one doesn't journey here for the physical challenge. At the nation's lowest state highpoint we walked the nature trail, picnicked, and posed for photos beside the summit marker.

It took five years and more than a half dozen trips to summit all the southern and southeastern highpoints, never reaching more than one per trip. But by following this deliberate pace, I was rewarded with fond and powerful memories—and a deeper understanding and appreciation of this complex region.

CHAPTER 6

A Real McCoy

The Central Appalachians

During my five year period of "highpointing denial," I visited few state summits outside of the south and southeast. One of these, however, was West Virginia, a state boasting itself as "wild and wonderful" and, like Mississippi, one that has struggled with hard economic times and a negative national perception.

A century ago, West Virginia was the southern flank of our nation's industrial heartland. Hardwood timber—oak, maple, hickory, and walnut—covered the mountainous landscape, while the nation's largest high-grade bituminous coal deposits lay beneath its surface. But it wasn't until the final decade of the nineteenth century that railroads cut deeply into these rugged mountains, allowing large-scale extraction of these twin pillars of West Virginia's fleeting prosperity. Yet workers realized little gain. When sawmills and factories closed, most people moved on; those who stayed endured some of the worst poverty in our nation.

Most factories have been shuttered for decades; many mines have closed and second-growth forests are reclaiming the once denuded landscape. Today, tourism and outdoor recreation are the state's main attractions.

En route to Spruce Knob (4,861 feet), West Virginia's highest point, Sheryl and I followed the New River north into some of the state's wildest and most rugged areas. The name New, however, is a misnomer. It is an old river—very old. Geologists believe it to be the planet's second oldest river (only the Nile is older), its winding channel pre-dating the uplift of the Appalachian

41

Mountains a half billion years ago.

The New's headwaters begin in the mountains of north-western North Carolina, the southerly of its twin forks flowing a half mile from my farm. A beautiful undammed river through my native state, it is one of the nation's longest unobstructed waterways.

However, it took a struggle to keep it that way. In the late 1960s, the Appalachian Power Company sought to dam the New near the Virginia border, creating hydroelectric power and two recreational lakes while inundating large portions of my home county. Determined local citizens—farmers and lawyers, housewives and journalists—fought to protect the river and their way of life.

The power company purchased the available land then sought to condemn the rest. But an influential Winston-Salem newspaper publisher, Wallace Carroll, championed the local cause. Through editorial persuasion and political power, the issue was brought before Congress, and in 1976 construction of the twin dams was blocked. The New remained free flowing, the North Carolina portion becoming one of the first federally designated Wild and Scenic Rivers.

On a warm June day, we followed the ancient waterway north to West Virginia, where over eons it has carved the deepest canyon east of the Rocky Mountains. Two thousand feet deep, the rugged landscape of the New River Gorge appears little touched by man. Only two bridges traverse the canyon while a solitary rail line parallels the river.

To experience this wild region more intimately, we descended the river via raft, a thrilling ride through spectacular scenery. Stately trees grew to the water's edge. Great blue herons stalked minnows in the clear water, while songbirds flitted nervously amongst shoreline vegetation. Hawks patrolled overhead. The early summer air was crisp and clean. The birds' spirited singing and harsh rasps of cicadas filled the air. But as rapids neared, the crescendo of rushing water intensified, its roar obliterating all other sounds, as paddlers and guide struggled to maneuver the inflated craft through rock-strewn rapids.

The river was clean; the canyon appeared pristine, and the ride was exhilarating.

The next morning, however, at the National Park Service's visitor center, I learned of the valley's human history. A century ago, the Gorge was a major industrial corridor. Company towns, often little more than hastily constructed shanties to house itinerant workers, crowded the riverside, while coal tipples and conveyors clung to steep slopes. Forests were felled for lumber, fuel, and housing; smoke from chimneys and industrial coking ovens filled the narrow valley.

After little more than two decades, however, the natural resources were depleted. New technology made the valley's coking process obsolete, and workers moved away. Nature began to reclaim the Gorge.

Today, ruins of this industrial past lay hidden beneath a leafy canopy. Following a trail cut by the Park Service, we walked nearly an hour to Kaymoor, one of the largest and best preserved of these sites. An abandoned coal tipple with rusting metal roof and decaying wooden sides perched against the steep hillside. Here, freshly mined coal had been screened and sorted then transported by conveyor to the coking ovens along the river's narrow flood plain, the canyon's only flat land.

Little is left of that conveyor today, just fragments of its frame scattered along a line that we followed downhill. Fifty feet from the water's edge, brush, vines, and saplings nearly obscured four parallel limestone structures, each a series of domed chambers covered with a large flat roof. Eight decades of accumulated soil and sand lay heaped against gray rocky walls. Two of the individual units, rounded rooms each twelve feet high, had been cleared and restored.

We peered into these beehive-shaped ovens where coal had been converted to coke, a fuel that burned hotter than wood, charcoal, or even coal itself. A dirty labor-intensive process was needed to produce this fuel, the only energy source that could generate the high temperatures needed for the blast furnaces of Pittsburgh's burgeoning steel industry. Each production run required from forty-eight to seventy-two hours. Coal was tightly packed into each oven, the door sealed, and the black rock heated without oxygen, driving off volatile gases and leaving the lightweight coke.

Tiny pieces of the porous gray fuel littered the ground as we crossed the rail line that had once hauled the coke north. At the river's edge I looked up at the canyon walls that would have held the gas, smoke, and soot in this valley. With each rain, treeless slopes would have eroded further, dumping tons of mud, garbage, and debris into the river. Briefly I imagined this industrial hell then chose instead to focus on nature's restorative powers and the beauty of the Gorge today.

From this canyon the river continues north, joining with the Gauley and forming the Kanawha before emptying into the Ohio. But we left the New, crossing the nation's longest single-arch steel bridge, a 1,700-foot-long span towering 876 feet above the water, en route to Spruce Knob, West Virginia's highest mountain.

Three state highpoints—Spruce Knob, Maryland's Backbone Mountain, and Pennsylvania's Mt. Davis—lie in nearly a straight line, eighty miles apart. Many highpointers summit all three in a single trip, some in a single day. But as in the southeast, Sheryl and I made separate trips for each.

Spruce Knob is the highest peak in the central Appalachians. Slightly less than a mile high, its summit is an alpine environment. Few deciduous trees survive here, and even hardy conifers are deformed—stripped of branches on their windward sides by fierce winter storms.

On a mild afternoon juncos foraged beneath a cover of low-lying vegetation. Mosses and ground-hugging flowers surrounded blueberries and huckleberries, stunted plants in full summer bloom. The landscape surrounding Spruce Knob looked pristine, but like the New River Gorge had been heavily logged—and had recovered remarkably

We ascended the square summit tower, alone atop the state, and enjoyed quiet solitude and magnificent views as a vulture rode thermals high above the peak. The mountaintop was rugged and isolated, the surrounding terrain steep and undeveloped.

No one joined us during our stay. From the open observation deck we looked across West Virginia at a nearly unbroken woodland where, except for the chestnut which was nearly exterminated by blight, most of the plant species present when Europeans arrived can still be found today. And although these trees have yet to reach the size and grandeur of those that met the logger's saw, nature is reclaiming West Virginia's natural beauty. We descended from the 25-foot-high platform to better see the alpine environment and tiny flowers surrounding the tower's base. For much of the afternoon we explored Spruce

Knob's summit, enjoying a peak—and an environment—as wild and wonderful as the state motto claims.

In hindsight The Dream began long before I stepped from the emergency department the final time. The opportunity for extended excursions began that night. So did the freedom, absence of schedules, emotions of "non-employment", and associated financial uncertainties. But before that last exit, as work conditions spiraled downward, diversions including travel and highpointing became ever-more important. As I tried to bridge a widening gap between reality and hope, thoughts of The Dream often sustained me.

During one crisis, Sheryl bought a now-long-lost magazine featuring a state highpointing article. Over the past decade, I had reached less than a dozen state summits—most of them in the southeast—and never more than two in one year. But this article described highpointing's unique difficulties in a lightly irreverent style and made attaining all fifty summits seem a worthy challenge.

I read and re-read the article, recalling my high school teacher's climbing ambitions, the pleasant memories of the state summits I had achieved, and the search through the atlas in an Iowa motel room after Jon and I had summited that state's unusual highpoint.

An epiphany occurred. Previously a vacation sideline, state highpointing could be a unifying theme—and goal—of The Dream. As my employer's financial condition grew ever weaker, and I believed that my job would soon end, highpointing trips became more frequent, yet work obligations kept them to little more than a week in length.

Two months after this personal revelation, Sheryl and I drove into the heart of coal country to Black Mountain (4,139 feet), Kentucky's highest point. No longer in "highpointing denial," I was now a serious highpointer on a quest that I hoped would take me to the top of each state in our nation.

Noisy trucks, trailing fine black coal dust and dark clouds of noxious diesel smoke, rumbled past strip mines and through hardscrabble Appalachian towns. The land appeared tired and spent, bulldozed and logged, stripped of its most obvious natural resources. But any wealth from decades of exploitation wasn't apparent. Aging houses and shuttered storefronts dominated slowly decaying towns, while mine tailings tumbled down deforested hillsides.

En route to Black Mountain we descended into the Tug Fork Valley, an isolated region dominated by the Tug Fork, a swiftly flowing mountain stream that here delineates the Kentucky-West Virginia border. In the 1880s, however, this river also separated two feuding clans—the Hatfields and McCoys. Though popular culture has portrayed the feud as a fight between two hillbilly bands, both families were large, solidly middle-class, and well respected in their communities.

No one is certain why the first killing—the 1882 stabbing of Ellison Hatfield by three of Randolph McCoy's sons—occurred, but the feud intensified after Ellison's brother, Anderson "Devil Anse" Hatfield, an ex-Confederate guerilla leader, executed the three perpetrators. Visiting journalists embellished facts as the violence continued for a decade, claiming twelve lives. The feud was already a legend when in 1897 a photojournalist posed the Hatfield clan, guns drawn and ready, in front of their rough-hewn barn. Thought a joke by the prosperous Hatfields, this tightly framed photo made it appear as if this aging structure was their home instead of the well-constructed two-story frame house in which they lived. Whether a joke or carefully crafted deception, this sensationalized photo has become the feud's defining and most enduring image.

Today, Matewan, a small West Virginia community that serves as the valley's commercial center, is a quiet town; Hatfields and McCoys reside together peacefully. But even after the last victim, a McCoy, was killed in 1890, violence again visited this isolated enclave.

I had come to learn more of this later event, the Matewan Massacre, a bloody incident of the West Virginia "mine wars" and one of the deadliest episodes in American labor history. But unfortunately the town's storefront museum was closed and looked as if it had been for some time. The downtown was nearly deserted late this pleasant weekday morning. Save for a bank, a hardware store, and some second-hand shops, few businesses remained.

I pressed my nose to the glass and peered into the darkened museum, hoping to see a schedule or attract the attention of someone who might let us in. Like much of Matewan the museum looked dated with few displays and no posted hours. As we turned to leave, fearing that our efforts would yield nothing but a quiet community and shuttered museum, I saw a smartly dressed woman in a neatly tailored business suit and high heels walking toward us. She looked out of place in this run down town.

Greeting us warmly, she asked if we wished to tour the museum. Despite our affirmative reply, she said that her boss, the bank president, had the only key and would not return until "after lunch." In the interim she suggested we tour Matewan, a town five blocks long and two wide.

Near Matewan's southern limit, where mountains, the Tug Fork, and a railroad squeeze the town's two streets ever closer, a brass plaque on a bullet-scarred wall marks the site of the gun battle known as the Matewan Massacre. I photographed these large caliber holes then crossed the "back street," for a larger view of the scene.

Then I noticed him, a short man, shirttail out and ball cap pulled low over his eyes, walking with a slight limp, slowly but steadily toward us. Half an hour earlier, we had searched downtown for someone, anyone with information about the museum and gun battle. But now, on the back street of a town that receives few visitors, I wasn't eager to engage in any lengthy discussions.

I tried to ignore him, but he limped directly toward me. "Hi," he said, extending his hand, "I'm Buster. Buster McCoy. A real McCoy."

I took his hand, acknowledging his greeting with a simple "hi." He appeared unkempt but friendly.

"Where you from?" he inquired forcefully.

"North Carolina," I said flatly. I knew little of the Matewan story and was uncertain how townspeople felt about their historical notoriety, especially when outsiders inquired of it.

"North Carolina," he repeated slowly, the words tailing off, half stating, half questioning. "I got a friend there," he blurted excitedly. "Statesville, you know. I drive through Mt.

Airy—Andy Griffith, Mayberry, you know."

I knew.

"Where you live?" he questioned.

"In the mountains." I never say Crumpler. No one has heard of it. No one can spell it. No one believes that a town still exists with a single frame building—post office, general store, and gas station combined—and that town signs for both directions are on the same signpost.

"I have relatives there," he said, referring to the mountains. "Where you live?" he again demanded.

"Ashe County, Jefferson, Crumpler." I ran the words together.

"Yea, I know." He became more excited. "My relatives, they left here. No jobs, you know. Doing good there. Insurance, real estate."

Now *I* was interested. "George McCoy?" I inquired, referring to one of our local businessmen.

"Yeah, he's my cousin—twice removed."

"And Elmer?"

"He's from here too," Buster said.

He then told of this valley's economic decline, as mining mechanization resulted in a slow but steady loss of jobs. With no other major industries and few nearby jobs, people were forced to move away. But despite prodding, Buster never revealed why he stayed.

"See the bullet holes in that building?" he asked, motioning toward the bullet-ridden brick wall I had just photographed. "Matewan Massacre," he declared.

"I am interested," I began, but Buster continued before I finished my sentence.

"Right here in Matewan, right by these railroad tracks," he said, pointing to the single rail line five feet behind me. He proceeded to detail the 1920 shootout between miners, local police, and armed "detectives" of the Baldwin-Felts Company, a private security firm employed by mine owners to enforce stringent company rules. After evicting six mining families from company housing, the hated detectives—thirteen in all—prepared to leave Matewan aboard the southbound train. An angry crowd gathered; a shot rang out and an hour-long gun battle ensued. When it ended, two miners and seven detectives lay dead, the town's mayor mortally wounded.

"Downtown there's a museum," Buster said, abruptly ending his narrative. "Go to the bank. They have the key."

I thanked Buster for the information and advice then asked if I could take his picture. "I want a picture of a real McCoy," I told him. With obvious pride, he graciously obliged.

After saying goodbye to Buster, we walked two short blocks returning downtown, where we met Sam McCoy, the bank's president and an authority on local history. Although he didn't elaborate if he was a "real McCoy," he detailed West Virginia's "mine wars" of the early twentieth century as we entered the rather spartan museum.

Coal was then America's chief energy source, he told us, as vital and profitable as oil is today. Supply threats, including attempts to unionize mineworkers, were harshly suppressed. But the miners labored in some of the nation's most difficult and dangerous working conditions and chafed under the owner's control, forced to live in company housing and paid in company scrip, a monetary substitute redeemable only at overpriced company-owned stores.

Violence had smoldered throughout West Virginia's coal-fields for a decade, but when the miner's hero, Matewan police chief Sid Hatfield, was gunned down on the McDowell County courthouse steps by Baldwin-Felts detectives in 1921, the state's miners erupted with rage. Led by World War I combat veterans, workers and owners organized private armies, recruiting volunteers from across the state. Miners seized company stores, commandeered trains, and at one point controlled 500 square miles of southern West Virginia. With thousands of men each, the armies constructed crude fortifications, dug trenches, and prepared for battle.

State police and militia could not suppress the unrest. Skirmishes broke out; pitched battles ensued. Owners dropped crude bombs from biplanes onto miner's positions. Still the workers held firm.

As the fighting intensified, President Harding ordered the U.S. Army into West Virginia to restore order. With the arrival of thousands of federal troops the violence abated, and both sides dispersed without the army firing a single shot. But little changed for the miners. It would take much of the next two decades, Sam told us as we finished touring the museum, before pay and working conditions significantly improved across this region.

The Matewan Massacre
This bloody episode of West Virginia's "mine wars" is depicted on the town's flood wall.

Leaving Matewan, we drove west up the winding road out of the Tug Valley and into Kentucky. Grass and saplings tried to cover scars on the recently mined landscape. The number of coal trucks increased as did the mines that gashed the mountainous terrain. Here the coal industry is modern, mechanized, and remarkably efficient. Even conventional strip mining is being replaced by the faster and more destructive process of "mountain-top removal," whereby much of a mountain is leveled to extract the coal beneath.

Black Mountain (4,139 feet), Kentucky's highest point, is still intact but on private land—coal company land. Written permission is now required to visit the highpoint, but when we turned off U.S. Hwy. 19 and followed a gravel road to the summit, there were no limitations.

The rocky peak was rough and uninviting. Scrubby trees blocked distant views while a communications tower jutted skyward from just below the highest point. There were no engraved markers or observation platforms, interpretative signs or picnic facilities. Only a solitary USGS disk embedded nearby denoted the state's summit.

Many highpoints were similarly unadorned a few decades ago with no monuments, markers, or registers. Early highpointers struggled to determine the correct mountain, obtain permission to enter private land, then climb to frequently unmarked summits, all without guidebooks or maintained trails to follow.

As I thought of these early highpointers and the challenges they faced, a pick-up truck, its company logo nearly obscured by dirt and coal dust, drove up the narrow gravel road, breaking the silence and ending our solitude. A lone workman wearing a clean gray uniform stepped out and walked briskly toward the tower, neither acknowledging our presence nor returning my wave. We chose not to linger, but again traversed the summit, this time returning to our car.

Descending from atop Kentucky, we looked across a scarred landscape. But the human scars I had learned of on this trip—and of those in Mississippi and Selma, Alabama—can be deeper and more difficult to heal than physical or ecological damage. These human stories, like others I would learn about while touring the nation, are well-known locally, if little-known nationally. But all are part of our national fabric—of fits and starts and mistakes made as we forged a nation. Some, like the bullet-ridden wall in Matewan are marked by simple plaques. Others, perhaps yet too difficult or painful to interpret, remain unmarked but not forgotten, still vibrant legacies in their respective regions.

CHAPTER 7

SILENCE

The Lower Mississippi Valley

On a muggy July night, I received the call adult children fear. My father was unresponsive and receiving CPR. Seventy-three, trim, and physically active, he had never been hospitalized in his life. However, he was the first male in his family to live past age sixty-five.

The code was over before I reached the hospital, an hour's drive away. The man who had been my friend, mentor, and role model, who had guided and advised me, even through my adult life, had passed on.

The loss seemed incomprehensible. My parents had been exceptionally close; during the fifteen years following my father's retirement I had never seen them apart. And they had frequently helped me, especially during my travels, handling finances and paying unexpected bills.

Shortly after my father's death, my mother asked me, an only child, to temporarily refrain from climbing. "I can't handle any more losses right now," she explained.

She didn't need to ask. I had no heart for climbing.

Time is the best, indeed the only, healer. But it is a terribly slow and painful process. A parental death is a permanent and irreplaceable loss. I have endured divorce, but healthier, happier relationships followed. However, a parent's unconditional love, present since before birth, can never be replaced.

I struggled with the loss—and its suddenness. There had been no warning, no anticipatory grieving, no thank-yous or goodbyes. But I held to the fact we had been happy, had visited two days earlier, and that my dad hadn't suffered.

52

Like each seemingly inconsequential step climbing a mountain, each day brought slow, almost imperceptible healing as I reluctantly realized and painfully accepted that life was forever changed. During the ensuing weeks and months, cherished memories of my father slowly filled the void of his passing.

Meanwhile I functioned mechanically—working as scheduled, completing necessary tasks, surviving each day but experiencing little joy. My job provided structure and stability but little solace as the hospital twice needed to be rescued from near-bankruptcy, once just a week from closing its doors.

As a new year began, I resumed highpointing—to Hawaii in January then to Louisiana, Arkansas and Missouri two months later. Plans for The Dream were now carefully crafted; with the financial woes faced by my employer, only its "official" starting date remained in doubt.

Spring is the south's finest season. Azaleas and dogwoods bloom as the frequently damp and cloudy weeks of winter give way to fresh, clear days, a brief delightful respite before summer's intense heat and humidity.

In March I drove to Louisiana and the Lower Mississippi Valley. Here highpointing is only slightly more challenging than in the southeast; drive-ups are replaced by short hikes such as the ¾-mile walk to Driskill Mountain, Louisiana's highest peak. Remarkably, however, it took two attempts to summit this 535-foot-high hill.

A year earlier, while returning from a medical conference in New Orleans, I had detoured to touch the state's highest point. However I had forgotten my guidebook, yet reasoned that Louisiana's lowly state summit should not be difficult to find. But the state's northwestern corner, where the highpoint is located, is hilly, the rolling landscape covered in scrubby pine forests. There was no dominant mountain or any sign indicating the state's highest peak. As memories of Iowa flashed through my mind, I began asking for directions.

Everyone I asked had heard of Driskill Mountain, and again, no one seemed shocked by the question. Directions to the unmarked "trailhead," the Mt. Zion Presbyterian Church parking lot on Route 507, were consistent but hiking instructions from there varied widely. Sans guidebook or map, I drove to the church, hoping that the trail, or at least the general path to the summit, would be apparent.

At first it was. An abandoned logging road traversed a recently timbered ridgeline toward a wooded, gently rounded hill. But shortly after entering the forest, the path split; the road continued downhill while a well-used but unmaintained foot-path ascended steeply to the right, leading to the highest nearby terrain.

I ascended past scattered beer cans and assorted litter to an unmarked forested summit. Grass and vegetation beneath the trees had been flattened, but there was no summit sign or survey marker. All surrounding land was lower, and although views were partially blocked by trees, I could see no higher hills nearby. Disappointed by the unmarked, nondescript summit, I took a photo then mentally checked Driskill off as my thir-teenth, and thus far least interesting highpoint.

During the following months, however, the uneasy feeling that I might have climbed the wrong hill persisted. Some high-pointers are sticklers for details, arguing which point of a sum-mit expanse might be a quarter-inch higher, or if a particular mound of dirt was formed naturally, qualifying it for highpoint consideration or man-made, rendering it ineligible. Many of these discussions I find trivial. Atop a mountain, I always touch the highest obvious point, but do not worry if, on an otherwise flat summit, I fail to step upon the highest speck of dust, or trample the highest plant or prettiest flower. But I do want to top out on the correct mountain. Had I missed Driskill entirely?

Months later I found summit photos on the Web. A stone cairn and wooden sign marked the state's highest point; a sum-mit register was nearby, and the entire area was surrounded by a litter-free area of packed red earth. I had driven hundreds of miles, sought directions, and hiked forty-five minutes—and had not even been on the correct mountain.

I vowed to do better. For my second attempt I brought not one but two guidebooks, having recently purchased Paul Zumwalt's *Fifty State Summits*, plus photos and maps downloaded from the Web. In the church parking lot, I loaded my pack with food, water, compass, jacket, maps, and guidebooks, determined to find the correct peak.

The logged landscape appeared unchanged from the

previous year. Dry, brittle pine branches lay scattered, their needles long lost. A few hardy blackberry bushes and scrawny vines struggled to survive in the dry, bleached soil. No animals or birds—and very few weeds—survived in this barren environment.

The scrubby pine forest seemed inviting after passing this lifeless debris. Songbirds chirped shrill alarms before flitting deeper into the woods. Following guidebook instructions I turned left—downhill—along the logging road, bypassing the trail I had ascended the previous year.

Within a few yards I encountered a parked SUV. Nearby, a young couple, Nan and Steve, with their two pre-school-aged daughters wandered the rutted path. This was their first highpointing vacation they told me, proudly relating that Driskill would be their fifth state summit of the week. Both adults appeared tired, unable to locate the summit trail. "This is our hardest highpoint yet," Nan said, breathing rapidly, "much more difficult than I ever expected."

As we talked I noticed a sign, nailed ten feet over their heads, pointing towards Driskill's summit. When the couple asked for directions, I confidently pointed to the sign, not having the heart in the fading afternoon light, to tell them that this was my second attempt. As they rested I hurried up the trail, found the summit and shouted back the news.

This summit was well marked and neatly maintained, far different from the litter-strewn knob that I stood upon the previous year. Steve, Nan, and the children soon topped out, the parents flushed and perspiring from exertion, the children excited at having climbed a "real mountain."

After summit photos, including one prominently displaying the all-important guidebooks, we shared snacks and discussed highpointing. Highpointers are a diverse group—aging baby-boomers and physically fit retirees, families seeking outdoor adventure, and experienced hikers and mountaineers attempting new challenges. Most are congenial, out-going and non-competitive, striving for personal goals and pushing individual limits, often with no thought or desire of climbing all fifty state summits.

I showed my guidebooks to Nan and Steve and told them of the Highpointers Club, a 2,900-member national organization that I would join within the year. Like many others, this young couple had begun highpointing as a family activity as they toured the country. Unaware of the challenges posed by the tall western peaks, they hoped together to reach as many state summits as possible.

We talked until the sun nearly touched the western horizon. The family wished to linger and enjoy the hard-won summit, but I needed lodging for the night. It was a straightforward 200-yard descent to their vehicle but a ¾-mile walk to mine. I wished them well in their travels and highpointing then started down. After rounding the trail's first bend, just out of the family's sight, I heard a young voice call plaintively, "Mister, please don't leave us. We'll die out here."

I took a few steps back, again in view of the family. Nan and Steve, embarrassed and red-faced, were laughing. After reassuring their youngest daughter that she had two excellent mountain guides, she smiled and relaxed as I resumed descending.

The next morning I met a family friend in Murfreesboro, Arkansas, at the Crater of Diamonds State Park, the nation's only diamond mine. Fifty years earlier "Uncle" Dave had met my parents while he and my father attended National Cash Register's technical education school in Dayton, Ohio. Although never living closer than 800 miles, the friendship flourished through letters, visits, and further corporate training. Uncle Dave knew me as an infant, visited as I grew up, and kept in touch during college and medical school, nurturing my interest in Native American culture, Civil War history, and rock collecting. He and his wife paid an unexpected visit a week after my father's death, bringing solace and even a little cheer during that dark time. A youthful 70-something retiree, he still possessed the indomitable optimism necessary for rock hounds and for years had invited me to "come look for the big one" at the world's only public diamond mine.

The "mine" was far different than I had expected. There were no rock outcroppings, mining equipment, shafts or excavations—only thirty acres of bulldozed Arkansas earth plowed into giant furrows. Heavy rain had made the field a muddy wallow; a steady drizzle made it even softer and more slippery. Fortune seekers crowded beneath open-sided metal roofed shelters washing buckets of dirt looking for small "greasy-appearing" pebbles, the typical appearance of an uncut diamond.

But this nondescript field is the heavily eroded surface of an ancient volcanic pipe where, under intense heat and pressure, diamonds were formed deep within the earth's crust. Following eons of uplift and subsequent erosion, the first was discovered here in 1906. Seventy thousand have been found since, averaging a respectable quarter-carat each. Twenty percent are gem quality including the largest, a 40.23-carat beauty named "Uncle Sam," unearthed in 1924.

Uncle Dave and I talked and shared memories as we washed away mud, sifting for diamonds. Three hours later we had accumulated a dozen promising-looking pebbles. Showing them to a park ranger, an identification expert, we hoped to hear the shrill siren that signaled a diamond discovery. Only once all morning had the siren sounded. Unfortunately we did not hear it again.

Vowing to return some day for the elusive "big one," we said good-bye, and I drove west toward Magazine Mountain (2,753 feet), Arkansas' highest point. Here in the west-central portion of the state, the Ouachitas, a series of mountain ranges barely 100 miles long, rise steeply above broad river valleys. Picturesque and heavily forested, they are among the few North American ranges with an east-west orientation.

The road to the summit cuts deeply into the steep, rocky flank of the long ridge that is Magazine Mountain. A well marked hiking trail gently ascends the final half-mile to the broad, forested summit, also known as Signal Hill.

Soft light filtered through still-bare trees this early spring day warming the tan earth. Except for the occasional singing of a lone sparrow atop the forest canopy, there was silence—no wind, no leaves rustling or insects chirping, not even the sound of a chipmunk scurrying along the forest floor. Nor were there human sounds—radios, traffic, or the crescendo whine of distant chainsaws—that frequently drift into all but our most isolated wilderness areas.

Instead there was silence—absolute, profound silence. After the sparrow flew off, I was alone atop Arkansas. Propping my backpack against a nearby tree I sat down, marveling at the absence of sound. I loved the intense quietness and did not move to avoid snapping twigs, moving dried leaves, or even creating the soft scratching of coarse fabric rubbing against itself. An expected short summit visit lengthened to a half-hour, then an hour, as I sat enveloped by the sound of silence.

I don't know how long I might have stayed, transfixed by this rare phenomenon, but I gradually became aware of a distant, guttural rumble that slowly, steadily grew in intensity. The tranquility broken, I was startled to realize these sounds were from construction equipment ascending the road to the trailhead.

There were plans, I later learned, to develop this peak and surrounding state park into a multi-use recreational area with campgrounds, paved parking and a $20 million conference center. Development, proponents claimed, would make the park more accessible, increase tourism, and provide the region with a much needed economic boost.

But once more, silence will be banished—permanently.[5] As I returned to my car, walking toward the increasing din with a sense of unease bordering on anger, I was thankful to have summited this peak before "improvements" had been forced on it. I had seen Magazine Mountain at its best, enjoyed a spring morning with glorious silence and was deeply moved by this simple yet rare event. A straightforward walk-up had resulted in a remarkable experience—and thus far my most memorable state summit.

Before leaving Arkansas I wished to learn more of two native sons, Bill Clinton and Sam Walton, who loomed large on the world stage during the last quarter of the twentieth century. From Magazine Mountain I made the short drive to Hot Springs, Arkansas, boyhood home of the forty-second president and a town famous for hot water—850,000 gallons of it—that pours from the base of Hot Springs Mountain each day.

A prosperous retirement community and horseracing mecca, this area was first visited by Europeans in 1542, Hernando De Soto writing in that year of soaking in these naturally heated waters. Three centuries later, and predating the creation of our first national park by four decades, these springs were desig-

---

[5] Silence was indeed banished. The Lodge at Magazine Mountain, an upscale facility with swimming pool, fitness center, and in-room internet access, opened May 2006. Nightly rates range from $129 to $429. With thirteen adjacent cabins, the project's final price was $33 million.

nated the country's first "reservation," protecting them from private exploitation and ensuring public access. Their popularity soared, and by the second half of the nineteenth century, tens of thousands of bathers came each year for relaxation, recreation, and the purported curative powers of the hot mineral rich waters. Ornate, Victorian-styled bathhouses were built beside the springs, structures that today are being restored as part of the Hot Springs National Park.

William Jefferson Clinton, born in the small southwestern Arkansas town of Hope, moved to this city at the age of six, spending his formative years here before graduating from the local high school. Yet I saw no signs or public acknowledgement of the President's roots. Residents seemed reluctant to discuss Clinton, the years he lived here, or his tenure as Arkansas' governor. It was even difficult to learn the location of his boyhood home.

With directions from the National Park Service, I eventually found the large, privately owned but now vacant two-story frame house. Perched atop a prominent hill not far from bathhouse row, it is marked by a small plaque, barely visible from the busy street. Standing on the front sidewalk I photographed the well maintained structure. No passersby stopped; no one seemed to care; and at no time during my visit to Hot Springs did anyone show pride in, or a desire to discuss, their famous native son.

In Bentonville, however, a small town in the state's northwestern corner, there was civic pride and even personal affection for the late Sam Walton. "Mr. Sam," as he was commonly known, purchased his first store, a Ben Franklin 5- and 10-cent store on the town's main square, in 1950. By treating customers with fairness and honesty, his business prospered. During the next decade he expanded to larger stores in nearby cities en route to creating Wal-Mart, today the world's largest retailer. That first store in downtown Bentonville is now a museum chronicling the growth of Wal-Mart and describing the retailing innovations and famously modest lifestyle of Sam Walton.

However, the most interesting and ironic story about the retail giant's early years came not from the museum but from my friend, Uncle Dave. Four decades earlier, while installing cash registers at a new store, he had met Sam Walton. Minutes before the store's grand opening, Mr. Sam told the gathered

Birth of an Empire
This Bentonville, Arkansas building, formerly a Ben Franklin 5-and-10, was Sam Walton's first store. Today it houses a museum documenting the life of "Mr. Sam" and Wal-Mart, the retailing giant he created.

employees that this was his fifth and probably final store.

He was wrong—by more than 6,700.

From Bentonville I drove north into Missouri, bypassed the commercial development, neon lights and country music of Branson, and traveled to Taum Sauk Mountain (1,772 feet), Missouri's highest peak. Deep in the heart of the rugged Ozarks, Taum Sauk could be called the epicenter of state highpointing.

Here lived the late Jack Longacre, founder and first president of the Highpointers Club. "Guru Jakk" (with 2 k's), as he was fondly known to club members, was the seventh person to reach all 50 state summits. After climbing Wyoming's Gannett Peak, Jack wrote a letter published in 1987 by *Outside* magazine stating his accomplishment and inquiring if there were other "highpointers." The response was modest, but the following year Jack and seven others formed the Highpointers Club. He served as president, treasurer, membership chairman, and newsletter editor—all at the same time.

Unfortunately, when I visited Taum Sauk Mountain I knew little about, and was not yet a member of, this club. Driving to the summit I passed a hand-lettered wooden sign stating "Highpointers Club" with an arrow pointing to a rutted dirt road leading into the woods. As a non-member, I was afraid I might be unwelcome. I had yet to learn of Jack and his legendary hospitality. Regrettably I never met this remarkable climber who for years welcomed visitors to this mountain, encouraged highpointers, and removed litter from beside the summit road. Jack Longacre died of cancer in 2002.[6]

Today a Missouri state park, Taum Sauk's summit is the nation's most elegantly designed and tastefully developed state highpoint. A gracefully curving, wheelchair-accessible concrete walkway leads from the paved parking area up a slight incline to the forested summit. A gray rhyolite boulder surrounded by fine gravel, its exact altitude—1772.68 feet above sea level—inscribed on a polished granite plaque, marks the state's highest point. To the side, a shaded bench permits rest and repose atop Missouri's state summit.

Otherwise the hilltop remains in its natural state with no large monuments, observation decks, or communication towers—and no conference center. Sitting on the bench five feet from the summit boulder I ate lunch, enjoying the scenery and surrounding forest. Other "summiters" strolled up, more out of curiosity it seemed than a determination to reach Missouri's highest point. Many were RVers, some on their annual migration north from their Texas wintering grounds, others touring the Ozarks en route to Branson. After exchanging a few pleasantries they returned to their homes on wheels, walking along the same paved path, their feet never stepping upon the Ozark earth.

Though little time remained before needing to return home, I wanted to experience the rugged beauty of the undeveloped Ozarks. Leaving the smooth concrete pathway I descended to the Ozark Trail, crossing exposed boulders and weathered scree down Taum Sauk's southwestern flank.

The landscape was rugged and wild; forested peaks rose steeply above deeply cut valleys. Once more I was alone with nature—the RV crowd, pavement, and concrete half a mile

---

[6] Even death did not stop Jack Longacre's highpointing. "Guru Jakk's" final request was that his ashes be scattered atop the fifty state summits, a project completed by club members in 2004.

behind but a world away. Insects buzzed loudly this cloudless spring day, while a flock of crows took flight upon my approach. The trail was rocky, surrounding vegetation sparse and stunted, struggling for its very existence in the thin soil that covered the steep slopes. The air was brisk and clean, while the sun provided pleasant warmth.

Below the summit the dark rhyolite was replaced by pale weathered limestone. Bleached by sun and time to a cream color, these sedimentary rocks and surrounding low vegetation gave the slope an arid appearance. Beneath the bright sun the area seemed more a desert park than a trail in the often rainy Ozarks.

One hundred yards later, however, I heard sounds of falling water, a foot-wide stream cascading down a series of boulders and steeply angled steps. Cool mist drifted through the air; ferns and mosses flourished beside the water. Here at Mina Sauk Falls, named for a legendary Indian chief, I rested, enjoying the warm sun, soothing sounds and tranquility of nature, and the wildness and solitude of the Ozarks.

I wished to linger, but couldn't. It was time to return to North Carolina. Although I looked forward to seeing Sheryl and enjoying the Appalachian spring, I knew as I returned to my car and began the journey home that I was facing a very uncertain future.

CHAPTER 8

DOWNHILL

The Northeast

For seven years I enjoyed professional success and personal happiness in this small rural North Carolina hospital that now struggled to survive. Improved roads, medical specialization, and regionalization of healthcare made this institution that had served community needs for a half century obsolete. Like an elder with an incurable disease, its demise was imminent. Gloom prevailed as insolvency neared.

Although lives would be disrupted, there was little bitterness, instead resignation and anticipatory grieving as patients and staff chatted freely. The depth of emotion and gratitude, even when family members recalled deaths of loved ones, amazed me, and such reminiscing increased as the hospital's closure approached.

As emergency department medical director, however, I remained point man and buffer between physicians and corporation, a national firm that still sought to balance its ledger and correct past investment blunders at the expense of its physicians. Financial difficulties and contract revisions had left raw emotions and strained relationships. Scheduling nightmares, payment disputes, and administrative issues took ever-increasing portions of my day—and my energy. Each week brought further problems, each payday renewed anxiety about if, or how much, we would be paid.

Beneath a calm façade, I felt anger and grief, doubt and fear.

Yet the hospital survived months longer than I had expected. I delayed climbing Alaska's Mt. McKinley and cancelled a planned excursion to Oregon's Mt. Hood. Finally in June, I opted for a shorter trip to New Jersey and New England, timed to follow this region's infamous "mud season" and allow Sheryl, on summer break from teaching, to join me.

"Mud season" is more than an aesthetic inconvenience. From late April until early June, rain and melting snow turn trails into wallows and rocky ravines into small creeks. Newly hatched swarms of mosquitoes and biting flies add to the miserable conditions. To reduce erosion and protect fragile environments, hiking and climbing during this period are strongly discouraged, and some trails, including those to the state highpoints of New York and Vermont, are temporarily closed.

Three miles east of the tri-state junction of New York, Pennsylvania, and New Jersey, we exited Interstate 84 and drove a short distance to the Garden State's highpoint. Alone among state summits, it carries the simple moniker of High Point, and not surprisingly, is located in High Point State Park. Despite the unimaginative name and New Jersey's reputation as a heavily populated and industrialized state, this region, fifty-five miles west of New York City, is rural, hilly, and forested.

The park is tastefully developed and well maintained. Lake Marcia, a crystal-clear lake, fills the valley beneath the gently rounded mountain. A paved road skirts the water's edge then ascends steeply up the 1,803-foot-high peak. Atop the summit, a 220-foot-tall granite obelisk, the tallest monument on any state highpoint, honors New Jersey's wartime veterans.

The air was still and clear this warm June day. Forested mountains, more like the southern Appalachians and Ozarks than any I had expected in this populous region, extended west to the Poconos and north to the Catskills. The Delaware Water Gap, one of America's great river corridors, lay hidden in a forested valley three miles away.

Atop New Jersey we touched the monument, a 1930 gift from Anthony Kuser, a philanthropist and former president of the South Jersey Gas and Electric Lighting Company. But the 70-year-old spire was closed for repairs, restoration, and sandblasting. As we strolled around its base and enjoyed the scenery and early summer sun, I noticed a slightly built man struggling with

High Point State Park
The nation's tallest state summit structure, a 220-foot-tall monument,
stands atop the New Jersey hill named High Point.

a small camera atop a flimsy tripod. Dressed in business attire
sans tie, he looked out of place in this rustic park.

I volunteered assistance, an offer readily accepted. He too
was a highpointer, having driven two hours following an early
morning business meeting in New York City to reach this, his
sixth state summit. But he was in a hurry and never introduced
himself, requesting just two snapshots in front of the monument. As he quickly packed tripod and camera to return for a
midafternoon flight to Illinois, he related his goal of climbing
all fifty state summits. "I wish to visit all the states," he told
me, "and I thought reaching each state's highest point would be
an easy way to remember which I had visited." Then without
another word, wave or good-bye, as thoughts of Rainier, Hood,
Denali, and many easier methods to remember states flashed
through my mind, the businessman scurried off.

Less than half a mile from New Jersey's summit is a high-
altitude wetland, home to the most northerly stand of Atlantic
white cedar. Shafts of sunlight cut through the forest canopy and
reflected off the water's dark surface as we walked along a path
of wooden planks. This mountaintop swamp was a strange land.

Insect-eating plants thrived in acidic, nitrogen-depleted soil; mosses and ferns clung to tree trunks, hung from branches, and rose from the damp muck; and cedars, some a millennium old and among the oldest trees east of the Mississippi River, towered above all. And around everything was the water, clear and glistening brown, and seldom more than a quarter-foot deep.

We followed the shifting walkway, a mile-long path three boards wide. Each trio was wired to the next half a foot away, and each sank gently beneath the weight of our footsteps, creating gurgling sounds as wood pushed into the underlying muck. Noisy bumblebees and large dragonflies droned across our path; a lone blue jay's shrill call pierced the air. Dark water, stained by tannin from decaying vegetation, reflected the lighter-colored cedars, blue sky, and cumulus clouds.

We walked quietly through this land of sedges and carnivorous plants. Diminutive sundews grew where hummocks of soil pierced the water's surface, and glistening droplets clung like early morning mist to the plant's rounded leaves. But this shiny gelatinous substance is a lethal trap, a sticky secretion that entices, ensnares, and ultimately digests hapless insects. North America's largest insectivorous plant, the pitcher plant, also thrived in this environment and was in full bloom, its foot-tall flowers attracting insects seeking water and nectar. But after entering the vertical yellow blossoms, its victims cannot escape up the smooth tubular sides. Exhausted they die and are digested in the flower's base, providing the plant with vital nutrients.

This was the most unusual mountain hike I've ever taken. Less than sixty miles from our nation's largest metropolis, we moved alone through this primal landscape, an environment probably little changed since dinosaurs walked upon the planet.

I am not a "city person." I enjoy museums and art galleries, nice restaurants, and inspired architecture, but detest the noise, traffic, and hyper-retailing that characterize most metropolitan areas. However, en route to New England, we planned one detour into New York City's vast metropolis—the Hudson River Valley.

Once America's most important river, this valley was home to many of the young nation's renowned writers and artists. Washington Irving and James Fenimore Cooper wrote here, setting their classics *The Legend of Sleepy Hollow* and *The*

Leatherstocking Tales in the Valley. Here too, in a style later known as the Hudson River School, Thomas Cole and Asher Durand, Frederick Edwin Church and Albert Bierstadt painted dramatic landscapes. And here, early New Yorkers sought nature and solitude at what they considered the edge of the American wilderness, a half-day horseback ride upriver from New York City.

Today, aging towns line the lower Hudson, the river recovering from decades of pollution and industrial abuse. In Newburgh, a decaying city sixty miles upriver from New York City, we exited the interstate, descending to the water's edge. Once-glorious brick houses, many now abandoned, gutted, or boarded up, lined the bluffs overlooking the town's waterfront. The scene was depressing and uninviting, the gloom worsening as twilight deepened and evening fog settled.

There is little to remind visitors of Newburgh's storied past. But during the spring of 1783, in one of our nation's most pivotal moments, General George Washington met here with his fellow officers. The soldiers were disgruntled, angry about delayed pay, and sought Washington's approval to overthrow Congress and establish the general as king.

During the emotional discussion, Washington listened without saying anything. The aging warrior then rose and strode slowly to the front of the crowded room. He enumerated reasons why he wouldn't assist the conspirators, nor accept a monarchy or military dictatorship. As the men listened intently, Washington took a carefully folded paper from his pocket, a letter from the Continental Congress explaining the young nation's near insolvency. He struggled to read the document, then stopped, and with great theater slowly put on a pair of glasses.

"Gentlemen," he continued, "you will permit me to put on my spectacles, for I have not only grown gray but almost blind in the service of my country." Few but Washington's closest aides knew the general now required reading glasses. This, the first sign of their leader's fraility, stunned subordinates. But the general's words and dramatic presentation produced the desired effect; the conspiracy collapsed, saving the republic.

North of Newburgh, the Hudson is wide and straight, more a ribbon-like lake than a river nearing the sea. From Albany to the Atlantic, 140 miles, the Hudson drops just five feet, its negligible current reversed by twice-daily tides, the effects of which reach upriver past Albany. South of Newburgh, however, the river narrows, squeezing through the Palisades and Highlands, short chains of heavily eroded hills that rise steeply above the water. Yet even here the Hudson deviates little, its erosive powers having leveled nearly everything in its path.

But a flat-topped hill a dozen miles downstream from Newburgh never yielded to the water's power. Here at West Point Americans built their most strategic Revolutionary War fort, a lynchpin to keep the British from seizing the Hudson Valley and cutting the fledgling nation in two. The fortress was nearly impregnable; as warships slowed to negotiate the river's bend, they were exposed to cannon fire from three sides.

In the spring of 1778, engineers added yet another obstacle. With military genius, or perhaps desperate ingenuity, a 1,500-foot-long chain was stretched from West Point across the Hudson to Constitution Island. This barrier of 800 wrought iron links, each weighing 125 pounds, was floated atop forty log rafts to keep it at the water's surface.

The strategy succeeded. The chain was never seriously challenged, and the British never captured the Hudson Valley.

West Point, today the site of the United States Military Academy, is the army's oldest continuously commissioned facility. Patches of fog, yet to be consumed by the midmorning sun, hovered over the river and clung to forested hillsides when we arrived. Except for a solitary powerboat cutting white arcs in the water below, river and valley looked soft, quiet, and undeveloped, perhaps little different from when Henry Hudson sailed past here in 1609 searching for a water route to the Orient.

But forged bronzes and sculpted granites stood atop Monument Point, a stark contrast to the soft hazy forms near the river. Surrounded by carved spheres and weathered cannon, the Western Hemisphere's tallest polished granite shaft reached skyward. Known as the "Battle Monument," this elaborate memorial honors West Pointers' service (at least those remaining loyal to the Union) during the War of the Great Rebellion, as nineteenth century northerners termed the Civil War.

Nearby, an iron chain surrounded a small pile of broken stone atop an otherwise empty concrete pad. Shiny with black enamel, the metal appeared as though it had once encircled a now-missing sculpture. But these thirteen links, one for each of the original colonies, are the only surviving remnants of the great chain that blocked the Hudson during the Revolutionary War. Few visitors slowed to look at this simple shrine; fewer paused to learn its history. Yet among the heroic sculptures and towering memorials, I found this monument the most moving—a tribute to the ingenuity, resourcefulness, and resolve that secured our nation's freedom.

Before leaving the military academy, I wanted to see one more monument, the memorial most visited by cadets especially before exams. Honoring John Sedgwick, a divisional commander killed during the Civil War, the sculpture is small by West Point standards. But spinning the rowels of the general's spurs is believed to bring good luck. Though not particularly superstitious, when no one was looking I reached up and gave the worn discs a spin.

We were now ready to cross the Hudson and ascend New England's highpoints.

Encompassing six states northeast of the Hudson River, New England is geographically compact, its area smaller than Missouri's. Three of this region's state highpoints—Connecticut, Massachusetts, and Vermont—form a nearly straight line east of the Hudson Valley.

We began in the southern Berkshire Mountains, seeking Connecticut's highest geographical point, the nation's only state summit reached by walking downhill. Yes, downhill. Unique among state highpoints in not being at least a subsidiary peak, this unnamed point 2,380 feet above sea level is where the Connecticut state line traverses the south slope of Mt. Frissell, whose summit, 100 feet higher, is located in Massachusetts.

Connecticut certainly doesn't boast of this dubious distinction. Bear Mountain, five miles away and sixty-four feet lower, is correctly claimed as the state's highest *peak*, shown prominently on state maps and well marked by road signs. However, highpointers do not seek the highest peak but the highest geographical *point*, so to the nondescript "green stake on the south side of Mt. Frissell," we went.

Two hiking routes lead to the stake: one, a partially overgrown footpath passing near the tri-state marker (New York,

Connecticut, Massachusetts); the other, a well-maintained trail traversing Mt. Frissell's summit then descending to the high-point. We opted for the latter, a delightful hike through forests still sporting late spring's light green leaves. Songbirds sang in the early morning coolness. Forested slopes appeared pristine; oaks and maples, birches and hickories grew tall and straight, as though these mountains had never heard a logger's saw or seen a factory.

But in these northwestern Connecticut hills, the colonial iron industry had flourished. In pyramidal stone ovens four stories tall, locally mined iron ore was melted, purified then cast into slabs. Forests were felled for lumber and fuel. Crudely built dwellings housed itinerant workers, creating "camps" that differed little from those of the Appalachian coalfields a century later. But when natural resources were exhausted, the ovens were abandoned and workers moved on. As in West Virginia's New River Gorge, nature reclaimed this former manufacturing region.

Ascending Mt. Frissell, we hiked through one of these recovering forests. Trees were closely spaced, but few trunks measured a foot in diameter. This young forest was vastly different from the woodlands recorded by early European chroniclers who wrote of widely spaced trees with trunks up to five feet in diameter, open forest floors, and a leafy canopy so dense that a squirrel could travel 100 miles without touching the ground.

Mt. Frissell is neither Massachusetts' nor Connecticut's highest point, but the rocky peak did have a summit register. Atop the mountain we rested, perusing the lengthy notebook. Many entries were from highpointers, most either disparaging Connecticut's highpoint or boasting of totals achieved. A peculiar exchange began after one man reported climbing all twenty-two state summits west of the Mississippi River. "What should I do now?" he wrote. Answers—some thoughtful, others inane—were inscribed by subsequent hikers, although there was no evidence the original writer ever returned to read the responses.

We signed our names and walked downhill to the state "summit." The trail was little more than a thin corridor through brush and forest, its surface packed by hundreds of feet tramping a narrow path. A tenth-mile later, a piece of faded survey tape hung limply from a nearly buried brass stake. There was no monument, register, or USGS marker. Two steps from the trail I placed my foot atop the metal post marking Connecticut's highest point.

There was no rush of exultation or sense of jubilation; neither poetry nor beautiful prose filled my mind. The highpoint was a rough looking site dug from the rocky hillside, views blocked by dense brush and stunted trees. Here the forest was shorter and thinner than in the cove through which we had ascended; twisted trees eked out an existence on a thin veneer of coarse tan soil wedged between closely spaced gray boulders. Vegetation and soil appeared tired and spent. Yet we stood atop another state, a highpoint remarkable for its barrenness and unique in its topography, a site scratched from the earth by fellow hikers, unmarked and unmaintained by the state.

We did not linger. After snapping a few photos, we walked to a nearby rocky outcrop to relax and enjoy the view across Connecticut. Forested hills, like receding waves, stretched south to the horizon. No farms or villages, houses or clearings were seen, hidden by a nearly unbroken canopy of trees. The air was crisp, but the morning sun warmed the rocks around us as we enjoyed the peaceful solitude of Mt. Frissell's southern flank.

Whenever practical I descend via a different route, returning through varied landscapes, facing new challenges but experiencing more of a mountain's environment. Already partway down Mt. Frissell, we continued along the alternate route, a rocky trail that ultimately deteriorated to little more than a slash through tall vegetation. Looping slightly, this path passed within fifty feet of the tri-state junction of New York, Massachusetts, and Connecticut.

In the United States there are sixty-two points where three states touch. Thirty-eight are on dry land, the rest beneath rivers, lakes, or reservoirs. And, like state highpoints, 14,000-foot-high peaks, or state capitols, there are enthusiasts who seek to reach them all. Jack Parsell is the best known among them. The tenth person to summit all fifty state highpoints, he became the first to also reach each state's lowest point. Seeking additional challenges, he journeyed to each of the "dry land tri-state corners," as he called them, completing all by 1999 and publishing a guidebook the following year.

Although I have little interest in these corners, I couldn't resist a 50-foot detour. But like Connecticut's highpoint, this tri-state site was unusual, its four-foot-tall stone marker erected in 1898 engraved with only two state names. Citing colonial land grants, Connecticut claims a more distant boundary and has yet to officially accept the widely recognized state line—or allow its name carved onto this granite shaft.

After touching three states, we returned to the car and left Connecticut, its disputed tri-state junction and unusual state highpoint behind. Following Route 7 we continued through the Berkshires toward Mt. Greylock (3,487 feet), Massachusetts' highest point. The Berks, as they are commonly called, are among the world's most picturesque mountains, a short chain of gently rounded and heavily forested hills extending from northwestern Connecticut to southern Vermont. Interspersed with broad valleys filled with horse farms, covered bridges and quintessential New England towns, this region has been home to writers, artists, and intellectuals. Suffragette Susan B. Anthony was born here; Daniel Chester French, sculptor of the Lincoln Memorial, worked here; and Oliver Wendell Holmes, William Cullen Bryant, and Herman Melville all wrote here.

But Norman Rockwell is the area's most famous figure. The twentieth century's leading commercial illustrator, he is best known for his *Saturday Evening Post* covers—323 in all—published over forty-seven years. For a quarter-century Rockwell lived and worked in Stockbridge, a prosperous community midway between the state highpoints of Connecticut and Massachusetts. The town still appears to be a snapshot from the artist's era, its downtown little changed from "Main Street, Stockbridge," a Rockwell painting of forty years earlier. There was no urban decay or suburban sprawl, few strip malls, and fewer national chains. Yet the town is thriving, benefiting from the arts and the throngs of tourists the Rockwell legacy attracts.

Mt. Greylock, Massachusetts' highest peak, dominates the skyline north of Stockbridge. Half a billion years old and once 20,000 feet high, the mountain has eroded into today's gently sloping form, its forested flanks topped by a prominent saddle-back and gray rocky summit. Herman Melville, from his home near Pittsfield a dozen miles away, saw in the mountain's contours the shape of a giant whale. My imagination wasn't as fertile. Melville, however, had whales on his mind, writing *Moby Dick* while living in the Berkshires.

In 1898 Mt. Greylock, although heavily logged during the

nineteenth century, became Massachusetts' first state park. Today a paved road leads steeply through second-growth forest to a mountaintop lodge and restaurant. A 93-foot-tall lighthouse tops the rocky summit.

This unusual structure wasn't designed for Mt. Greylock, planned instead for the mouth of the Charles River in Boston Harbor. But in 1931, plans for an artificial island needed for the lighthouse were scrapped. The already-cut blocks of Quincy Granite had no home. Instead the lighthouse was assembled here, dedicated as a war memorial, and topped with a rotating beacon visible for seventy miles.

Around the monument's base, a network of hiking paths including the Appalachian Trail cross sub-alpine terrain. Winds can be harsh, storms fierce and unexpected. Thoreau visited here and was caught unprepared, writing later of piling boards atop himself for warmth while enduring a frigid night on the mountain.

However, our visit was blessed with light breezes and clear long-distance views. Forested mountains extended in all directions. Four ranges—the Taconics, Greens, Hoosacs, and Berkshires—can be seen from Greylock's summit. But as in New Jersey and Connecticut, little of this region's development spoiled the view.

This was not the New England I had expected. Instead of sprawl and commercial development with congestion and high population density, this region was rural, wooded, and peaceful, life's pace slower and more relaxed. Homes and villages nestled among sugar maples gave a sense of peaceful rural gentility. From Mt. Greylock's summit even the larger cities—Adams and North Adams—were mostly hidden beneath leafy canopies in deep valleys.

We touched the monument and circled its base, then stood in a short line for an unobstructed photo of the mountaintop lighthouse. The summit was a busy place this summer week-end; daytrippers, picnicking families, and heavily burdened AT hikers all enjoyed the sunshine and warmth. Again blessed with good weather, the storms endured on Rainier and other high-altitude peaks seemed a distant memory as state highpoints were almost effortlessly checked off.

From Mt. Greylock, Highway 7 continues north into Vermont and the Green Mountains, an area I had visited in the

Mt. Greylock, Massachusetts
Designed as a lighthouse for Boston Harbor, this monument was
instead erected as a mountaintop war memorial in 1931.

1980s and a region I remembered as a scenic rural environment much like my North Carolina mountain home. But the past two decades haven't been kind to rural Vermont. Although there were luxury condos, expensive vacation homes, and new resorts for the well-to-do, the countryside seemed otherwise depleted, its economy struggling. Aging barns and cheap manufactured housing stood in stark contrast to the opulence of elite homes and gated resorts.

Throughout my travels, I had seen these dramatic differences in wealth. But as in much of the nation, I had seen little other rural prosperity, just varying levels of decline. Through the south, this hadn't surprised me; the region's agricultural economy has struggled for a century. In the southeastern mountains I had expected to see poverty, the term Appalachia synonymous with hard times. But here in an area portrayed as progressive and even prosperous, and so near the affluence of the Berkshires, I was shocked.

Twenty miles from Vermont's tallest mountain, however, is one of this region's few economic success stories. In 1978, after taking a five-dollar correspondence course, Ben Cohen and Jerry Greenfield began commercial ice cream production in a renovated gas station. The company used only local dairy products raised in an environmentally sensitive manner. Producing innovative ice cream flavors with quirky names, Ben and Jerry's prospered; the friends' $12,000 investment grew to be worth $326 million before the company was sold—to one of the world's largest multinational corporations.

Naively I had expected to join a handful of people touring a small manufacturing facility. But Ben and Jerry's is big business and, I later learned, Vermont's most visited tourist attraction, drawing 300,000 people annually.

The carefully orchestrated tour was disappointing—barely fifteen minutes long, the first seven watching a slickly produced "moovie" about the company and its founders. After being shepherded along a glass-enclosed catwalk overlooking production facilities and given a tiny sample of ice cream, we were deposited in the gift shop as though it was the primary destination. Although a few of the store's food products were produced in Vermont, nearly all the souvenirs had been manufactured overseas, differing little from the typical plastic items found in similar venues. In less than half an hour, I'd had my fill of commercialism and longed for the mountains.

Mt. Mansfield (4,393 feet), Vermont's tallest peak, is located in the heart of the Green Mountains, a chain named for the color of its rock, not its vegetation. The state's summit juts nearly 1,000 feet above timberline, its eastern flank, home to Stowe Mountain Resort, heavily developed. But the summit and rocky ridgeline remain an unspoiled alpine environment, windswept and natural.

Called the "Great Stone Face" by early American writers, the mountain's two-mile-long summit ridge appears from the east as a giant facial profile. Prominent landmarks are named accordingly—the Forehead, Nose, Chin, and Adam's Apple.

I wanted to ascend via the Long Trail, a 272-mile-long footpath completed in 1930 and said to be the inspiration for the Appalachian Trail. Extending the length of Vermont, it is one of New England's premier walking routes and the nation's oldest long distance hiking path. But the weather forecast was discouraging. Steady rain and thunderstorms were predicted as an approaching cold front was ending our streak of good weather.

We arrived early the next morning, paid the 12-dollar toll as soon as the collector unlocked the gate, and after receiving stern warnings about road conditions and risks, drove our ten-year-old Ford Taurus up the steep, winding gravel road. Ski trails, rocky slashes cut through coniferous forests, crossed the roadway then plunged down mountain slopes and over steeply angled cliffs.

But instead of the mountain's most challenging route, a 2.3-mile-long ascent gaining 2,800 feet, we opted for a ridgeline walk along a more southerly portion of the Long Trail, hoping to beat the storm. When we arrived at the trailhead, however, a cold northwest gale was already raking the exposed crest. To the west, dark clouds hovered over New York's Adirondack Mountains; Lake Champlain was barely visible through fog and haze below. We quickly began walking, traversing bare rock and skirting alpine vegetation, following the 1.4-mile-long path from Nose to Chin.

A thin layer of wind-driven clouds passed over the mountain. Frigid water droplets chilled our exposed faces. Although the fog cleared, the winds didn't abate, the gusts feeling colder on damp skin and through moistened clothing.

Halfway to the summit we met the "monitor," a young

woman retreating from the storm. Such workers are stationed atop Mt. Mansfield and other popular northeastern peaks from June to October. Although some are paid, many volunteer their time seeking to protect and educate visitors—and to keep them off fragile alpine vegetation. As the wind loudly flapped nylon hoods and parkas, the monitor shouted a few sentences that were carried off by the wind. Yet she continued down and didn't turn us back. We advanced as fog returned, this time followed by steady drizzle.

Minutes later we scrambled up a final promontory to the Chin, Vermont's highest point. We knelt, barely able to stand against the tempest. I had read warnings of summer storms atop New England's tallest peaks. But this storm's intensity shocked me. Except for my cotton denim jeans, we were well prepared, wearing hats, gloves, rain jackets, and multiple insulating layers. Yet the drizzle and unceasing wind chilled me deeply, my body warmth quickly carried off through porous cotton pants. Sheryl had dressed appropriately; I had not. Within minutes I began shivering.

Cotton clothing—blue jeans, sweats, flannel shirts—seem warm but are useless insulators when wet, even when dampened only by perspiration. In the eastern United States, more people become hypothermic during summer than any other season, not because of extreme temperatures, but due to wind and rain. "Synthetic underwear," a guide told me, "will not keep you dry, but it will keep you warm. You will be wet, but at least warm and wet."

We spent little time atop Vermont. After a half dozen photos and less than ten minutes, we started down, Mt. Mansfield earning the distinction as the stormiest summit I would visit.

With renewed activity, the shivering ceased but the descent was cold and damp. We moved quickly—for warmth and to leave the exposed ridgeline before thunderstorms might develop.

My shivering returned after reaching the car as I fumbled with the keys and began removing wet clothing. I was dangerously near hypothermia due to one clothing error. But with protection from the wind, warmth from the car heater, and dry clothes, I recovered quickly. We had been lucky to reach Mt. Mansfield's summit and fortunate to return safely.

Descending is the riskiest portion of a big climb and, I learned, of driving mountain roads. We had been warned of the steep descent and the risk of burning brakes. Although driving in second gear and stopping frequently, the acrid smell of over-heating brakes wafted into the car as we descended the final hill. I downshifted further, the engine straining to hold the auto back, as I tapped increasingly useless brakes. Wisps of light-colored smoke drifted from behind the front wheels. There was no place to stop; I wasn't even sure I could.

A cloud of foul-smelling smoke enveloped our aging vehicle as we coasted to a stop at the mountain's base. We got out and watched helplessly, afraid the vehicle would catch fire.

"Came down the toll road, huh?" inquired a passerby.

I nodded affirmatively, glancing at the cloud of smoke.

"Happens all the time. Don't worry; no damage done," he said.His nonchalance surprised me. I was a thousand miles from home and it was *my* car in that gray cloud. But I thanked him for his reassurance as he strolled on without slowing.

This had not been one of my outstanding mornings.

It took twenty minutes for the smoke to clear. While the brakes cooled I called home, only to learn of new issues at work. We had only been gone a week, had summited just three New England state highpoints, and hadn't ventured more than forty miles east of the New York state line. Yet I now needed to cut this already abbreviated trip short.

After determining the brakes hadn't been damaged, we drove south, following the eastern shore of Lake Champlain. Beneath leaden-gray skies we left New England. The clouds didn't help my somber mood. I was returning to more than the worry and uncertainty of the previous six months. I knew this would be the final act in a drama that I had allowed to continue too long.

CHAPTER 9

SOLITUDE

The Upper Midwest

Returning from New England, I tendered my resignation, anxious to depart before further losses. Although the hospital would remain open a few more months, I was ready to go, having lived with insecurity and wondering each month when, how much, or if the physicians would be paid.

The finality of the inevitable was a relief. I confirmed travel plans, scheduled guides, and made reservations. Planning was exciting, realizing that for the first time in my adult life I could fill hours and days as I pleased.

"What will this do to your career?" colleagues and recruiters asked when told that I intended to take up to a year off. "Can you afford that? Will you be able to return to medicine?"

These questions spoke to my doubts and fears. Despite a confident façade, I was filled with uncertainty for I had no mentors or role models for guidance and knew no other physician who had taken such a lengthy leave.

The final days were filled with emotion. Colleagues, friends, and patients thanked me. We reminisced and laughed, recalling challenges and discussing uncertainties facing the hospital, its staff, and me.

As I left the emergency department that last night, I never looked back.

Apprehension was quickly replaced by the youthful hope and optimism that had conceived The Dream—and sustained it during a quarter century. And although I now realize that this journey of growth and discovery had begun years earlier, it had received only partial commitment. But with neither the obligations nor security of full-time employment, I was now free to explore—and face the accompanying risks, challenges, and opportunities.

Nearly all state summits can be reached as part of driving loops. Eagle Mountain (2,301 feet), Minnesota's highest point, is an exception. A dozen miles north of Lake Superior, the peak is located in Minnesota's "arrowhead," a triangular piece of our nation wedged between the Great Lakes and Canada, its tip at Grand Portage.

One week after leaving the emergency department, I met my son Jon at the Minneapolis airport. Since our muddy foray to Iowa's loftiest point years earlier, we had together reached just two additional state summits, South Dakota's Harney Peak (7,242 feet) and Illinois' Charles Mound (1,235 feet). On this trip we hoped to increase our total by standing atop Eagle Mountain and the highest points of Michigan and Wisconsin.

Armed with maps, guidebooks, and two large bottles of insect repellant, we drove north from Minneapolis into Minnesota's northwoods, an ecosystem I had imagined as an unspoiled wilderness, a primal place with dense forests and populated by moose and wolves and bears. Instead we found hilly terrain with light-colored soils and coniferous forests with little understory vegetation. Lakes dotted the landscape. The Canadian Shield, a mineral-rich remnant of the earth's early crust and one of the planet's oldest geologic formations, under-lies this thin veneer of forest, soil, and water.

At the southern edge of the Mesabi Range near Mountain Iron, signs advertised public mine tours. Instead of primal woods and howling wolves, we were near one of the world's largest open pit mines—and Minnesota's largest industrial site.

The source of much of the nation's iron ore, this complex is a massive operation. Cranes with scoops a dozen feet across and eight feet high lift 50,000 pounds of ore at a time, loading it into dump trucks, each with a 170-ton capacity. Rocks up to five feet in diameter are transported to crushers and, in a series of rotating cylinders, reduced to a fine powder. The iron is removed magnetically, heated, then combined with limestone, silica, and bentonite into gray marble-sized pellets to be shipped to the blast furnaces along Lake Erie's southern shore.

The scale was impressive; the operation never ceased, working around-the–clock even through northern Minnesota's bitterly cold winters. But discovering industry instead of solitude, I now wondered where this area's reputed wildness—that glorious sense of rugged isolation in an untamed land—could be found. We drove north to Ely, a thriving four-season tourist destination. But although surrounded by what is popularly known as "wilderness"—in this case large tracts of land recovering from logging—I failed to find wildness or solitude here either.

Perennially one of the nation's coldest locations, Ely serves as the outfitting center for most Boundary Waters excursions and commercial hub for much of the Arrowhead. Tourists sporting the latest outdoor fashions walked between pricey galleries and upscale shops, their feet never touching the damp Minnesota soil. Restaurants and bars lined Main Street, the entire town showcasing a rustic northwoods theme. Expensive SUVs and late-model foreign luxury cars occupied nearly every parking space.

We opted for an early dinner but despite the hour, nearly every table was occupied. The restaurant's inner walls were of shiny recently shellacked pine logs, bark removed but knots protruding. Seats, benches, and tables matched the walls, unstained but heavily shellacked. Above the door a trophy moose head, antlers wider than the door frame, stared with shiny glass eyes, the animal's huge size out of proportion to this small room, its mournful look contrasting with the diners' noisy chatter.

After eating we fled the crowds, driving toward Eagle Mountain. The next morning, beneath deep blue skies and a Canadian high-pressure system, we began the 6½-mile roundtrip hike to Minnesota's highest point. A light wind stirred the cool August air keeping mosquitoes at bay.

A well-maintained trail led toward the peak. For two miles we walked through coniferous forests, traversed soggy depressions, and crossed seasonal rivulets. Near the mountain's base the route turned, skirting Whale Lake, a large, shallow pond ringed with forested hills. Long reeds, sunlight glistening off wet tubular shafts, floated offshore. A decaying log lay submerged. Light breezes stirred the water's surface, creating scallop-edged reflections of nearby mountains.

We rested, enjoying the view and watching ever-changing patterns across the rippled surface. For the first time in Minnesota, we had found a sense of wildness and, although just off the trail, a degree of solitude. The quiet was remarkable—few insects or birds, no splashes or rushing water, only the occasional scuff of hiking boots along the nearby footpath. We lingered, enjoying this wonderful and unexpected place.

Yet the trail's steepest portion remained. From Whale Lake the route ascended through scrubby pines then crossed exposed granite, there overlooking the unbroken forest I had expected. We paused to savor the view. But the summit was too close to linger. The trail turned sharply, reentered the woods then rose steeply to a small, deeply fissured rocky outcropping surrounded by brush and pines. A small stone cairn above an engraved metal plaque marked the state's highest point.

Atop Minnesota, we congratulated each other.

We snapped triumphant photos, but with the breeze blocked by surrounding vegetation and the late morning sun reflecting off light-colored granite, the summit became uncomfortably warm. Retreating to a nearby overlook, we rested and snacked while enjoying the refreshing coolness and expansive views.

The mountaintop was a busy place. A dozen and a half people summited while we were there—experienced backpackers and casual day-trippers, solo hikers and families with young children. For some, this was the biggest mountain they had ever ascended.

The number of people atop this relatively remote peak surprised me, as had the popularity of many state highpoints. On only a handful of state summits had I met no other hikers. These were often the easiest or least scenic "peaks"—Florida, Mississippi, Connecticut—while the higher, more remote, and most challenging summits had the largest crowds.

From our airy perch, I looked across a rolling landscape. Minnesota's highest point is located near the southern edge of the Boundary Waters Canoe Area Wilderness, a million acres of undeveloped hills, forests, and lakes. In this preserve, the largest such federally designated area east of the Rocky Mountains, water challenges the land for dominance. Many of Minnesota's "10,000 lakes" (officially the state claims more than 15,000) dot this landscape, separated only by thin strips of hilly terrain.

This area is also home to some of the best canoeing in the

nation. Jon and I gazed across this watery landscape and discussed out next adventure; the following morning, armed with more enthusiasm than experience, we stepped into a canoe and pushed off.

Soon, however, we discovered one reason for the Boundary Waters' famed solitude—the portage. Portaging, the transporting of paddles, gear, and boat between lakes, often across hilly forested land, was a new challenge. It was not fun. Perhaps to trick the novice canoer, portage distances are measured not in feet, meters, miles, or any familiar measure of distance but in rods, each rod 5½ yards long. Denoted on maps by a single unlabeled number, a portage of, say eighty-five, doesn't sound too difficult—until one calculates its quarter-mile length.

Gear transport between lakes is awkward. Canoeing backpacks, although waterproof, are little more than haul bags, lacking compression straps and internal stays, causing loads to shift frequently. But transporting the canoe is the biggest challenge. Our experienced outfitter demonstrated the preferred technique: One person lifts the boat, much as a weightlifter executes a clean and jerk, then rotates and balances the craft upon their shoulders. Wearing the boat like an oversized hat, the paddler walks along a narrow wooded trail while an experienced partner follows, carrying food, backpack, life preservers, and paddles—all in one carry.

Reaching our first portage, I realized the impossibility of a single haul. Thankfully the distance was short. On the third try I hefted the canoe onto my shoulders, its bow extending eight feet in front, its stern a similar distance behind. But my vision was nearly blocked, and the slightest twisting of my torso made the boat swing wildly.

I met more than one tree during that short walk. After colliding with one trailside resident, which had obviously occupied its location many decades, I tried lifting the boat's front end to see better and promptly ran into an equally unyielding low branch. After a third collision we changed strategies, completing the portage by each carrying one end of the canoe then making two more carries to transport gear.

Not surprisingly, following this portage, we didn't see another person. Battered and bruised, we had at last found both wildness and solitude.

A second portage, executed little more gracefully than

the first, brought us to a half-mile long, crescent shaped lake. Conifers extended down steep hillsides to the water's edge; a gray rocky cliff, twenty feet high, rose from the lake's far end. A pair of loons, black and white symbols of the northwoods, floated a hundred yards from shore.

We paddled briefly but soon stored our oars, awestruck by the quiet magnificence. Only the soft splash of diving birds broke the silence. We drifted. The birds, unafraid though not oblivious to our presence, resurfaced nearer the boat. Bright red eyes contrasted with the loons' black heads. From fifteen feet away, I could see individual feathers, each plume glistening, clean and dry. After each dive, water beaded quickly then fell effortlessly from the bird's head and back. The loons rode low in the water, bodies mostly submerged, heads raised prominently. We remained quiet as the birds continued to dive and feed, moving ever closer, this remarkable display continuing half an hour as they hunted, swam, and showed off before slowly drifting away.

Throughout the afternoon, we enjoyed the long-sought solitude and wildness, never seeing another human being. Our companions were sun and silence, the latter interrupted only by birdcalls and the soft sound of water stirred by our paddles. We traveled across four lakes, endured three portages, and enjoyed a magnificent wilderness.

The next morning, before leaving Minnesota's Arrowhead, we followed Lake Superior's northern shore forty miles eastward to Grand Portage. Here at the tip of the Arrowhead is a busy border crossing, a large casino on a small Indian reservation, and a reconstructed fort administered by the National Park Service showcasing the French-Canadian fur trade.

For centuries Grand Portage has been a commercial crossroads. Voyageurs, eighteenth century French-Canadian fur traders, established a major trading center here. Supplies and trade goods transported across the Great Lakes by canoe arrived from Montreal, while furs and buffalo hides were brought from west-central Canada. And from here, adventurers followed the Pigeon River north, trading and establishing commercial networks with native peoples, exploring much of central Canada, and returning with thousands of beaver pelts annually.

But Grand Portage, French for "great carry," was also a bottleneck. To avoid dangerous rapids along the lower Pigeon

The Portage
The author carrying the canoe correctly—after much practice.

River, all items—boats, trade goods, beaver pelts—had to be hauled by the rivermen overland between Lake Superior and Ft. Charlotte, a distance of 2,500 rods. Eight and one half miles long, this route crossed a 700-foot-high ridge. Supplies were packed into 90-pound bundles, each man expected to carry two bundles at a time and complete two trips daily. Yet company records reveal that Voyageurs frequently transported double (360-pound) and occasionally triple loads.

Recalling our difficulties carrying a Kevlar canoe and one day's supplies, I felt humbled. It was time to return to the mellow world of twenty-first century highpointing.

We returned to Duluth following State Route 61 and Lake Superior's northern shore then turned east. Along Wisconsin's heavily industrialized lakefront, both beauty and prosperity had long vanished. Roads were heavily potholed, bridges grimy and crumbling. Decaying piers and rusting ships' hulls littered the shoreline, while once-elegant brick buildings, now boarded up, lined the main thoroughfare.

We stopped briefly to survey the economic carnage. A rusted car rattled into the adjoining parking space, the vehicle's bumper sporting a faded sticker with an angry, obscene message. The two female occupants glared at us, never smiling or acknowledging my head nod and wave, looking as downtrodden as this decrepit waterfront.

From this depressed port city we continued across northern Wisconsin and into Michigan's Huron Mountains, home to that state's highest point. But *which* mountain is Michigan's loftiest summit was contested throughout the twentieth century. Today Mt. Arvon (1,979 feet) is believed the tallest but is the nation's least certain state summit. A 1982 survey determined this peak to be eleven inches taller than neighboring Mt. Curwood, for two decades considered Michigan's loftiest mountain. But Mt. Curwood had only claimed the distinction in 1963; before that, Porcupine Mountain was thought the state's highest. The issue is far from settled. Many of the mountains in this region are nearly the same height and some have yet to be surveyed.

Determining a state's highest geographical point can be an inexact science. In June 1909, *National Geographic* listed forty-nine state and territorial highpoints (omitting Hawaii). Eleven were as yet undetermined, listed only by state region or mountain range. Of the remaining thirty-eight, eleven have changed, replaced with taller peaks after subsequent surveys.

A mountain's height is not the only uncertainty. State boundaries are also disputed. In 1909 two highpoints, those of Maryland and Nevada, were located in disputed regions. Litigation, not surveying, established Maryland's state summit. But Nevada's highest point is still contested; the current highpoint, Boundary Peak, is located in a narrow strip of land claimed by both Nevada and California.

The greatest challenge in summiting Michigan's Mt. Arvon is reaching it. Much of the 27-mile-long route from the L'Anse Indian Reservation winds through a maze of unnamed, unnumbered, and unmaintained logging roads, frequently impassable due to mud or snow. For years local guides were hired to lead highpointers to the trailhead. But as highpointing's popularity has increased, the route has been marked by a series of light blue, diamond-shaped blazes.

The walk from trailhead to summit is still easier than the drive. A straightforward, half-mile-long footpath follows a deeply gullied logging road, a recently cut scar through scrubby pine forest. Light-colored rocks and exposed subsoil reflected the midday sun; with breezes blocked by trees, the air was uncomfortably warm as we walked to the top.

Mt. Arvon's summit, thus far, has been spared the logger's chainsaw. Forested but cleared of underbrush, the shaded summit is open and airy. Two logs provide "summit seating;" a nearby blue mailbox contains the register. We stepped between the logs, located the nearby USGS marker, then congratulated each other. We were atop Michigan.

Due to its remote location, Mt. Arvon receives few casual visitors. While we rested, snacked, and enjoyed the cool shade, Jon and I perused the summit register. These logbooks can be fascinating documents, revealing not only the number of people summiting, but also how they are affected by the experience. Entries follow patterns—boastful, inane, or profound—but once begun, the similarity persists for pages, if not the entire book. Content and style seem unrelated to the mountain's difficulty, geographical region, surrounding beauty, or the writer's home state. Some entries curse or belittle the mountain beneath them and criticize trails, maps, and rangers, while others feature beautiful poetry and elegant, deeply moving prose.

Mt. Arvon's register, a fraying, dog-eared spiral notebook, was a dry compilation of facts. Ten days earlier a Boy Scout troop had hiked here; fourteen boys signed beneath their troop number and leader's name. Seven days later a pair of highpointers from Ohio had summited, "h.p. 31 and 29," inscribed after their names. Yesterday a Virginian summited. "Highpoint #28—on to Eagle Mountain," he wrote.

I neither wrote nor spoke of my accomplishments, nor of my goal of reaching all fifty. Instead, as always, I inscribed only my name and hometown; Jon did likewise.

Of my completed state summits, only Mt. Rainier ranked among the most difficult. As I closed the book and returned it to the mailbox, I thought of the challenge ahead. I firmly believed that I possessed the skill, ability, and stamina to reach any state highpoint. But to touch all the remaining summits during the next twelve months would require more than skill and stamina, more than remaining uninjured and healthy. It would also require luck with scheduling, permits, and especially the weather.

Four other highpointers, a recently retired couple and two individuals, soon joined us atop Michigan. The banter was casual as we discussed other state summits.

The graying couple was from Pennsylvania. Traveling by RV and peak-bagging—reaching a series of summits quickly with little sightseeing or exploration between—they wanted to know if Harney Peak's trailhead in South Dakota was RV-accessible. (It is.) A trim middle-aged man from the Pacific Northwest was driving east and inquired if there were state summit access problems in either Ohio or Indiana. (There aren't.) From the other individual, a sandy haired backpacker from Colorado, I learned that Wisconsin's Timms Hill, our next goal, was easy to find and required only a short stroll up a paved path.

After summit photos, the others descended but Jon and I lingered, enjoying the shade and solitude. However, when Jon learned of my next planned stop, a restaurant claiming itself "home of the world's largest sweet roll," he too was ready to go. We returned to L'Anse, driving through the maze of logging roads, following faded tire tracks and guessing at turns, then searching behind us for the blazes that marked the uphill route.

Reaching town we stopped at the Hilltop Restaurant, a tradition among highpointers, an appropriately named glass and brick structure overlooking the small city. "A single sweet roll will feed you both," our waitress claimed. I was doubtful. Jon was a teenager and we both were hungry. But she was right. The confection was huge—three inches high and the diameter of a dinner plate—and satisfied both our appetites.

L'Anse is also home of the Ojibwa, formerly known as the Chippewa, a native woodland people that once ranged from the Great Lakes to the Dakota grasslands. Following contact with Europeans—French fur traders and American settlers—the Ojibwa were forced to adapt and assimilate. They also had to change many cultural practices including their burial customs.

With the exception of my father's grave, I seldom visit cemeteries. However, the energetic woman staffing the town's visitor center strongly recommended a visit to L'Anse's "Indian Cemetery." She spoke of "interesting burial practices," but wouldn't, or couldn't, elaborate. Her reticence concerned me; I even wondered if she had ever been there. But she assured me the cemetery was open to the public, again emphasized it was "most interesting," and said that visitation was not considered offensive by the Ojibwa.

My interest piqued, we drove east five miles to what appeared a miniature village surrounded by a dilapidated fence and tall deciduous trees. Small houses, seemingly placed at random, were in various stages of decay. Footpaths worn to bare dirt led from the missing gate, weaving amongst the wooden structures. This was the cemetery, each "house" protecting a single grave.

Dating from the second half of the nineteenth century, none of these graves were individually identified. Earlier the Ojibwa had buried their dead on the mountains overlooking Lake Superior. But with the arrival of white settlers the Indians interred the dead in this cemetery, constructing the small structures to protect the dead during their journey to the afterlife, a practice continued until the early twentieth century.

Although similar in style, none of the houses were identical. All were of sawn pine, each measuring approximately five by two feet. Sides were low, less than a foot high. A triangular roof with tightly fitting gables covered the structures; one gable of each house remained intact, the other interrupted by a diamond or hexagonal-shaped opening carefully sawn into the wood.

Moss clung tightly to the aging boards.

We walked quietly through the cemetery. There was no directional orientation of houses or openings, nor family groupings of graves. Grass and flowers grew beside the small wooden structures, some of which had been recently reconstructed. It was a quiet, reverent—and "most interesting"—place.

I wished to further explore the Porcupine Mountains and Michigan's Upper Peninsula, but Jon's vacation was ending; school would begin within days. The next morning beneath heavy gray clouds and in a light drizzle, we left for Minneapolis where Jon was to meet his mother.

En route we detoured to Timms Hill (1,951 feet), Wisconsin's highest point. We walked up the wide, gently sloping paved trail, touched the USGS marker at the hill's apex then climbed the summit tower into the clouds and light rain. We congratulated each other but remained atop Wisconsin less than five minutes.

Although necessary due to schedules and weather, Timms Hill became the first highpoint that I had simply "bagged." It felt like a hollow accomplishment. As I continued south through Wisconsin, seeing little but traffic and rain—and learning nothing of its history or people—I thought of Internet reports boasting of "Nine highpoints in five days", "Fourteen summits in eight days," even nighttime visits to increase state totals more rapidly. If I had any doubts, this bagged summit had convinced me that touring the area, meeting people, and learning of a region's history and geography was as important—and often more interesting—than non-stop climbing.

Jon would return to school; with changing interests, busy schedules, and extracurricular activities, he would be unable to join me again during my quest. In Minneapolis we said our goodbyes, and I flew home to repack for a western climbing trip. For the first time since my father's death, I would resume technical mountaineering—attempting the two most challenging state summits in the contiguous forty-eight states.

CHAPTER 10

ROCK!

Wyoming

I stepped from the terminal of Las Vegas' McCarren Airport into 107-degree heat. Toting 120 pounds of climbing gear, cameras, and supplies, I scanned the desert parking lot looking for a white Dodge Neon, a rented car that would be my mobile "base camp" for the next month. Plans were to climb first in the northern Rockies, attempting the highest points in Wyoming, Montana, and Idaho, then traveling south, touring and climbing as weather, time, and energy permitted.

There would be challenges. This summer was already the most destructive fire season in decades, and dozens of fires still burned, threatening several western highpoints. It was also late August—the high country winter wasn't far away.

I had flown into Las Vegas only because of modest airfares and the nation's lowest rental car rates; I had visited here before, and the city held no interest for me. Anxious to begin climbing, I left promptly, beginning the two-day drive to Jackson, Wyoming.

When I conceived my highpointing plan, I thought of potential hazards and necessary skills: rattlesnakes, scorpions, and water shortages in the desert; avalanche, crevasse, and rock fall risk on alpine peaks; and the need for excellent map-reading, navigational, and route-finding skills on all mountains. However, I gave little thought to the biggest danger on the western highpoints—thunderstorms.

"Mountains create their own weather," climbers are taught. This is true, summer and winter. From mid-July to mid-

91

September, prevailing southerly winds, the monsoon, bring relatively humid air to the southwest. Cooling as they rise over mountain ridges, these moist breezes spawn thunderstorms that are frequently accompanied by lightning, heavy rain, and flash flooding. And although these storms are the greatest risk faced by summertime hikers and climbers, this is also the best, and sometimes the only, climbing season.

Less than an hour after my arrival, I encountered such a tempest. Above the desert flatness, the western sky darkened and the wind freshened, first bringing welcomed relief from the searing heat but quickly followed by torrential rain and a further 30-degree temperature drop. Drivers pulled off the road as high-speed wipers couldn't keep up against the deluge. Water covered the highway, and I recalled warnings of dry desert ditches becoming raging rivers.

But ten minutes later the downpour ended as quickly as it had begun. The sun emerged, dramatically illuminating the thundercloud's trailing edge; steam rose from the dark asphalt and the desert heat promptly returned.

The route to Jackson necessitated following interstate highways much of the way, one of the few times during my nearly 25,000-mile highpointing odyssey I would use these superhighways. Begun in the 1950s, the modern interstate system is both wonder and curse. One can drive border to border or coast to coast never stopping for a single stoplight, traveling from New York to Los Angeles in less than forty-eight hours. But one can also cross our nation experiencing little of our regional cultures or geographic variation. Interchanges everywhere share familiar vistas of fast-food restaurants and mega fuel stops peddling items from bottled water to velvet Elvises. This may be the new America—consumer-friendly, homogenized, and prepackaged. But it wasn't the America I had crossed a continent to see.

In Evanston, Wyoming, I escaped the interstate. Turning north and following State Route 89, a two-lane road paralleling Wyoming's western border, I drove through Almy and Sage, Cokeville and Smoot, high altitude hamlets nestled in lush valleys. Yet even here, surrounded by remote peaks, commercialism reigned as scores of billboards extolled Yellowstone's attractions hundreds of miles to the north. And I passed through tiny Afton, home of dairy farmer Rulon Gardner who shocked the world during the 2000 Summer Olympics by upsetting previously undefeated Russian heavyweight wrestler, Aleksandr Karelin. Gardner earned a gold medal and Wheaties box cover for his efforts—and fifteen minutes of fame for Afton.

Traffic increased the final forty miles as the state route joined three U.S. highways funneling tourists toward Grand Teton and Yellowstone National Parks, and to Jackson, an upscale community located near the parks' southern entrance. Bill Clinton regularly vacationed here while president. Vice-President Dick Cheney owns a home here. Alan Greenspan, Ben Bernanke, and world economic leaders frequently meet here. And I paid dearly to sleep here, the $128 room at the Super 8 the most expensive night's lodging throughout my highpoint travels.

Twice before, I had visited Yellowstone's sprawling ecosystem, the largest wilderness in the contiguous forty-eight states. During this trip, however, I would remain south of the parks, hiking and climbing in the Wind River Range, attempting Gannett Peak (13,804 feet), a remote glaciated mountain that is Wyoming's highest point and one of the three most challenging state summits.

Tom Torkelson of Jackson Hole Mountain Guides would accompany me. A thirtyish, slightly built athletic man, Tom had spent most of the previous decade climbing and guiding. Insightful and intellectual, he possessed an intensively inquisitive mind. He had earned a bachelor's degree, studied pre-law, and later told me that he "had bought a suit for law school interviews."

He has yet to wear that suit. Instead he took time off to travel and climb, trained in Europe as a mountain guide, then led climbers throughout the Alps and later the Andes. This was his first summer guiding in the northern Rockies, but he had already made multiple ascents of Gannett Peak and nearby Granite Peak, Montana's highest point.

We briefly shared adventure travel and climbing experiences then began two of the most important skills for expedition mountaineering—gear selection and efficient packing. Pack weight, especially at high altitude, is critical. An 80-pound pack is not twice as difficult to haul as a 40-pound load; it is four or even six times more strenuous. Unnecessary items such as excess clothing, superfluous gear, even candy wrappers and food packaging, add needless bulk and weight.

During the nine years since my introduction to climbing on Mt. Rainier, I had learned to pack more efficiently and carry fewer items. Instead of an aluminum frame Kelty backpack with multiple small pockets, I now used a large internal frame pack, an ergonomically designed stuff sack shaped by internal supports and held tightly by external compression straps. Gone was my fastidious concern of keeping clothes neat and unwrinkled, replaced only by the desire to keep everything dry. And, like all expedition climbers and long-distance backpackers, I had learned to save weight by wearing clothes multiple times—and learning to tolerate disagreeable odors from myself and others.

Tom and I divided group gear—tent, stove, fuel, and climbing equipment—with Tom, like most guides, carrying the larger portion. The heaviest and least used equipment went into the packs first, low and near the spine, while lighter items such as snacks and jacket were placed higher and more peripherally. With years of hard-earned experience I found room for everything, and after cinching the pack's compression straps, created a large but stable mass weighing sixty pounds.

Dew clung to fragrant pine needles as we began the approach to Gannett Peak early the next day. Twenty miles long and gaining 7,000 feet in elevation, this approach is the longest and most strenuous among the contiguous state highpoints. It is, however, a beautiful hike. For a dozen miles the trail gently climbs through forests of towering pines and past clear lakes—Eklund and Hobbs, Seneca and Little Seneca—before reaching timberline at 10,000 feet. After skirting Island Lake, we ascended into the Titcomb Basin, a glacially carved valley ringed with towering peaks. Jackson and Fremont, Sacagawea, Warren, and Woodrow Wilson, all more than 13,000 feet high, rose steeply above the rocky valley. Gannett Peak, tallest of all, was yet to be seen, blocked at the Basin's far end by a steep, rocky headwall, still a day's walk away.

We camped on a gently sloping hill overlooking a small pond midway between Island and Titcomb Lakes. Fremont Peak's image, bathed with the soft glow of the late afternoon sun, reflected off the water's surface. Shrubby willows, four feet tall, crowded damp, shallow depressions, while blueberry bushes, ten inches high but loaded with ripe fruit, clung to the grassy hillside.

We had walked seventeen miles; removing the pack felt

liberating. Setting the burden aside I descended to the pond, a shallow body of clear water, its bottom a jumble of rocks. Sharply angled boulders protruded from the calm surface, piercing reflected images of nearby peaks. The only sounds were of moving water—a small stream trickling into the lake's upper end and excess liquid spilling over polished granite along the opposite shore.

I lingered beside the pond until the sun sank below the horizon then slowly walked beside the stream, a narrow waterway bordered with a thick mat of sedges, grass, and moss. This spongy carpet contrasted with the steep, rocky walls surrounding the valley and the hard-packed trails over which we had walked. Alpenglow, a warm, soft, reddish light seen only at higher altitudes, bathed the scene in an otherworldly glow.

Climbing, for me, is more than summiting mountains. It is both process and journey and, although challenging and difficult, is accompanied by moments of peace and beauty. This was such a moment. The alpenglow intensified to a deep red as the sun sank lower beneath the horizon. After the sun's rays no longer touched the upper atmosphere, the alpenglow vanished, the sky darkened quickly, and the evening's first stars shone above now-silhouetted peaks. Dusk deepened and the valley's rocks gave up the last of the day's warmth as I slowly walked back to the tent, stepping softly and moving quietly, wishing not to intrude upon the silence.

The next morning I crawled stiffly from the tent, feeling each of the previous day's seventeen miles. The ascent to Dinwoody Pass (also known as Bonney Pass), our goal at the far end of the Basin, appeared much steeper this morning, its sharply angled 2000-foot headwall now seeming an impossibly high vertical barrier. I surveyed our gear. We had consumed a small amount of food and fuel; packs would be lighter—fifty-eight instead of sixty pounds. I wanted to crawl back into my warm sleeping bag.

From past climbs, however, I knew not to focus on the totality of a day's efforts. The thoughts were too overwhelming. Instead the day would be thought of in smaller, more manageable portions: cooking breakfast; breaking camp and packing; walking over the first hill; hiking around the next. With tents down and packs loaded, I hefted the burden onto my back. It pulled on my aching shoulders, feeling much heavier than yesterday. Thankfully my knees didn't buckle. Of course not, they couldn't. They could hardly bend. Then we began walking—slowly—in the morning chill, moving steadily toward the headwall and pass.

The walk beside the Titcomb Lakes was relaxing and peaceful. A soft breeze stirred the slowly warming air. Flanked on the right first by Fremont, then by Sacagawea Peak, the path hugged the shoreline, following a soft dirt trail worn into low-lying vegetation. Talus slopes, formed by millennia of rockfall from the great peaks, created a steeply angled transition between lakeside greenery and bare granitic mountains.

The trail rose little as we walked beside mile-long Lower Titcomb and the slightly smaller Upper Titcomb, broad shallow lakes that cover most of the Basin's floor. At Upper Titcomb's far end, the shoreline was indistinct, the clear water merging with a rocky marsh that extended another hundred yards. Then marsh and all plant life ended abruptly, the trail steepened, and the ascent to Dinwoody Pass began. From here to the pass's summit, nearly a half mile above, there is no water, no snow, no shade, and no campsites.

The route ascends steeply up a huge talus slope, a shifting pile of irregularly shaped rocks ranging in size from gravel little larger than golf balls to boulders the size of minivans. To a climber, these unstable hills seem a devil's creation. Occasionally a compacted path winds among the rocks, but generally one must "boulder hop," jumping from rock to rock, each unstable boulder shifting upon landing and take-off. Unnerving with normal ambulation, it is truly frightening wearing a heavily loaded pack.

There is no way to prepare for this experience. In the east, roots and soil stabilize rock fields, creating steep but sure-footed scrambles. In arid climates and at extreme altitudes where plants cannot survive, however, soil is washed away, leaving bare loosely stacked boulders.

From shifting rock to shifting rock we scrambled, moving ever higher. The view of the Basin below was spectacular. Titcomb Lakes, their surfaces stirred by a light wind, sparkled beneath the midday sun. Green rings of vegetation encircled each lake, while the tall peaks surrounding the valley appeared a faded tan beneath the intense high altitude light. We struggled up the talus, measuring our progress not by deceptively angled slopes and false summits above but by landmarks on neighboring mountains. The ascent was laborious, the rocks less stable the higher we climbed.

Often the summit of a mountain, headwall, or pass isn't apparent until the climber is nearly on top. Instead of another false summit followed by yet one more incline, the land drops away, the sky arches to the horizon, and a new and often spectacular view is revealed.

Cresting Dinwoody Pass, I saw the grandeur of Gannett Peak for the first time. Here was a magnificent mountain, its flanks partly snow-covered, interspersed with deep, icy couloirs and long exposed rocky ridges—ideal lines of ascent. A deep valley and heavily crevassed glacier separated us from this beautiful giant, a peak with elegant, challenging climbing routes worthy of any mountaineer.

Although just 800 feet below the summit, we yet needed to descend to the valley and cross the glacier before ascending the peak, a grueling round-trip trek that would require a full day. So despite the midafternoon hour, we made camp on a rocky surface little larger than our tent and carefully studied the mountain, analyzing risks and estimating challenges. "Is the rockfall danger of that wall too great?" we asked. "Will that chimney go? Can we get around that huge crevasse?"

Tom, who knew the mountain well, asked me to detail potential climbing routes. I saw three possibilities: 1) A snow climb up Gannett's eastern flank, a route that required a long approach; 2) A rock scramble along a prominent ridge (the standard climbing route I later learned), a path made more difficult by loose rock and lack of snow cover; and 3) An ice couloir that looked deceptively short but was a 40-45 degree, six-pitch (nearly 800-foot) technical ice climb. After discussing the risks, challenges, and advantages of each, Tom asked for my choice.

When I began highpointing, I had decided to seek routes that were interesting and challenging, though not necessarily the easiest. However, as I looked across the valley at Gannett's steep sides, I realized that if we failed on a difficult route, time and weather might not allow a second attempt via the standard line. But ice climbing is my favorite mountaineering style and the steep couloir too inviting. With Tom's agreement I opted for the icy route, fully cognizant that if this line proved impassable, then the two-day-long approach and ideal weather conditions would have been squandered.

Wake-up time was 2:00 a.m., sleeping in compared with the 11:30 p.m. start years earlier on Mt. Rainier. Alpine starts, as these nighttime departures are known, are an unpleasant facet of mountaineering. Cold temperatures and fatigue, stiffness, and grogginess make for a challenging start to a long, physically demanding day. But as hot drinks and a light breakfast are consumed, packs loaded and ropes uncoiled, the excitement begins and the adrenaline flows. Joints and sore muscles loosen; the senses awaken. Stepping from the tent, I looked up at the multitude of stars, inhaled the clear thin air, and felt Gannett's presence, even though the mountain formed only a dark silhouette this moonless night.

By headlamp we descended the rocky northern flank of Dinwoody Pass, reaching the glacier by our 4:00 a.m. goal. Before stepping onto the ice we roped up and prepared for the precise choreography known as glacier travel—walking single file with a steady speed and using identical foot placements, all for safety. On these icy surfaces each climber must be constantly vigilant, ready to stop, or "arrest," a teammate's fall before that climber's momentum yanks the entire group off the mountain. When only two climbers are roped together, the individual responsibility is magnified.

Crevasses, however, present the greatest risk. Formed where glaciers cross irregular surfaces, these cracks may be inches wide or expand into gashes 30 yards across, 150 feet deep, and a quarter-mile long. During winter and spring, most of these scars are covered with deep snow, giving the glacier's surface a smooth, clean appearance. Up to a dozen feet thick, these bridges of snow are surprisingly strong, many able to support an entire climbing team's weight. But with summer's warmth these bridges weaken, often collapsing without warning.

Now in late August, both bridges and snow had long melted, leaving the glacier's surface hard and icy and dirty, covered with fallen rocks and fine soil granules blown from the surrounding peaks. Guided only by headlamps and our recollection of the glacier's topography, we attempted to cross the crevasse field, a jumbled maze of yawning, frequently interconnected cracks in the ice. We traversed the upper side of a long crevasse, its sides plunging into an abyss too deep for our headlamps to illuminate. For 200 yards we walked, rope nearly taut, forcing our crampons firmly into the icy surface just three slippery feet above this gaping hole. We then reached a sheer dead end where the crevasse joined another huge rent in the ice. We retreated, following the lower edge of this second crack until jumbled masses of fallen ice blocked our path. We worked around these obstacles, only to be stopped by yet another crevasse.

For two hours we struggled, trying to reach the couloir's base, succeeding only after daybreak—and after retreating nearly to our 4:00 a.m. location. Delayed, we could rest little, snacking as we approached the long icy chute, still hoping to complete the climb before daytime warming loosened ice-bound rocks.

At the gully's base, I looked up at an 80-foot-wide river of ice that appeared much larger than it had from our camp atop Dinwoody Pass and much steeper than the 40-45 degree angle cited in guidebooks. Rocky walls lined the channel, but the rock was cracked and loose, offering few protection placements and no rappel anchors. This would be a committing climb. Once begun there could be no retreat. The only way out would be up and over.

We looked at each other. Thumbs up. We rechecked gear and harnesses then began ascending.

The couloir was a beautiful line, challenging but not over-whelming. Ice axes and crampons bit deeply into a firm surface the consistency of dense Styrofoam, giving solid placements as we climbed. By midmorning we were halfway up the channel. Below us the icy ribbon plunged so steeply that I could no longer see its base, the ice curving into a void beyond which lay the crevasse field that had bedeviled us. Above, the rope led 140 feet to Tom, who appeared as a small red mark on the white surface, a glistening path that extended upward further than I could see. Alone in this wilderness, we overlooked dozens of rocky peaks jutting above glacier-cloaked bases.

A small pebble, no larger than a marble, bounced down the ice to our right, breaking the tranquility. A shiver of fear shot down my spine. Such a pebble cascading down this steep slope could crack a climbing helmet. Without speaking a word our pace quickened. The crevasses had delayed us, and now the sun's warmth was loosening the rocks along the gully; the couloir would channel any falling objects towards us.

Minutes later another tiny rock tumbled past. I began to glance upward much more frequently, not to measure our progress, but to see if other stones were falling.

"Rock!" I screamed seconds later as a large object bounced wildly down the gully directly toward us. Tom, who had been searching the icy surface for tool placements, heard me and looked up as the foot-wide projectile hurtled past, head high and a yard to his left. The rock gathered speed, touched the channel only once and sailed past me—six feet above the ice and to my *right*.

Tom looked back, yet nothing was said. Guide and client were both experienced and, although shaken, knew what needed to be done. The leader's pace quickened further, while I followed, lungs straining and heart racing. Showers of icy bits flew from the frozen surface with each crampon kick and tool placement.

I train diligently for climbing by running, hiking, and working on my farm year-round, hoping to have "something extra" if needed. Only once during a decade of climbing had I needed to tap that reserve. But today the physical conditioning again combined with a fear-induced surge of adrenaline to hurry me higher. Icy granules, knocked loose by our climbing, tumbled down the slope. Pebbles bounced past as we ascended the couloir's steepest and most exposed portion. But even after the slope moderated and rockfall risk lessened, we slowed little, maintaining a lung-searing pace to the top of the gully and to safety.

There we rested, speaking only briefly of the dangers encountered, recalling instead the firm ice and challenging line of ascent, again able to enjoy the magnificent view. Higher than the surrounding mountains, we now overlooked peaks that stood like rocky islands above a sea of ice in a region as rugged and beautiful as any I had seen in the "lower 48."

From the top of the couloir a straightforward path followed a rocky ridge to the summit. A half-hour later, we stood atop Wyoming.

A deep blue sky arched over the Wind River Range; calm winds and stable weather allowed a relaxed summit stay. I touched the mountain's highest point, a boulder perched precariously atop others, then retreated to the register box, a sturdy metal container wedged in a crack five feet below. There

Above the Couloir
The steep, icy chute ascended by the author is shown at the lower left.

a computer-generated banner had been left by a previous team. "Gannett Peak—13,804 Ft.—Aug, 2000—TOP OF WYOMING," it proclaimed. With paper in hand, I scrambled back to the state's loftiest rock, unrolled the sign, and held it high while Tom shot triumphant summit photos.

Few climbers remain long atop major peaks. Once the summit has been reached and a handful of photos taken, climbers descend before conditions worsen or weather deteriorates. Ironically, the highest and most challenging peaks necessitate the shortest summit visits.

But the mild weather allowed us to remain atop Gannett for forty-five minutes. The time passed quickly as we enjoyed the warm sun and splendid panorama, snacking and chatting as we rested, preparing for the challenging descent. After a final look across the Wind River Range's full expanse, we began the long walk back.

Descents are seldom fun. The summit has been reached, but the ultimate goal of a safe return has yet to be accomplished. And descents can be deadly. More accidents occur on the way down than during any other segment of a climb.

We returned via the standard route, the Gooseneck, a long rocky rib covered with deep snow much of the year. But the snow, which provides a more sure-footed descent, had long melted leaving a thin veneer of loose stones covering solid bedrock. With the confidence of walking on a marble-covered ramp, we inched downward, roped together for safety. Only after rappelling to the glacier below could crampons again provide firm footing as we worked our way through the crevasse field one final time. Elated but exhausted, we reached camp 12½ hours after departing.

There we relaxed, enjoying hot drinks while watching the setting sun cast rich light and lengthening shadows across Gannett Peak. The weather held one more day, time spent exploring the Titcomb Basin and retracing the path to our lake-view campsite. Cirrus clouds, harbingers of weather change, streamed across the afternoon sky followed by evening lenticulars that hovered over the tall peaks. The next morning we awoke to a cold, steady rain that would accompany us all seventeen miles out.

But even the rainy weather did not dampen my spirits. My confidence was high. I had summited one of the most difficult state highpoints via a challenging and elegant route. The climb had been beautiful, even if a little scary. And perhaps this widespread precipitation would douse the forest fires that blocked access to Montana's Granite Peak, that state's loftiest mountain and my next highpointing goal.

Yet it was not to be. In Pinedale we learned that the Forest Service had decided to prohibit all access to Granite Peak for the rest of the season. My goal of reaching the highpoints of Wyoming, Montana, and Idaho, three of the nation's most remote and difficult state summits, would not be realized this year. As we shared a celebratory feast in a Pineville restaurant, Tom and I discussed the third peak in that northern triumvirate, Borah, located in south-central Idaho. I had hoped to attempt this challenging peak, the most difficult state highpoint that can be summited alone, after climbing the other large mountains. But with Montana's summit closed and winter rapidly approaching, I was advised to try Borah next.

Later that evening Tom returned to Jackson for his next guiding assignment. I stayed in Pinedale to wash clothes, dry gear, and study both the road atlas and guidebooks.

For now, a change of plan was necessary.

CHAPTER 11

HEADING SOUTH

The Rocky Mountains

I couldn't bask long in the glory of summiting Gannett Peak. The sudden weather change and season-ending closure of Granite Peak, my next planned goal, necessitated a new strategy, a quickly conceived modification of my carefully crafted itinerary. Sitting on a wobbly plastic chair in a laundromat, I ran my finger along red and blue lines in the atlas adding up distances: nearly 600 miles to White Butte, North Dakota's highest point; less than 200 to Borah Peak, Idaho's loftiest summit.

White Butte had not been on this trip's itinerary. Borah had, but it scared me. Located in south-central Idaho's Lost River Range, Borah Peak (12,662 feet) is the most challenging state summit that can safely be climbed unroped, and a mountain feared by many highpointers. Its primary route is a steep rocky ascent along an exposed ridgeline with the anxiety-provoking name of Chicken Out Ridge. This strenuous ascent is rated a third- to fourth-class scramble—safe for experienced climbers yet sufficiently difficult and dangerous that many novices rope up with a guide.

A solo attempt would be even more demanding. In the east I had frequently hiked alone, finding the quiet solitude exhilarating, but had yet to solo a major western mountain. Before this trip I had sought advice from Jackson Hole Mountain Guides, a company which leads climbs up Borah, and from Forest Service personnel who manage and patrol the peak. I consulted guidebooks, talked with other climbers, and read trip reports posted on the Internet. Although some highpointers with little technical mountaineering experience voiced concern, all others concurred that, although challenging, an experienced climber could safely solo the peak.

But did I have sufficient experience? As Tom and I hiked through the rugged expanses of Wyoming's Wind River Range, I thought of the responsibilities that even a single-day climb in a remote region entails—route finding, hazard evaluation, weather forecasting—and the ability to survive illness, injury, or a fall. On tall western peaks there are no painted white blazes or rustic wood-burned signs detailing color-coded routes with distances measured to the tenth mile. Instead climbers are expected to follow natural "lines" of ascent—ridge crests and rocky spurs—that are often unmarked save for occasional stone cairns.

I had hoped to do more climbing to increase confidence and better acclimate before my first solo attempt. But as cold rain splatted against the laundromat's window I knew that time was not an ally; winter was nearly upon the northern Rockies. A mellow hike up North Dakota's White Butte was not an option. So the next morning, beneath blustery skies, I left Pinedale, driving toward Borah.

A leisurely drive through Wyoming's arid grasslands brought me to State Route 28, a modern roadway paralleling the Oregon Trail and Big Sandy River. Historical markers lined the route. Here in 1847, Jim Bridger met Brigham Young, urging the Mormon leader to abandon plans to settle near the Great Salt Lake and telling him that Utah's land was so poor that the renowned mountain man "would pay $1,000 for the first bushel of corn grown in that valley." Another marker commemorated the graves beside the Oregon Trail, final resting places for some of the thousands of pioneers who never lived to complete their journey, while a third detailed a planned federal invasion of Utah, an 1857 fiasco led by General Albert Sidney Johnston. The general had orders to replace Brigham Young as territorial governor; however Utah militiamen attacked the poorly defended federal supplies. With the army delayed, negotiations commenced, ultimately averting bloodshed.

West of Kemmerer I turned north through Pocatello and the Ft. Hall Indian Reservation then entered the Idaho National Engineering and Environmental Lab, a sprawling nuclear research facility covering over 500 square miles. Recent range fires had scorched a quarter of the facility's grasslands; flashing signs warned of dust storms. With car windows rolled up tightly, I drove on.

At the southern terminus of the Lost River Range I entered Arco, population 1,000, a town that prides itself as the nation's first community lighted by atomic power. This was not my first visit here. Six years earlier while touring Craters of the Moon National Monument and EBR-1, the first atomic reactor to produce electricity, I had stayed here. Arco had changed little since that visit. Aging buildings lined Main Street, many predating the night in 1951 when the town's lights were first powered by split atoms. Small "mom and pop" motels advertised "clean, air-conditioned rooms" with "in-room television and telephone," while Pickle's Drive-In, at the town's south end, proclaimed itself "Home of the Atomic Burger."

I turned into the empty lot beside the small motel in which I had stayed half a decade earlier. Surprised by the lighted "No Vacancy" sign, I entered to inquire about other lodging. Rooms, however, were still available. "It's been a really slow day," remarked the resident manager, who seemed disinterested when told of the lighted sign. The motel's small rooms were as advertised—neat and clean with a private phone, a coffee maker, and an aging television that received two channels and all for a quarter the price of my Jackson Hole accommodations.

After registering I did not tarry long, instead following U.S. Highway 93 and the Lost River north, scouting the route to the trailhead before evening darkness. The strenuous hike up Borah, climbing more than a vertical mile, required a pre-dawn start; I didn't want time wasted searching by headlamp for the trailhead.

North of Mackay I turned onto a gravel road and drove three miles to a dusty clearing. The parking lot and nearby campground were both empty; a frightened ground squirrel scurried across the parched landscape. A rocky wall and precipitous 14-foot drop cut across the valley near the mountain's base. Surface fissures, some a foot wide and forty yards long, split the surrounding terrain.

The Lost River Valley is one of the nation's most seismically active regions. Borah, through a series of earthquakes, has been lifted 8,000 feet during the past five million years. The most recent quake, a 1983 jolt measuring 7.3 on the Richter Scale, killed two

Borah Peak
From the Lost River Valley

people in this sparsely settled valley and created the 14-foot-high escarpment near me, a rift extending twenty-one miles.

I looked up at the mountain, a rocky behemoth towering a mile above. As I searched for the trailhead and followed the path a short distance into the forest to ascertain the route, I reconsidered plans to climb alone. I had climbed many mountains and visited remote areas but always as part of a group. And, although frequently alone to photograph, enjoy solitude, or explore, I had the safety of others knowing my whereabouts and expecting my timely return.

Tomorrow would be different. I would be responsible for everything—safety and food, route-finding and weather evaluation, all while attempting one of the most demanding state summits. But before returning to the parking lot, I had reached my decision: I would try. If the mountain was too big, too dangerous, or too isolated, if I became uncomfortable or scared, I could retreat. I could accept a failure to summit; I could not forgive a failure to try.

No stars were visible as I left the nearly empty motel parking lot at 4:00 a.m., the no vacancy sign brightly lit as it had been since my arrival. Ten miles up the Lost River Valley, the clouds were lower, touching the mountaintops. Five minutes later a cold drizzle spattered against the windshield. Turning onto the dirt road leading to the mountain's base, dust and drizzle mixed into a nearly opaque glop that was smeared by the wipers into messy semicircular streaks.

The parking lot, deserted yesterday, was abuzz with activity. Nearly every space was occupied; around each vehicle groups of climbers, barely seen save for their headlamps, donned raingear and repacked backpacks, adjusting for the unexpected weather. Stepping from the car, I was shocked by the low temperature. I quickly put on Gore-Tex raingear, tightened bootlaces, and cinched my pack, anxious to begin the ascent.

Dozens of climbers traced a path from the trailhead into the forest. This was not the wilderness experience I had hoped for, nor the risky isolation I had feared. Instead I was one of nearly a hundred climbers walking into a cold rain on a holiday weekend, hoping to reach the top of Idaho.

The trail rose quickly; exertion drove off the morning chill. One of the steepest highpointing routes, this trail climbs 5,750 feet in less than 3½ miles. Falling into a steady rhythm with steps and breathing synchronized, I gained 1,000 feet before earliest light made headlamps unnecessary.

However, I was puzzled. Two hundred feet ahead, the ground appeared white. An illusion, I reasoned, probably due to the dull early morning light. But minutes later, my fears were confirmed. Snow had begun to fall.

It was September 2. At 8,500 feet above sea level, I was entering a snowstorm. Four thousand feet of mountain loomed above, hidden by clouds that cloaked the treetops. I had no rope, no crampons, and no partner. Desire and determination pushed me on as I hoped that the storm would abate.

Soft blobs of heavy wet snow clung to pine branches and fallen logs, but the trail, although increasingly muddy, remained snow-free. A quarter-hour later, however, the precipitation intensified and the wet flakes began covering both ground and trail. Climbers slowed, reassessing conditions. One couple turned back. As the snow deepened, nearly obscuring the increasingly slick trail, I advanced more slowly, hoping for a break in the weather, a change that seemed ever less likely.

Optimism, for a climber, is as necessary as desire, physical conditioning, stamina, or skill. To arise at 4:00 a.m., walk into cold darkness, then climb for six, ten, perhaps fourteen hours, hoping to touch an isolated speck of earth, is an act of faith. Confidence and a sense of possibility, tempered by a realistic evaluation of danger, are essential.

But doubt and worry seeped into my mind. The snow was accumulating rapidly and fresh flakes quickly blurred footprints. Clouds reached the ground; visibility was limited by fog and snow to sixty feet.

At timberline, 3,500 feet below the summit, I approached a huddled group of climbers in the midst of an animated discussion. All faces showed worried expressions.

"I've climbed Hood," I overheard one strongly built young man say, as I stepped to the edge of the group, "but these are the worst conditions I have ever seen."

"Last month I climbed Rainier and the guides called me an animal (a compliment about personal toughness). I want to push on," said another.

Three climbers, ascending as a team, glanced at each other. "I have a rope," one of the men stated boldly, as he reached into his pack. But instead of a standard 160-foot climbing rope, the "rope" he proudly displayed was a nearly useless 15-foot length of one-inch webbing. His wife, wearing only a thin Lycra top beneath her unzipped jacket, shivered as he spoke.

Their companion had summited Denali. "It is pointless to move higher in these conditions," he stated.

All eyes turned to me, until now only an observer. More than half a foot of snow covered the large, irregularly shaped rocks that would be our path to the summit. The snow was falling rapidly; visibility was near zero; and no one had rope, harness, or crampons. Under these conditions any mishap, however minor, could necessitate a difficult and high-risk rescue.

Following the others' pattern, I first related a major climbing accomplishment, that of summiting South America's Aconcagua, before sharing my opinion. Then disappointment swept over me as I softly said, "I am going down."

Heads nodded in agreement. A half-inch of snow had fallen during this short discussion, covering our footprints. Even the "Animal" understood the danger and futility of going higher and opted to descend with us.

Falling snow, low clouds, and minimal visibility accompanied me to the parking lot as did the Animal, a likable, retired serviceman from northern Utah. Al had recently begun mountaineering and possessed a determination and passion for climbing that rivaled mine. Though not a true highpointer, he hoped to summit many prominent peaks including most of the western state summits. As we descended, he shared his extensive knowledge of the region's topography and weather patterns.

The information was not encouraging. Kings Peak, Utah's highest mountain, would also receive this storm's heavy snowfall, Al said. So would Granite—and all the northern Rockies. Reiterating information I had read in guidebooks, he told me that with this, autumn's first major snowfall, the year's climbing season was over. A week and a half into my grand excursion, fire had denied even an attempt on Granite Peak, and now an early-season snowstorm was forcing me off Borah. Even summiting Kings Peak this year would no longer be possible.

The snow line had dropped to the parking lot; an inch covered the cars when we arrived. Al quickly took down his tent, tossed soggy gear into his van and followed me to Arco. He too had seen the no vacancy sign, and assuming the motel full, drove to the trailhead campground, there enduring a cold rainy night in a leaky tent. But rooms were now available—he could even have mine. Although unsure of my destination, I was leaving, heading south before being stranded in Arco by snow.

Wet snowflakes mixed with cold rain as I packed the car, bid Al goodbye and left the motel, passing the still lit no vacancy sign. Following the Lost River south toward the Snake River Plain, I felt lost too. Gray skies and cold drizzle added to my somber mood as the waters of the Lost River slowly disappeared into the ground, its waters percolating between chunks of volcanic rock where mountains and Plain meet.

Six weeks earlier I had left the emergency department to embark on The Dream, a journey I had envisioned as filled with hope and promise and discovery. Discovery, I knew, was not always accompanied by clear skies and gentle breezes, but now both climbing and touring plans were unraveling. If I failed to summit only one of these northern peaks, I had reasoned, I could climb it the following summer. But as I drove westward,

I realized that three state highpoints, three of the nation's most difficult, would remain unclimbed this year.

I tried to focus on the scenery as I crossed a stark volcanic landscape shrouded by fog and drizzle. A broad flat expanse across southern Idaho, the Plain is like a giant inverted arch, 100 miles wide, traversing the state. The Snake River hugs the valley's southern boundary and is the region's only surface water. But between river and mountains, swaths of broken igneous rock separate broad expanses of rich volcanic soil. Center pivot irrigation systems feed mile-wide circles of agricultural bounty by tapping into an underlying aquifer, a slowly moving underground river seeping southward.

I followed the Plain's northern edge past the Craters of the Moon National Monument to Carey then turned south on Highway 93, traveling through Shoshone to Twin Falls. There I finally escaped the cold rain. But puffy white clouds, driven by a frigid northwest wind, blew over the arid landscape. The mountain storm, I learned, was predicted to last two more days, then following a 48-hour respite, another stronger storm was forecast.

In Twin Falls I stopped and rested, let clothing dry in the low desert humidity, and planned how this climbing excursion might be salvaged. There were two options: 1) drive southwestward to the White Mountains and Sierras, attempting the highest peaks of Nevada and California; or 2) travel southeast, hoping to top out in Colorado, New Mexico, and perhaps Arizona. Both options were fraught with uncertainty. Colorado and New Mexico, although easier climbs, lay in the storm's predicted path. And although the westerly peaks currently enjoyed stable weather, they were remote, more challenging, and beset with access issues and logistical difficulties. The decision was critical. Neither my schedule nor confidence could accommodate another failure.

Sometimes the best choice is a "non-decision." In Idaho's fourth-largest city, I took a 24-hour break and waited for the storm's movement before deciding between competing strategies. It was a welcomed reprieve.

East of town I visited Shoshone Falls where the Snake River plunges down a 212-foot-high cataract. However, this September the falls were nearly dry, the upstream water dammed and diverted for irrigation. Instead of the thunderous cascade that once spanned this canyon, only thin ribbons of water trickled over the rocky precipice. A nearby interpretative sign showcased irrigation and the "blooming of the desert," a process requiring the equivalent of sixty inches of rainfall annually to yield agricultural crops. And the sign boasted of how little water was "wasted" by being allowed to flow downstream.

West of Twin Falls I followed the Snake River Canyon twenty miles to Hagerman and Thousand Springs. Geologists believe that this canyon, a steep-walled gash in the earth hundreds of feet deep, is not the result of eons of slow erosion, but instead the product of a cataclysmic flood 30,000 years ago. Lasting perhaps just two weeks, this inundation occurred when Lake Bonneville, a huge shallow lake that once covered much of northern Utah, overflowed its banks, cut a rapidly enlarging swath through soft bedrock, and released nearly one cubic mile of water—140 billion gallons in all—into the Snake River.

Today, torrents of water, the southern terminus of the Lost River, gush from fissures lining the canyon's northern wall, refilling the Snake's nearly dry riverbed. Decades earlier this water had flowed off Borah Peak and past Arco, then slowly seeped south beneath the Snake River Plain to re-emerge cold, clean and well-oxygenated. With a year-round temperature of fifty-eight degrees, this water is not used for irrigation but for fish hatcheries, supporting a local industry that supplies 70 percent of the nation's trout hatchlings. At Thousand Springs, I had "found" the Lost River—quite unexpectedly—at nearly the same time I decided on highpointing plans.

Feeling less hubris after summiting only one of the highpoints in the northern Rockies, I opted for the easier hikes in Colorado and New Mexico, hoping to beat the winter snows. My first goal would be Mt. Elbert (14,433 feet), Colorado's loftiest peak and the second tallest mountain in the contiguous 48 states. Sixty-one feet lower than California's Mt. Whitney, it is a physically demanding but straightforward, non-technical day hike. Hundreds of hikers reach its summit on busy summer days. Hockey's Stanley Cup, a silver trophy three feet high and weighing thirty-five pounds, has been carried to Elbert's top. And Keegan Reilly, a paraplegic climber, pushed himself to the summit in a specially-designed wheelchair, an endurance feat that required five days.

But as I drove south from Idaho, I scanned the sky and worried. Little had gone as planned. Now I was bypassing sights I had hoped to see—Dinosaur National Monument, Arches National Park, Colorado National Monument—trying to reach Leadville, near Mt. Elbert's base, before dark. In mid-afternoon I entered Colorado's high country—Vail and Aspen, Glenwood Springs and Independence Pass—and more 14,000-foot-high peaks than anywhere else in the contiguous United States. The skies were gray but lightening, there was no fresh snow on the high peaks, and the forecast promised one day of good weather before the next storm. Maybe, I thought, maybe my luck was changing.

The next morning, beneath starry skies, I began ascending Mt. Elbert, following a well maintained trail that rose 5,300 feet in 5½ miles. At this early hour I was the only hiker on this often crowded path. As day broke, I walked through open coniferous forests. Steller's Jays and Clark's Nutcrackers, nearly ubiquitous birds of western montane forests, sounded shrill alarms at my approach. Squirrels scurried away, temporarily retreating from autumnal nut gathering.

It was a pleasant hike. The layer of pine needles covering the soil allowed quiet, soft walking, while the wide trail did not require constant attention for foot placements. The mountain air was crisp and clean; scents of pine wafted on the gentle breeze.

Two and a half hours after starting, I reached timberline, here slightly above 11,000 feet. At this uppermost altitude where trees can survive, there is little transition, no gradual thinning or shortening of the forest. Instead the forest ends abruptly and one steps into a high alpine environment, an environment dominated by lichens, mosses, and ground-hugging vegetation. Bare rocks are the tallest features of this landscape; vegetation crowds between and behind them, seeking protection from both the intense high-altitude sun and the bitterly cold winter winds.

But these hardy plants, able to withstand some of the planet's harshest conditions, are amazingly fragile. Eroded trails, some nearly a foot deep, cut narrow brown swaths through low-lying vegetation. No blazes or signs are needed here, one only needs to follow the deeply cut ruts uphill.

The wind and sun took turns taunting me on this exposed

slope. When the wind stirred, the thin mountain air was cold; when the breeze abated, the sun was uncomfortably warm. Several clothing adjustments later, the trail steepened and vegetation thinned. A flock of plump ptarmigans, pigeon-sized avian residents of Arctic and alpine environments, foraged among scattered grasses beside the trail, the birds displaying mottled brown summer plumage, a feathery coat that would soon be replaced by one of solid white for winter camouflage.

Seven hundred feet below the summit, a magnificent vista spread before me. Mt. Massive, its snow-streaked summit only twelve feet lower than Elbert's, lay across the valley to my right; Twin Lakes shimmered far below to my left; and directly ahead, Mt. Elbert's summit loomed large against the deep blue sky. The air was crisp and, save for a few wispy clouds, the sky clear. Hiking alone on a mountain so large and high was a new and exhilarating experience.

Surrounded by light breezes, sun, and wildness, I walked on, through ever-thinning air. Yesterday I had considered Mt. Elbert a consolation peak, but now, as I neared the summit, it was THE peak, and a wonderful mountain for my first solo ascent.

The trail's upper portion was its steepest, ascending stepwise through a rocky field. Plant life was left behind; even lichens and moss couldn't survive the extreme conditions at this altitude. I coordinated slowing steps with more rapid breathing. Two steps per breath slowed to one per breath as I labored up the rocky incline. The trail crossed boulders and bedrock, not loose scree; footing was firm and solid.

Then the trail turned sharply to the right and leveled off. With each step, the rocky profile of Elbert's summit sank nearer the horizon. A dozen breaths and a similar number of steps later, I stood atop Colorado.

I had done it!

Alone, I gazed at the state's high country spread below. Rugged peaks, many sporting vestiges of last winter's snow, extended in all directions. Deep valleys, green with coniferous forests, separated the bare, mostly brown peaks. Only to the east did the land flatten, there forming the Arkansas River Valley.

I walked around the summit, a rocky but mostly level area nearly thirty feet across, enjoying the majestic view and wild solitude. Many minutes passed before I sat down to inscribe my name in the summit register. After signing I leafed through the notebook, a mostly uninteresting document, but quickly put it back in its container; the scenery was too spectacular to ignore.

Half an hour after topping out, I heard labored breathing and the scratching of boots against rock. At the summit's far end two hikers slowly appeared, torsos lifting higher with each labored step. The men paused and waved, resting and hyper-ventilating, finding the thin air as challenging as I had.

Todd and Dave, two Texans in their mid-20s, had ascend-ed an alternate route, a slightly shorter path from near Twin Lakes. Experienced hikers and backpackers, they had recently graduated to mountaineering. Oregon's Mt. Hood was the only technical peak they had climbed, but on this trip, to gain experi-ence at altitude, they had hiked to the top of three of Colorado's fifty-four 14,000-foot-high peaks. This was their fourth state highpoint, and although they did not share my goal of reaching all fifty were intrigued by my quest.

We chatted and shared climbing tales as other climbers moved toward the summit. Half an hour later, eight people stood atop Colorado, while two dozen more labored upward. Today would be another busy day atop Elbert.

Todd and Dave needed to return to Texas, and work, by morning. I wished them safe travels and successful climbing as they began descending, then after a final look from the sum-mit of Colorado, I also began retracing my steps. The descent was peaceful and without incident. Throughout the afternoon clouds gathered, not the dark thunderheads common in sum-mer, but a thickening layer of gray, heralding the approaching winter storm.

But this time, I didn't worry. I had summited Elbert—and done my first solo western peak. As I walked down the gray rocks, followed the well-worn ruts through alpine vegetation, and again provoked alarm calls from forest birds, I felt a sense of peace and contentment. Thrilled to have summited Elbert, I was proud to have done it alone—and relieved to have beaten the snow.

The next morning, clouds obscured the mountains and a steady drizzle dampened Leadville. The bank's time and tem-perature sign read forty degrees. The hour didn't matter; it was again time to head south.

Like a refugee fleeing an advancing force, a storm that

would bring an early winter to Colorado's mountains, I drove through the Arkansas River Valley, past Buena Vista, the Great Sand Dunes National Monument, and Alamosa. Growing up in Colorado, I had visited these areas and, although I wished to see how they had changed during these three decades, I feared delay might trap me in a snowstorm.

I drove the entire day, reaching a windy and chilly Taos, New Mexico, shortly before nightfall. Four days earlier I had been in Idaho's Lost River Range, 500 miles from the Canadian border. Now I was 300 miles north of Mexico, still trying to avoid this series of storms. In Taos I planned to rest and wait, hoping that the next storm would bring only rain—and that the unusual weather pattern would change.

CHAPTER 12

CATHARSIS

The Southern Rockies

In Taos, the Weather Channel predicted that unsettled weather would spread across northern New Mexico the next day. After that, the smiling anchorwoman said, strong thunderstorms and heavy mountain snows were likely. In a pattern typical of winter, the jet stream was plunging south across the Rockies, from Washington to New Mexico, before turning east. Like an airborne conveyor belt, these high-altitude winds were bringing a series of rapidly moving storms along, and to the north of, its path. This pattern, she said, would persist at least another week.

I was tired, hoping for a rest. During two weeks, I had driven from Las Vegas to the Montana border, west to Idaho then south to New Mexico—3,000 miles in all—but had summited only two state highpoints. Stormy weather was again predicted. Now twenty miles from the base of Wheeler Peak (13,161 feet), New Mexico's tallest mountain, I had but twenty-four hours before an early season storm might make the trails impassable until spring. Rest and touring would have to wait; there was a mountain to be climbed.

Hispanics, Anglos, and Native Americans, each comprising approximately one-third of the population, give New Mexico a vibrant cultural mix. Pueblo Indian communities such as Taos that are located in the state's northern third are among the most intact and traditional indigenous societies in the nation. Before European contact, these were settled peoples who farmed the

Adobe Church
Taos, New Mexico

Rio Grande Valley and lived in compact cities of multi-storied adobe houses.

Some of these villages pre-date the Anasazi, builders of Mesa Verde, Chaco Canyon, and dozens of other sites in the Four Corners region. Sky City, a Pueblo village on the Acoma Reservation, is believed to be the oldest continually inhabited location in North America. Evidence documents human settlement atop this rugged butte since at least 500 A.D., half a millennium before the Anasazi flourished. And although the Anasazi mysteriously abandoned this region around 1200 A.D., the Pueblo people remained.

During an earlier southwestern excursion, I had visited Sky City. Fewer than two-dozen people, mostly elders, still reside there, living in two-story stone and adobe dwellings. There is no running water or electricity, and photography is not allowed. Water is brought daily to the residents, and if needed, generators can be used to power life-saving medical equipment. But the day I visited, accompanied by the required tribal guide, the only sounds were of the wind blowing across the high exposed butte. Residents quietly carried out daily tasks, never acknowledging my presence, living much as their ancestors did a thousand years earlier, yet within view of modern Acoma and Interstate Highway 40.

Today, however, most Native Americans reside in mobile homes or small single-family dwellings, much like working-class people throughout the state. These communities—Acoma, Santo Domingo, Santa Clara, Jemez, and a dozen others—appear as compact modern towns. But each represents a separate tribe; each has its own laws and government; and the economy of each depends heavily on tourism and the accompanying gas stations, convenience stores, tobacco shops, and casinos that bring jobs and varying levels of prosperity.

The Pueblos are one of the few native groups to have retained their ancestral lands. In contrast to the nomadic Plains Indians and the wide-ranging mountain tribes, these people were farmers, using irrigation to grow corn, beans, and squash near their villages. Despite conflict, the Spanish accepted the land claims of a sedentary people, granting ownership titles recognized even after the United States gained possession of New Mexico in 1846.

Thirty-six hours after summiting Mt. Elbert, however, I was not sightseeing but wandering through Taos Valley Ski Resort's parking lot looking for a trail leading to Wheeler Peak's summit. My late arrival and sudden change in plans had precluded scouting the trailheads during daylight. Instead, after a short night's sleep in Taos, I was wasting valuable time searching for them in pre-dawn darkness.

Two routes ascend Wheeler Peak. One follows ski runs, traverses undeveloped Forest Service property and climbs steeply up a long rocky gully to the summit; the other requires a longer but more gradual ascent along an exposed ridgeline. According to guidebooks and trip reports, both routes are beautiful. And both are listed among the nation's most challenging highpoint hikes.

I had planned for an early start, hoping to reach the summit via the steep gully then return along the scenic ridge. But at the ski area there were no maps, signs, or markers for either trail. As the eastern sky lightened, and after a half hour of fruitless searching, I would have taken either route, any route, to reach the summit before the predicted afternoon storms. Even the guidebooks weren't helpful, and at this early hour, the parking lot remained deserted.

A jogger approached and I waved, hoping he would slow as I shouted out my query. But his pace never varied. "I don't live here," he yelled as he shrugged his shoulders and ran on.

I drove around the expansive parking lot, past shuttered shops and restaurants. Surely one of these businesses must be preparing to open. But the only people I met were an older couple walking a small poodle. The trailheads were several miles up the mountain, they said, but were uncertain which roads led there.

Sunlight touched the highest peaks. It was 6:40 a.m. An aging dust-covered pickup truck rattled into the parking lot. I waved the driver down. "Yeah, it's up the mountain a ways," the burly man said, "but it's hard to find." He paused. "Follow me. I'll take you there."

We ascended steep roads, made multiple turns, and passed neatly maintained vacation homes. The pavement ended but we continued until the bumpy road dead-ended into an empty gravel parking lot. "There it is," the man shouted over the truck's low rumble, pointing to a small sign at the lot's far end as I retrieved my pack. "Good luck."

I yelled my thanks as he turned and left then began walking, hoping to make up for the late start. The hiking was easy, but the scenery disappointing as the well-marked route traversed a maze of ski trails and logged terrain. Fallen trees and sawn limbs littered the mountainside; this was not the beautiful hike I had expected.

A mile later the route left the privately owned resort and entered the Wheeler Peak Wilderness Area. In this pristine landscape, as in all such federally designated areas, the trail was unmarked. But the path was evident, a narrow brown line trampled through thin vegetation between ever more sparse trees. Decades had passed since this land had been logged, and although the high-altitude forest was thin, the trees appeared youthful and vigorous. Surrounded by dramatic scenery, the trail rose gradually, and forty-five minutes later I stood at the head of the valley beside Williams Lake.

Mountain images, bathed in the golden glow of early morning light, reflected from the lake's dark, still water. A small grassy plain, wet with dew, extended eighty feet from the shoreline. Mountains ringed the lake on three sides. Deep in the early morning shadow of Wheeler Peak, valley and lake were cold, calm, and quiet.

I removed my pack and sat on a log near the water's edge. Eleven thousand years ago a river of ice had filled this valley, smoothing and rounding the terrain, as it moved slowly downhill. But at the glacier's head, the ice had deeply gouged the mountainside creating a cirque, a steeply walled natural amphitheater that cut into Wheeler's flanks.

I looked up at these rocky walls, searching for the best route to New Mexico's highest point. A steep gully, filled with a jumble of tan and gray rocks, provided the only practical line. Alongside this thin route, extending the full breadth and nearly half the height of the cirque's walls, dew-slickened grass mixed with loose scree, making ascents elsewhere all but impossible.

The high altitude and cold morning temperature lessened the risk of snakes, but I approached the gully cautiously and remained vigilant as I started up, especially when reaching toward a rock. From the lake these stones had appeared loose and randomly scattered, another line of shifting scree. But centuries of rain, frost, melting snow, and ice had repositioned them, creating a stable path 2,000 feet up the steep wall.

The sharp angle and irregularly placed rocks, some the size of a small house, required strenuous scrambling but permitted rapid elevation gain. There were few places to rest, so except for occasional glances back toward the still shaded cirque, I climbed on cautiously, possessing no illusions that this was a heavily trafficked route. Since leaving the trailhead, I had not seen another person nor heard another human sound—and had no expectation of meeting anyone before the summit ridge.

Yet I did not find the isolation scary. Soloing is much different than group hiking or climbing and may at first seem risky and dangerous. But each facet of such an ascent can be an asset—or liability—depending upon personal, weather, or climbing conditions. The experience can be exhilarating if the weather is good, the route well marked, and the climber strong.

But even the most trivial problem can quickly escalate into a major crisis. There is no one to help scout for trail markers or changing weather conditions, to cook or obtain water, or lighten the pack of an exhausted climber. A turned ankle or twisted knee can result in a frigid night outdoors waiting for rescuers.

Groups, however, can breed a false sense of security. Strong individuals can assist injured, ill, or weak members. But many parties are composed only of inexperienced, poorly prepared climbers. When difficulties arise, groups often split with the strongest individuals frequently forging ahead leaving the least prepared and least experienced members to fend for themselves.

I understood and accepted the risks of hiking alone and tried to mitigate them. I carried extra water and food plus iodine tablets, knife, map, and compass. For warmth I packed an extra layer of capilene and always took hat, gloves, jacket, and rain pants, believing that if misfortune befell, I could survive, albeit uncomfortably, a night out. With the additional weight of cameras and lenses, my pack often weighed thirty pounds when I left the trailhead.

However, I did not carry a cell phone. In the mountains reception is frequently poor, often limited to summits and exposed ridgelines. Many times their use requires a considerable hike and prior knowledge of where reception is possible. If I was healthy enough to reach an exposed ridgeline, I reasoned, I should be healthy enough to walk out. Another rationale was philosophical: I enjoy wildness and solitude and, although phones can be turned off, I did not wish to feel electronically tethered to the world below. Instead I arranged a contact person—a family member or park ranger—who would summon help if I failed to make a timely return.

Alone above Williams Lake, I worked my way up the rocky gully. The air thinned but the route remained steep—nearly forty degrees—forcing a gradually slowing pace. After two hours of steady exertion the channel widened; the rocks became smaller and looser. The slope's angle lessened and the skyline was dominated by a long ridgeline ascending gently to the right.

At the ridge, I rested. Sunlight filled the cirque below, sparkling off the lake's wind-stirred surface. The morning sun felt pleasantly warm, but a light breeze intermittently chilled the air. The sky was clear and the views spectacular.

A rocky path followed the prominent crest directly to Wheeler's summit. It was an easy stroll to the top of New Mexico. At 10:45 a.m. I completed the final steps and stood atop Wheeler Peak.

Mountainous terrain fell away in all directions. A deep blue sky, now broken by white cloud wisps above the highest peaks, arched over the landscape. The rocky summit was void of vegetation. A round canister, appearing like a spent artillery shell, was chained to the mountain and nestled into a deep rocky hole. A nearby metal plaque memorialized the mountain's namesake, Major George Wheeler, who for a decade during the late nineteenth century led scientific explorations throughout the American southwest.

Leaning against the warm, tan-colored stone, I removed a frayed notebook from the heavy container and scanned the entries. Most were a mixture of machismo, profanity, and drivel. But one stood out, speaking directly to my heart. "We thank the Earth, the Creator, and all creation," it said, "and all those who have come before and gone on."

Memories of my father and feelings of inestimable loss overwhelmed me. Alone atop New Mexico, I broke down and cried. The full power of the loss of a parent, a mentor, and yes, a friend, overcame me. I wept openly, a deep sobbing cry.

Two years had passed since my father's death. I had already cried and grieved and hurt. Why again? And why now? It suddenly felt as though I had never grieved. Had all the pain accomplished nothing?

I glanced down the trail, hoping no one was ascending. No one was, but if someone had appeared, I am uncertain if I could have stopped this emotional outpouring, for this was a catharsis, an involuntary and spontaneous expulsion of suppressed grief.

Minutes later the sobbing stopped, the emotional abscess drained. I re-opened the register and turned to a blank page. "To those who have gone before," I inscribed, "with love and thanks." Then, as always, I wrote my name and town.

Closing the notebook, I looked up. The white wisps had expanded into large cumulus clouds with dark underbellies. Today thunderstorms would arrive early.

After a few self-portraits, I photographed my backpack beside the plaque, visual documentation of my accomplishment. (However, I was never asked for such evidence. The Highpointers Club, I later learned, operates strictly on the honor system.)

Less than half an hour after topping out I started down, following the exposed ridgeline, a route traversing three named peaks—Mt. Walter, Frazer Mountain, and Bull-of-the-Woods Mountain. Horseshoe Lake, a high alpine pond, lay to my right as I neared the first of these peaks, then a short distance later I stared down the steep gully I had ascended from Williams Lake, a path that would be a slow and difficult descent. Downclimbing rock is much riskier than ascending, so despite the deteriorating weather, I hurried on, traversing Mt. Walter then descending toward the La Cal Basin, a route I believed would be safer. Nearing the shallow valley 12,000 feet above sea level, I met Eric, a stocky young climber and the first person I had seen on the mountain. We chatted briefly about the route and weather. He too had been watching the sky; the clouds were quickly gathering over the summit and he was as anxious to complete the ascent as I was to get down.

Minutes later the wind freshened and thunder rumbled, the deep guttural sound of a nearby storm. Looking right, then left, seeking potential shelter or escape along the ridgeline, I found none. Glancing back, an ominous dark gray cloud cap enshrouded Wheeler's summit.

I sped to a trot as sharp cracks of lightning were followed within two seconds by loud thunderclaps. The storm was close, less than half a mile away. I ran down the ridge into the La Cal Basin, but remained the highest point on this treeless expanse. With lungs straining and leg muscles burning, I skirted Frazer Mountain, a rocky mound rising above the large plateau. With each stride, my pack bounced and swayed. Briefly I thought of my cameras; this jostling certainly wasn't good for them. But then another crack sounded as lightning struck again.

Three seconds, four, five. The thunder was slightly delayed. Maybe I was gaining on the storm. I glanced back. The dark cloud still clung tightly to Wheeler's summit but hadn't grown; the sky over Frazer Mountain and other nearby peaks remained clear.

I slowed my pace. Frazer now stood between Wheeler and me, affording some protection from lightning, but blocking my view of the storm. Instead of a casual descent enjoying expansive views and the alpine environment, I hurried on to the relative safety of the forest, trotting and running nearly two miles—all above 11,000 feet.

Taking refuge beneath a single tree during a thunderstorm is extremely dangerous because it is often an area's highest point.

But a forest, its trees of nearly equal height, is safer than open terrain. Reaching the forest I rested and ate before resuming my descent, a descent completed at a more moderate rate.

Hours later I reached the car safely, although a little damp, impressed by the power of mountain thunderstorms and the suddenness with which they can develop. Wheeler had been a longer and more physically demanding climb than Elbert, and a mountain on which I had gained much confidence.

Returning to Taos, I learned that west of New Mexico a stable weather pattern, typical September conditions that in most years dominate the entire west, now held sway. For the first time since descending Gannett Peak two weeks earlier, my itinerary could be more than a rushed scramble before advancing winter storms.

Humphreys Peak (12,633 feet), Arizona's tallest mountain, was my next goal. Located north of Flagstaff and 350 miles west of Taos, it is arguably the least difficult of the western summits. Ascending a relatively modest 3,150 feet, the trail is well marked and measures just over four miles in length. Three major peaks, all dormant volcanoes in the San Francisco Mountains—Humphreys, Agassiz, and Fremont—are sacred to Native Americans. To the Navajo, this trio is the "Sacred Mountain of the West;" to the Hopi, the summit clouds are home to ancestral spirits that when properly honored bring rain to the land below. Aspen-filled valleys lie between mountains covered with ponderosa pine, but the major summits reach well above timberline and are snow-covered much of the year.

Twenty miles south of the San Francisco Peaks lies Flagstaff, northern Arizona's most populous city. Located 7,000 feet high on the Mogollon Rim, a lofty plateau extending across the northern quarter of the state, this city enjoys a climate more like Colorado's than the searing heat of Arizona's Sonoran Desert.

Nearing Flagstaff, however, I was worried; a plume of smoke rose from a forest fire burning near the base of Humphreys' northeastern flank. And although the summit trail ascends the peak's opposite side, I learned that closure of all hiking routes was under consideration. But it was midafternoon, far too late to begin an ascent. All I could do was wait, hoping that this fire would not add to my string of access problems.

Exiting the interstate I followed old Highway 66, today officially termed Business Loop 40, into Flagstaff. Called America's "Mother Road" by John Steinbeck, Route 66, however, is neither the nation's oldest highway nor its longest—but it is the most famous.

Commissioned in 1926, U.S. Highway 66 extended 2,448 miles from Chicago to Los Angeles, crossing portions of eight states and three time zones. Two hundred thousand people followed the road west during the Depression, leaving the Dust Bowl for better opportunities in California. By 1937 the road was completely paved; ten years later it was popularized in song; and in 1960 was the namesake for an eponymous TV series that aired for four years.

But by 1970 nearly the entire route had been supplanted by interstate highways. Route 66, however, was destined to be more than an historical footnote. The roadway had captured the nation's imagination and was lined with hundreds of individually owned businesses trying desperately to survive in towns bypassed by the superhighways. Segments, especially in the southwest, were converted to business loops and scenic bypasses. Preservation groups formed, guidebooks were written, and the Mother Road lived on.

I had encountered portions of this route in New Mexico, but the segment through Flagstaff was the longest I had followed. Drive-in restaurants, single-story motels, and converted service stations lined the street. Neon lights advertised "hot coffee," "in-room air conditioning," and "swimming pools." Except for a scattering of modern convenience stores, video-rental outlets, and pawnshops that jostled for visibility between the older yet generally well maintained structures, the scene looked very 50-ish. Shiny autos from that era cruised the wide thoroughfare. Only the drivers' appearances had changed from vintage photos; carefully coiffed gray locks now replaced the slicked-back hair of a half-century ago.

I inched along—speed limit twenty-five—seeming to stop at each traffic light. Half a century ago, before the interstate highway system, traveling this route, or any of America's highways, would have been equally slow. Today, however, I was in no hurry and followed Route 66's entire length through Flagstaff. It required half an hour to go six miles. As I idled at yet another stoplight, I remembered my parents recalling driving Dixie

Highway—U.S. Route 1—from New Jersey to Florida in 1949. The trip took four days. Driving 300 miles in a day, they said, was outstanding progress.

Although I wanted to stay in one of the rambling half-century-old "motor courts" that advertised "refrigerated air," I succumbed to practicality, opting for a modern chain closer to Humphreys Peak. The slow drive today had been interesting, but if Humphreys' trails were open in the morning, I wanted to be walking early, not stalled in heavy traffic.

Cooler nighttime temperatures and higher humidity prevented the forest fire from spreading. Although officially "uncontained," authorities believed the blaze didn't threaten the summit trail. So the next morning I was walking up Arizona's highest mountain before daybreak, hoping to beat the crowds, afternoon showers, and possible trail closure if the fire again flared.

With physical conditioning and acclimatization gained from ascending nearly 20,000 vertical feet in two weeks, I quickly climbed the well maintained trail to a rocky boulder field just above timberline. For an hour I worked my way among the rocks, following a broad ridgeline upward. Then 3½ hours after leaving the car, I stood atop Arizona.

The summit was rocky and, although less than a thousand feet above timberline, supported no vegetation. To the southeast a distant lake harshly reflected the morning sun while further north, far below the summit, a gray curtain of smoke rose from the fire's advancing edge. A light breeze stirred but mountaintop temperatures remained mild.

I took scenic photos and self-portraits then leaned back to rest and enjoy the view. Although hazy with smoke, the sky was cloudless. Today there would be no need to hurry off this mountain.

The morning sun felt warm on my face and contentment filled my mind. For a full hour I enjoyed Humphreys' summit. I thought of the last two weeks, hopscotching between fires and the snows that would both douse the flames and close hiking trails. Two weeks ago, not topping out in Montana, Idaho, and Utah would have been considered a failure. But now I felt no such sense, only feelings of accomplishment as I scanned the scenery of northern Arizona. Alone above timberline, the time passed quickly; solitude and tranquility were my companions.

After an hour atop the state, I started down, meeting no one above the forest edge, 800 feet below. The hikers there, the first of many I would encounter during the descent, were experienced outdoors people. Many had previously ascended Humphreys, and nearly all had hiked widely throughout the San Francisco Mountains. I spoke with some as I rested, exchanging tales, advice, and opinion. But two men in their mid-70s were the most remarkable. Each had ascended this mountain many times and, although physically fit and making good progress, told wistfully how "previous climbs seemed much easier."

Continuing down, the temperature warmed and the trail became crowded with the T-shirt and tennis shoe set. Dozens of people, many carrying only a pint of water and a granola bar, labored uphill, their facial expressions conveying a desire to be doing anything but walking up this mountain. Starting late, they would endure midday heat and possible afternoon showers. How many, I wondered, would return thirsty, hungry, and exhausted with tales of a miserable "epic"—and no desire to visit the mountains again?

The parking lot was full when I reached the trailhead. That evening in Flagstaff, I would again scan the atlas, but for the first time in weeks I had a blank slate. Hurrying to Elbert, Wheeler, and Humphreys ahead of snow and fire had given me extra time. Tonight I could dream how to fill it.

CHAPTER 13

THE TRAIL FORKS

Nevada

In 1962 London Bridge was falling down, sinking unevenly into the clay beneath the Thames River. Built in 1831, the latest in a series of bridges dating back 2,000 years, this arched structure was dropping an inch every eight years under its own weight and that of modern traffic. The British government wanted to replace it and sought to sell the aging span.

Robert McCulloch, chainsaw magnate and chairman of McCulloch Oil Corporation, submitted the highest bid, $2.4 million. His plan: disassemble the bridge stone by carefully numbered stone—10,276 in all—then reassemble the marked blocks in the Arizona desert. People were aghast, many thought it a joke. But McCullough, ever the entrepreneur, saw the bridge as a tourist attraction. People, he hoped, would flock to Lake Havasu City, a retirement community he was developing along the lower Colorado River, to see London's bridge, then remain as permanent residents.

Reconstruction began in the fall of 1968; by October 1971 it was completed. And the people came. Lake Havasu City flourished. Golf courses and businesses followed, and today more than a million people come annually to see the bridge, making it one of Arizona's most popular tourist attractions.

Searching the atlas in Flagstaff, my eyes fell upon the red dot in western Arizona labeled London Bridge. I recalled reports of its transport and reconstruction but hadn't realized its subsequent popularity.

As a child I had visited the Grand Canyon and decades later

129

toured nearby Hoover Dam. En route to an ice-climbing course in the Sierras, I hiked in Death Valley and reached Badwater, North America's lowest point, 282 feet below sea level. I was looking for something different. London Bridge fit the bill.

Driving west from Flagstaff, I followed Interstate 40 as it descended the Mogollon Rim, passed south of the Grand Canyon, and continued to the desert floor. Downstream from Hoover Dam and Lake Mead, the land flattened, its elevation neared sea level, and the temperature soared. Small cities that are among our nation's hottest locales dot this valley: Blythe and Needles, California; and Yuma and Lake Havasu City, Arizona.

Here the Colorado River, or at least its waters not impounded by upstream dams, flows south through the Mojave Desert toward the Gulf of California. Huge dams—Davis, Glen Canyon, Parker, and Hoover—block the river. So much water is lost to evaporation from the sprawling lakes behind these structures, and is diverted for agricultural irrigation and direct human use, that the Colorado dries to a trickle as its waters seep into the Mojave sands far from the Gulf. The nation's fifth longest river is completely drained and, as early twentieth century developers argued, "not a drop is wasted by flowing into the ocean."

Today this valley is one of the nation's fastest-growing regions. Yet, as in millennia past, life centers around and depends on the river's waters. Golf courses and parks, their lush grass irrigated by the Colorado's waters, line the river; modern homes with permanently sealed windows depend on hydroelectric power from massive dams to power air conditioners; and recreational boating, fishing, and water sports are year-round industries on the man-made lakes.

As I drove south looking for London's famous bridge, the mercury rose, and the car's air conditioner struggled to maintain a steady temperature. I passed signs advertising land for sale then larger signs touting ever-smaller pieces of the desert. Near Lake Havasu City the construction of planned communities with platted lots and paved roads had begun. Two-by-fours rose from the desert sand like noxious invading weeds as bronzed men assembled structures at a steady pace, seemingly oblivious to triple-digit temperatures.

Commercial development came next. Shopping centers, many only partly completed, vied to fill consumer's needs and desires. Garish signs painted in bright colors blocked views of the desert and familiar logos announced that corporate America had arrived in the Mojave.

The bank thermometer read 114 degrees as I neared downtown. Desert heat is a dry heat, but stepping into this, the highest temperature I had ever experienced, felt like reaching into a hot oven. The physical conditioning from miles of hiking and weeks of high-altitude acclimatization were useless under these conditions.

The bridge was easy to find, an incongruous span of five arches, 900 feet long, crossing a man-made channel cut through the town's center. Shops lined the waterfront and riverboats advertising dinner cruises moored nearby. I walked slowly over the span, past buttresses sporting royal crests and beneath ornate Victorian street lamps.

Not only the bridge seemed out of place; I was out of my element too. For nearly three weeks I had enjoyed nature, avoiding large cities and spending days alone. Now, surrounded by heat, traffic, noise, and urban bustle, I felt a loneliness never experienced in wild solitude. After crossing the bridge, I took a few photos then retraced my path to the car and left the urban desert sprawl.

North of Lake Havasu lies one of North American's harshest ecosystems. Of the southwest's four great deserts—the Mojave, Sonoran, Chihuahuan, and Great Basin—the Mojave is the hottest, driest, and lowest. Vegetation yields to rock and sand. Here it is too dry for the giant Saguaro cactus of Arizona's Sonoran Desert or the wiry sagebrush that covers much of Nevada's Great Basin.

Entering California near Needles, I had yet to choose my next highpointing goal. Two possibilities remained: Nevada's Boundary Peak or California's Mt. Whitney. Both bordered California's Owens Valley and both presented logistical challenges.

Mt. Whitney (14,494 feet), the highest mountain in the contiguous forty-eight states, can be ascended as a technical rock climb, a three to five day backpacking excursion—or a grueling 22-mile day hike. Either of the non-technical options requires a federally issued permit. But obtaining a permit, I learned, is a complicated process often requiring months of advance planning.

Fifty weeklong backpacking passes and 150 daily hiking

permits are issued for each date. These non-transferable permits are sold beginning March 1 each year and, except for early
spring and late autumn weekdays, all are claimed within the
first week. Depending upon the number of cancellations, however, a few may also be issued twenty-four hours in advance. To
receive one of these, it is necessary to arrive at the Forest Service
headquarters in Lone Pine, California, a day early. Hikers line
up before the office opens, but even an early arrival doesn't
guarantee receiving permission to climb California's tallest
mountain. Some climbers wait hours but are turned away when
the day's allotment is exhausted.

Nevada's Boundary Peak, however, has no overuse problems. Although less than 100 miles from Mt. Whitney, Boundary
is one of the nation's most isolated and least summited state
highpoints. Reaching the trailhead requires a high-clearance
four-wheel-drive vehicle and a challenging drive along a poorly
maintained gravel road, portions of which have washed away.

West of Barstow, I turned north on U.S. Highway 395
towards the Owens Valley. Two hundred miles long and thirty
miles wide, this arid valley is squeezed between two of North
America's tallest mountain ranges, the Sierra Nevada to the
west and the White Mountains to the east. Centuries before the
arrival of Europeans, Paiute Indians lived here, farming the valley floor and irrigating fields with water drawn from the Owens
River. Each autumn they hunted deer and elk in the surrounding mountains and gathered pinion pine nuts, a dietary staple.

By the mid-nineteenth century, however, European settlers
had displaced the native peoples. These newcomers continued
farming this productive land until the early twentieth century when William Mulholland and his agents began buying
rights to the valley's water. For a dozen years purchases were
made under the guise of a federal reclamation project. Then
Mulholland revealed his plan: to construct a canal and divert
the Owens River through an aqueduct to Los Angeles, then a
small coastal community whose growth potential was limited
by water. Local residents protested, but to no avail. The project,
an ambitious undertaking compared by contemporaries with
the construction of the Panama Canal, was completed; the
aqueduct opened in 1913; and Los Angeles prospered, while the
Owens Valley shriveled to an arid scrubland.

Shortly after entering this valley, I stopped at the Forest

Service office in Lone Pine to inquire about climbing permits for Mt. Whitney. Bulging backpacks leaned against the building's outer walls, while inside, hikers stood in line, gazing at aging photos of California's highest peak, waiting to talk with one of two harried rangers staffing this busy office.

It was not a pretty scene. Mt. Whitney, a half-day's drive from Los Angeles, is arguably the nation's most regulated highpoint. From behind a long desk inside the small building, rangers thrust pages of rules at each hiker, whether these individuals were picking up reserved permits or inquiring about obtaining one. The answers I received upon reaching the desk were brusque and bureaucratic: No, we don't know if any permits will be issued for tomorrow; no, it might be late afternoon but you must be here in person if any are issued; no, we don't know if any will be available later this week; and no, there is never a good time to ask questions, for we are always busy. Then the unsmiling ranger pushed a stack of papers detailing toileting rules, bear-avoidance rules, outdoor fire rules, and a three-part application for next year's permits across the desk, signaling an end to our conversation. As I walked away I scanned a nearby rack of Forest Service handouts then again thumbed through the papers given me. Nowhere was there information about Whitney's geology, biology, or ecology—only rules and regulations to manage people.

Stepping from the dimly lit office, I looked across the highway at the Sierras, their rugged eastern escarpment a dozen miles away, then peered through a mounted metal pipe that isolated Whitney's summit. It was a beautiful rocky peak, the tallest among a series of spires that glowed reddish-orange in the early morning light.

But my decision had been made: Whitney would have to wait. With time to attempt just one more highpoint, I did not want to delay, perhaps days, hoping for a permit through a process I did not understand and that no one seemed willing to explain. The weather remained good and a delay, I feared, might make an attempt on either state summit impossible. Instead I would climb Boundary Peak, then before next year learn more about Whitney's permitting process—and perhaps avoid it entirely by ascending the mountain's east face, a technical rock-climbing route considered among the classic ascents of North American mountaineering.

Ten miles north of Lone Pine on a windswept expanse of desert scrub, a small structure, appearing like an aging entrance to a failed desert community, stood beside the road. Cut flowers, small shoes, chopsticks, and cloth bundles surrounded its base; two large buildings rose from the arid flatness a short distance away. Years earlier, I had learned of this place, Manzanar, from rangers in Death Valley. It was fortunate I had, for here no interpretative signs denoted these ruins as those of a World War II internment camp.

During the months following Pearl Harbor, the U.S. government, fearing spies and subversive activities, confined nearly 50,000 first and second generation Japanese-Americans—and a smaller number of Italian- and German-American citizens—in geographically isolated locations throughout the rural west. Families were housed together, communities created, and the internment camps superficially resembled planned communities complete with sidewalks, stores, and movie theaters. But their residents were not free to leave, most confined for years until overseas fighting was nearly over.

One of ten such facilities from Wyoming to California, Manzanar is preserved as a National Historical Site and managed by the Park Service. But among Manzanar's buildings, only the gymnasium and cafeteria remain. When the camp was decommissioned, the houses were dismantled, their building materials used elsewhere.

In the desert heat, I walked the town site. Tumbleweeds, blown by a hot wind, bounced down abandoned streets and over crumbling foundations. Rock walls that once enclosed gardens rose above the dusty earth, and a few trees planted by residents more than half a century ago survive despite the arid conditions.

Although traffic sped past on Highway 395 and the desert wind blew unceasingly, I felt an eerie stillness walking among these ruins. Like other American tragedies—Selma, Wounded Knee, Sand Creek—little can be quickly said or easily printed on interpretive signs. Instead many of these locations remain unmarked, are seldom denoted on maps, and receive few visitors. But the silence of these places and the realization that our government, despite its checks and balances, can do great wrong is a powerful force. Chills ran down my spine despite 100-degree heat as I walked past the padlocked gymnasium and kitchen then paused at the entrance gate, gazing closely at the ribbons and shoes and flowers at this makeshift shrine, wondering about the stories and emotions behind each.

Then I drove north in silence. A dozen miles later near a town named Independence, a roadside sign describing bristlecone pines interrupted my contemplation. The Patriarch Grove, it said, home to Earth's oldest trees, was high in the White Mountains to the east and open to the public via a four-mile-long hiking trail. I looked at the sky; the weather was clear and the forecast promised at least two more days of good weather. Boundary Peak could wait. Today I would visit Earth's oldest citizens.

California claims the planet's tallest, largest, and oldest trees, all located within a 250-mile radius. Years earlier I had gazed up at a 347-foot-tall redwood, a tree taller than a football field is long—and a height two feet loftier than Britton Hill, Florida's highest point. During another climbing excursion, I detoured to the Sierra's western slope and stood beside the General Sherman, Earth's largest organism, a massive Sequoia with enough wood to build 1,000 homes. Now, I would visit the world's oldest known tree, Methuselah, a 4,700-year-old plant, older than Egypt's pyramids.

But California claims the oldest living tree only because of a tragic event. In 1964 a geographer, untrained in the thin-core technique of determining a tree's age, was given permission to cut one bristlecone pine in eastern Nevada in what is today Great Basin National Park. He chose Prometheus, a tree thought to be very old. But when the rings were counted—4,900 in all—it was realized that the oldest organism known to have lived on the planet had just been killed.

Methuselah, however, is guarded by anonymity, unmarked as protection from vandals and souvenir hunters. The hike to the Patriarch Grove is challenging—four miles, all above 10,000 feet elevation. The first bristlecones seen are "youngsters," a mere 800 years old, taller and more robust appearing than the wide, squat, heavily weathered ancients.

These pines need little to survive; only a thin strip of bark is required to sustain life. Many older trees have only a handful of actively growing branches, their weathered trunks appearing more as patinaed driftwood than living plants. Centuries, or perhaps millennia, ago most of their bark was lost; stripped from the trunks by wind-driven soil particles; rubbed off by deer and elk marking territories; or burned by one of this region's periodic natural fires. But the few remaining branches, many no longer than a handbreadth, sustain life.

At the far end of the trail, among the ancients of the Patriarch Grove, I found a rock, sat and ate lunch. Many of the trees were little more than stumps, some wider than they were tall. But for more than four millennia they have witnessed the rhythms of life, surviving individually and collectively despite storms, droughts, floods, and fires. And they have survived without moving, without technology, and without war. I felt privileged to share an hour of their lives.

At 5:00 a.m., I entered Nevada then turned south from U.S. Highway 6 toward Boundary Peak (13,140 feet), Nevada's highest point. Eight miles later I turned again, left the blacktop and began down the gravel road that Forest Service officials warned required a four-wheel-drive vehicle. Driving a Jeep Cherokee, I was now renting two cars, having spent half of yesterday arranging transportation to the trailhead.

Boundary is a challenging and isolated peak. Its poorly marked trail follows the mountain's natural contours, ascending more than 4,400 feet in less than four miles. Hoping to be walking by first light, I was driving toward the mountain in total darkness. The gravel road's first six miles were well-maintained, easily negotiable in any vehicle. Then the road steepened and narrowed; larger rocks replaced the crushed stone surface. I slowed, hoping not to puncture a tire or scrape the vehicle's bottom. Soon, however, the headlights illuminated a five-foot-high pile of dirt and debris blocking the roadway. I stopped, donned my headlamp, and got out to investigate.

It appeared the road had been destroyed, washed out by a flash flood that had cut a deep gash behind the debris. Tire tracks led into a chasm thirty feet wide and five feet deep then continued up this sandy wash a short distance to a firmer gravel surface. I walked part of this route, saw the tracks continue, and returned to my vehicle. But after driving less than a quarter-mile, the path narrowed, its walls of gravel and silt lining a channel that appeared more a dry creek bed than a roadway, its width little more than the Jeep's. Yet I continued. The road had been described as primitive but a hundred yards later it narrowed further while its walls remained high and steep. Further progress was impossible.

I got out and searched the darkness, looking for a way out—or a way back. But my headlamp's thin beam of light, excellent for nighttime climbing, was of little use seeking a vehicular route. I retreated, walking down the gravelly wash to the debris-blocked roadway, looking for a route to the trailhead.

Nearby an aging pair of tire tracks ascended a short but steeply angled turn. These tracks led to level terrain, possibly remnants of the roadway. But would this path also be a dead-end? As the eastern sky lightened, I decided to find out.

After carefully backing down between the steep walls, I turned the truck towards the tracks. Although the ruts rose only four feet, the path slanted sharply, and if not approached cleanly, could cause a rollover. In first gear and 4WD-low, with tires slipping and the truck tilting dangerously, I inched up the short incline and onto the flat, rocky surface. A short distance later, I realized I had found the roadway and that my previous path had been a dry arroyo, one of many such desert channels that fill with water only during cloudbursts.

But the road to Boundary Peak continued to deteriorate, becoming steeper and narrowing until only two ruts remained and encroaching vegetation scraped the truck's sides. Then the route leveled, ending in a flat parking area. Not surprisingly, mine was the only vehicle at the trailhead.

The 14-mile drive from the blacktop had taken two hours. The sun was up; insects swarmed beside nearby willows. A sign warned hikers of danger: bear attacks, wilderness risks, and lightning. After driving two hours up creek beds, through washouts, over road-wide boulders, and across nearly trackless vegetation, I was now being warned of danger ahead.

I didn't dwell on these risks but began walking along a path tramped into thin vegetation beside a tiny creek, a marshy environment of willows and sedges that is prime bear habitat. But no bruins were seen, and I was soon moving uphill through more widely scattered brush. There the trail fanned into diverging paths. Guidebooks state that the route leads right toward a prominent saddle. But the trail split into a half-dozen nearly parallel paths and two prominent saddles, or passes, loomed ahead.

I looked around. No one else was on the mountain or on the trails leading toward the peak. Delayed by the unplanned detour, I was starting late. A wrong choice of route now would not allow time for retreat and a second chance. I paused, studying the terrain, map, and guidebooks. Yet the choice remained unclear. The lightly worn trail to the right ventured miles from Boundary's summit, ascended a low pass then followed a long ridgeline. Although this crest appeared free of cliffs and large rock walls, I knew that many smaller obstacles, unseen from here even with binoculars, could block the route. Ahead the more traveled path also turned right, but an obstructing hillside prevented seeing the slope that led to the higher saddle near Boundary's summit. Intuitively this more direct route seemed correct.

Following imprints of horse's hooves and hiking boots, I began walking along a path of loose rocks and bleached, dusty soil. Near the head of the valley, I turned right. The trail petered out. Hoofprints vanished as the vegetation thinned further, and I looked ahead at a steep headwall, bands of crumbling rock cutting across its face. A hundred yards later, bootprints also vanished, and I stood alone before a trackless mountainside.

I thought of retreating. Anxiety and doubt mixed with anger as I tried to concentrate, searching for a potential line between rock bands and wondering if an improvised route was possible. Why couldn't a simple sign—even a rock cairn—have been placed on the valley floor to mark the correct direction? And what of safety? No one else was on the mountain, but even if others arrived, this waterless slope could not be seen from the parking area.

Yet I wasn't certain that this route was incorrect. Although no trail was evident, trip reports warned of experienced hikers retreating in the face of trackless isolation. Above me, 1,500 feet of scree, scattered vegetation, and flaking stone separated the ridgeline from the valley floor. But I began to notice ledges that could provide adequate footing and piles of scree that transected the cliffs. It would be a difficult scramble, but I decided to attempt it, cognizant of the risks, isolation, and intensifying late morning heat.

Alert for snakes and falling rocks, I moved up slowly. Sometimes a narrow path made by desert animals provided stable footing; in other locations, vegetation held the thin mountain soil, but most of the ascent was an exhausting scramble over shifting rocks.

Near the cliffs, the source of the stones slipping beneath my feet, I tried to move faster, minimizing exposure to fresh rockfall. But fatigue, frustration, and the heat took their toll. I wanted to rest, snack, and drink but this was the route's most dangerous portion. Then I looked down. Loose slabs of rock, perched atop smooth boulders, would make descending riskier than continuing this climb. Reaching a partially shielded ledge, I stopped. Fear and panic fought for my attention halfway up a mountain as I realized how alone a true solo climb can be—off route, in a waterless environment, and struggling to move higher but with an even riskier descent the only other option.

Following a short rest with some food and water, concentration and rationality regained control. First I studied the map, then weighed my options, concluding that the ridgeline above led directly to the summit. With food and water to last twenty-four hours and enough clothing to survive a night out, I needed only the strength and stamina to continue up the scree. I hadn't come this far to turn back. With a calm commitment and newfound confidence, I cinched the pack tightly against my back and scrambled higher.

It took another hour-and-a-half to reach the ridgeline and find a faint trail leading toward the mountain's crest. Here I rested, never happier at reaching a non-summit—and staring down at the steep rock pile I had labored three hours to ascend.

Twelve hundred vertical feet still separated me from Boundary's summit, "a straightforward ascent," according to guidebooks. This time they were right—and the route clearly evident. I joyfully walked upward beneath a cloudless sky. At this altitude pleasant temperatures replaced the valley heat; a gentle breeze stirred the air beneath a deep blue sky that arched overhead.

To the east, large valleys separated ranges of dusky purple mountains. White deposits, saline remnants of long-vanished lakes, covered the valley floors. But no rivers flow through here for Nevada's basin and range topography has no outlet to the ocean. Instead rainwater and snowmelt collect in old lakebeds, there to seep into the porous earth or evaporate into the desert air.

To the west, Montgomery Peak, slightly higher than Boundary Peak, dominated the view. Geographers claim Boundary is a subsidiary peak of Montgomery, but since the currently recognized state line places Montgomery in California and Boundary in Nevada, the lower peak qualifies as Nevada's highest point.

But whether this lower mountaintop is even in Nevada has been legally contested for a century. Based on conflicting surveys, the half-mile-wide strip of land that includes the summit has been claimed by both states. Now considered part of Nevada, if this thin wedge of land is ever awarded to California, Wheeler Peak—250 miles east in Great Basin National Park and bearing the same name as New Mexico's state summit—would become Nevada's highest point.

However, no thoughts of land claims or surveys entered my mind as I took the final steps toward Boundary's summit. Reaching the top, I gazed across the desert. Nothing moved save a lone raven that circled near Montgomery's apex. No human sounds drifted upward, and no one else was on the entire mountain. Alone atop Nevada, and perhaps the most isolated one can be in the contiguous forty-eight states, I removed my pack, knelt, and touched the USCGS marker then leaned back against the jumbled boulders perched atop Boundary's summit.

I signed the register but spent little time reading other entries, instead marveling at the solitude and feeling thankful to have reached the top despite challenges and miscues. The light-colored rocks that give the White Mountains their name reflected the midday sun, contrasting sharply with the dark blue sky. Following the strenuous climb, this rest was welcomed, but after just thirty minutes I knew it was time to descend. From here the correct route was clearly visible but it would be much longer, and to reach the paved highway before nightfall, I needed to leave soon.

The stillness was broken as I rose to retrieve my pack. I put it on slowly then adjusted it carefully, moving deliberately, not due to fatigue but to savor the views and mountaintop environment a few more moments.

With renewed strength I followed the ridgeline down, passing the location where I had reached the trail after my arduous ordeal. Scattered yellow asters, looking out of place on this arid mountain slope, bloomed in the dirt and trailside scree. Closely related to dandelions, these flowers would be considered weeds in any suburban lawn, but in this high-altitude environment any life or color was welcomed.

America's Loneliest Road

U.S. 50 through central Nevada has been called America's loneliest road. The region's widely-scattered towns and businesses tried to capitalize on this notoriety, yet very few people travel this isolated route northeast of Boundary Peak.

The standard route, which I descended, would make a challenging climb—but far less strenuous and risky than the one ascended. The trail passed through a small grove of bristlecone and limber pines as it dropped below the ridgeline and continued to the valley floor, there passing the unmarked confluence of paths where hours earlier I had made the errant choice. Reaching the parking lot, the truck started promptly, and as the sun neared Boundary's summit, I began the drive back.

Returning slowly and with much less stress, I noticed my surroundings: an abandoned mine, its tailings spilling like unnatural tentacles into the empty creekbed below; vegetation, sometimes dense and luxuriant, lining dry washes and shallow depressions near the mountain's base; and the desert floor, its rugged topography cut by canyons and seasonal stream beds. At the washout that had bedeviled me before sunrise, I was shocked to see the depth and ruggedness of the terrain I had navigated—and the hopelessly narrow creek bed I had tried to drive up.

In Mammoth Lakes, I returned the Jeep and retrieved the Neon. My travel time was nearly over. Whitney would have to wait as winter's grip would, within days, envelop the Sierra. Besides, there were obligations at home.

I had been gone nearly a month, climbed 25,000 vertical feet, driven 5,300 miles, endured winter storms and desert heat, and summited five of the nation's most difficult state highpoints. And I had done it safely, avoiding lightning, dodging falling rocks, not facing a poisonous snake or scorpion, and remaining healthy. The following day as I crossed the basins and ranges of south-central Nevada on one of the least traveled stretches of highway in the nation, I thought of the myriad sights and sounds experienced during these four weeks.

Once again, however, I would tempt fate. Returning to Las Vegas for a late night flight home, I passed near Area 51 and Nevada's Extraterrestrial Highway. But that night, the aliens were quiet. No UFO's were seen.

Approaching the Great One
Ascending the Kahiltna Glacier. Mt. McKinley (Denali), Alaska.

After the Tempest
Advanced Base Camp, Denali. Mt. Hunter is in the distance.

Mauna Kea, Hawaii
A native Hawaiian ceremonial
structure tops our fiftieth state.

Cheaha Mountain, Alabama

Mt. Sunflower, Kansas

Britton Hill, Florida
America's lowest state highpoint.

Granite Peak, Montana
The rocky summit soars hundreds of feet
above the snow bridge at far right.

Gannett Peak, Wyoming

Reflection
Williams Lake. From Wheeler Peak, New Mexico.

Lost River Range
From Chicken Out Ridge. Borah Peak, Idaho.

A Gathering Storm
Mt. Hood, Oregon.

**High-Altitude
Resident**
Marmot. Mt. Rainier,
Washington.

The Great One
Mt. McKinley (Denali), Alaska. From Camp Two, fifteen miles away.

Ancient Citizen
Bristlecone pine.
Patriarch Grove,
California.

Mt. Katahdin, Maine

West of the Pecos
El Capitan and the
Chihuahuan Desert
from atop Guadalupe
Peak, Texas.

Lofty Meadow
Lush vegetation surrounds a meltwater stream. Granite Peak, Montana.

Little Tahoma
From Ingraham Flats. Mt. Rainier, Washington.

CHAPTER 14

AN EARLY WINTER

North Dakota

T he Great Plains is a land of extremes. Covering the middle third of our nation, this transitional grassland extends from North America's eastern forests to the Rocky Mountain foothills and from Texas to central Canada. Summer temperatures frequently exceed 100 degrees Fahrenheit, while winter lows may plunge fifty degrees below zero. Great rivers that provided routes westward for pioneers and early explorers—the Yellowstone, Platte, Red, and Missouri—cut through this vast savannah. Herds of bison once freely grazed these prairies; sixty million lived here when Lewis and Clark sailed up the Missouri in 1804. But by century's end the herds had been exterminated, the species saved from extinction by a few hundred animals in protected enclaves.

Beneath the tall grass of the eastern prairie, Europeans found some of the planet's most fertile farmland. After Native Americans were displaced and the bison nearly eliminated, this land was fenced, turned with moldboard plows, and made to yield wheat and corn and soybeans. But west of the 100th merid- ian, a line bisecting the Dakotas and extending south through central Texas, the grass was shorter, the climate more arid, and the terrain frequently austere. Herds of cattle replaced the bison, and on some of the least desirable land, the Plains Indian tribes—the Sioux and Cheyenne, Crow and Comanche—were confined to reservations.

Five weeks after descending Boundary Peak, I journeyed to the Northern Plains to resume highpointing and to real- ize another long-held goal—providing medical care to Native

Sitting Bull's Grave

In 1953, the Sioux chief's remains were moved from Ft. Yates, North Dakota—near where he was killed by reservation police in 1890—to this site overlooking the Missouri River just outside of Mobridge, South Dakota.

Americans. Three months had passed since leaving the emergency department. I had traveled nearly half that time, reaching eight state summits, visiting a dozen national parks, and becoming ever-more comfortable hiking and climbing alone.

And this had been a grand adventure. Many people, upon realizing a life-long dream, find that reality falls short of expectations. But thus far, The Dream had exceeded mine. As expected, I enjoyed touring the country, learning of little-known historical episodes, and seeing remote pristine areas. But I was surprised by my sense of tranquility and the enhanced ability to quietly observe.

Psychologists claim that a ten-day break is required to fully unwind; during multi-week climbing and trekking adventures while employed, I had found this to be true. But over these past few months, I felt more relaxed than ever. This calmness and relief from stress allowed me to view the natural world more intently, watching varying light play across landscapes, observing animal behavior, and studying flowers, rocks, and geologic formations that previously I would have scarcely noticed. And I enjoyed the people I met and hearing of their stories, hopes, and fears.

However, I missed the personal contact of medical practice. Although relieved to no longer contend with insurance companies, staffing corporations, chart reviewers, or the myriad people who complicate a busy physician's already chaotic day, I missed the human interaction with patients, staff, and colleagues—and the camaraderie, structure, and purpose inherent in emergency medicine.

Three months earlier I had been departmental medical director, a skilled physician with two decades experience in high-pressure environments that required precise analysis and rapid decision-making. But as I contemplated a prolonged period of time off, I wondered: Would my judgment slow? Would my skills atrophy? And would I be able to reenter the physician workforce after my year of adventure?

Then I remembered an American Medical Association program that placed physicians on American Indian reservations. With youthful enthusiasm following medical school, I had considered such an opportunity. But I never found time.

After two decades of residency, private practice, and emergency medicine, my idealism had been sorely tested, yet thoughts of helping an underserved population and practicing medicine in a challenging and isolated environment still appealed to me. I discovered that this program, Project USA, still existed and needed physicians for short-term assignments at federal Indian Health Service facilities. It was an ideal opportunity combining challenge and professional growth while helping others.

I had hoped for two assignments, requesting a late autumn stint in the southwest and a springtime posting in the northern Plains. But staffing needs dictated the reverse; I was now scheduled to work two weeks at the Cheyenne River Sioux Reservation in north central South Dakota and have the "opportunity" to experience an early Dakota winter.

On a beautiful late October day, I drove north from Rapid City. Golden afternoon light bathed the buttes and badlands of western South Dakota, their tawny colors intensified by a year-long drought, one of the most severe on record. Years earlier, my son Jon and I had summited Harney Peak, South Dakota's highest point and, as South Dakotans proudly point out, the tallest mountain between the northern Rockies and the Alps. We had visited Mt. Rushmore and Wounded Knee, Custer State Park and the giant monument to Crazy Horse, the largest carving ever attempted and, sixty years after its inception, decades from completion. But on this trip I planned to tour North Dakota, perhaps our nation's least visited state, hoping to touch its highest point.

As the sun neared the horizon and cirrus clouds streamed overhead, I stopped briefly at an isolated hill north of Belle Fourche, South Dakota. There, scrambling past signs warning of rattlesnake danger, I reached a litter-strewn hilltop, the geographical center of the United States. Once near the Mason-Dixon Line separating Maryland and Pennsylvania, this calculated point has move steadily westward as our nation expanded. Following Alaska's statehood in 1959, this point, for the first time, moved west of the 100th meridian, a line long cited by geographers and ecologists as dividing east and west. Gazing over the arid plains of western South Dakota, I thought it appropriate after centuries of western expansion—geographically and demographically—that the nation's center is now physically located in "the west."

Hours later rain splashed against the motel window and splatted loudly onto the air conditioner. It was 3:00 a.m.; the record drought had been broken. By morning the heavy rain had ceased, but light drizzle and gray skies continued as I drove toward White Butte (3,506 feet), North Dakota's highest point.

An appropriately named mesa with eroding white flanks, the butte is on private property. Permission is required for access—as is a 20-dollar "donation." Following a short muddy drive along a deeply rutted road, I came to a small gray farmhouse and was met by a taciturn older couple who opened the door before I knocked. After a perfunctory greeting, the fee for "summit maintenance" was explained. Little else was said and, after payment, permission was granted and directions given to the trailhead parking area, less than a mile away.

"Walk two miles to the obvious highpoint," the printed instructions stated as I stood in the parking area and scanned a landscape of buttes and mesas, their tops hidden by an unbroken layer of gray cloud 100 feet above the prairie floor. No path was marked; no summits could be seen. Widely divergent trails led from the parking area toward cloud-shrouded hillsides. Waves of anxiety and memories of Nevada's Boundary Peak raced through my mind. Yet I was afraid to return to the farmhouse to ask for more specific directions. The fee, a compromise to permit continued access by highpointers, had recently been instituted and disturbing the couple again, I feared, might result in my "donation" being returned and access denied.

Recalling my errant ways in Nevada, I nevertheless chose the most heavily worn footpath, a muddy route through low brush that led toward a prominent butte. The trail ascended briefly then leveled, traversing a gently sloping but slippery white hillside of bentonite. A clay with many industrial uses, bentonite expands when wet, becoming very sticky but losing its cohesiveness. An inch-thick layer, I discovered, would adhere like glue to a hiking boot but provide little traction atop the remaining mud.

Every incline and traverse—and especially each descent—became an adventure. Sliding wildly, I left elongated footprints in the clay, some three feet long and half that wide. I tried to scramble across vegetation, but the leafy residue stuck to my clay-covered boot, allowing additional layers of white goo to accumulate. Removing the stuff was impossible; each attempt merely spread the muck while the freshly disturbed surface allowed yet another layer to accumulate. I slogged along, wondering if I could summit—and how much gear might be ruined in the process. Generally an easy straightforward hike, White Butte was becoming a demanding physical challenge.

An hour later, with pant legs crusted in thick white clay and hiking boots feeling the weight of lead, I scrambled up a steep ravine to a fog-shrouded plateau. A metal plaque, engraved with a cross and the name Buzalsky, rose above the flatness. A nearby register box confirmed this as the butte's—and North Dakota's—highest point. Atop the mesa, grasses bent low beneath the accumulated weight of rain and drizzle, seed heads nearly touching the wet earth. Rocks were piled beside the plaque. But this memorial to Lawrence Buzalsky, the late owner of White Butte, does not mark his grave. Contrary to popular belief, no one is buried at the summit although Indian graves have been found elsewhere on the plateau.[7]

I knelt atop the state and removed the soggy register from its container. As a steady breeze blew across the butte, I leafed through the spiral notebook, a log recording dozens of recent entries. Most commented on the barrenness or long-range views, vistas I could only imagine. Then with gloved hands holding a failing pen, I added my name and city to the damp document.

After a few photos, I needed to descend. Despite a Gore-Tex shell and appropriate layering, sweat from the strenuous ascent coupled with mist and wind began to chill me. It was time to go down.

Descending I slid down the hillside with even less grace than I had ascended. Following one prolonged slide that carried me off-trail, I nearly struck a pair of ring-necked pheasants, the startled birds taking off from the brush with a thunderous roar. Reaching the grassy parking area, I rested briefly, then for half an hour tried to remove clay from pack, pants, gloves, and boots, getting rid of some but spreading the rest. The fog never

---

[7] North Carolina and South Dakota are the only state highpoints with marked graves. Dr. Elisha Mitchell, for whom the Tar Heel State's highest point is named, is buried beside the summit tower while the ashes of Dr. Valentine McGillycuddy, the first white man known to have climbed Harney Peak, are entombed in a crypt near South Dakota's summit monument.

lifted, and I left without seeing White Butte's summit from the grasslands below.

From the mesas I drove north through one of the nation's most sparsely populated regions. For decades rural North Dakota has been losing population, the greatest loss in the state's western portion. As I passed through Amidon, county seat of Slope County where the highpoint is located, I briefly looked at this small town—very briefly—for with only 120 people, it is believed to be the nation's least populated county seat.

Four damp North Dakota days after summiting White Butte, sticky clay clung to the tires, undercarriage, and carpet of the car as I turned and drove toward Eagle Butte, South Dakota and the Cheyenne River Indian Reservation. One of five reservations in the state, these parcels had all been part of the Great Sioux Reservation, a tract of land promised the Indians by the 1868 Ft. Laramie Treaty. Under this accord, signed following a series of battles along the Bozeman Trail, the federal government relinquished territorial claims—the only such act during our nation's westward expansion— and agreed to dismantle a series of forts in eastern Wyoming. In return for allowing miners unimpeded access to Montana's gold fields, the Sioux were to receive all lands in the Dakota Territory west of the Missouri River including the sacred Black Hills

The Indian victory, however, was short-lived. Six years later, George Custer led an army expedition into the Black Hills searching for gold, violating the Ft. Laramie agreement. The Indian Wars resumed with unparalleled intensity, leading to Custer's annihilation at Little Big Horn in 1876 and the forced resettlement of all Native Americans onto much-reduced reservations shortly thereafter.

Eagle Butte, administrative center and most populous town of the Cheyenne River Reservation, was built in the 1950s to replace the "Agency," the former governmental center, when it, and most of the tribe's most productive farmland, was inundated following construction of Oahe Dam. Today the tribal headquarters is in Eagle Butte. So are the federal Bureau of Indian Affairs, a tribal college, a modern motel, two grocery stores, several restaurants, a half dozen churches, and the Indian Health Service hospital.

A sprawling brick building of typically-50s design, this hospital shared many similarities with the rural North Carolina facility where I had recently worked. It was aging but adequate, clean and unpretentious, providing basic health care to an isolated population 180 miles from most specialty services.

For two weeks I worked here, staffing the emergency "department," a tiny two-room facility that received 20,000 patient visits annually and assisting in the larger and even busier outpatient clinic. I lived in government housing, toured the reservation, and talked with tribal members. The needs were great and the resources limited, but during this time, I rediscovered the true joy of medicine.

While in Eagle Butte, winter arrived. For two days, an early November blizzard raged across the Dakotas, shutting down travel, touring, and highpointing. I would not return to White Butte on a clear day nor visit Nebraska's Panorama Point on this trip. But time passed quickly, and before leaving I agreed to a third IHS posting, a February assignment staffing an outpatient clinic in North Dakota.

On these windswept grasslands, I had discovered something important, an idea that wouldn't go away. For the first time in my professional life, I seriously considered working primarily with an underserved population. The experience in Eagle Butte had been challenging and the remuneration small, but the satisfaction felt had been among the greatest in my career. Over the holidays, while winter's icy grip held the mountaintops, I relaxed at home, enjoying farm and family, considering professional options—and planning springtime highpointing.

CHAPTER 15

A SNOWY PANORAMA

The Southern Plains

During the winter, I realized the enormity of the challenge. I had summited thirty-two highpoints; eighteen remained. Seven were drive-ups. Three others required modest walks. Four necessitated demanding daylong hikes, another a multi-day backpack, and the final three technical climbs.

Since they were widely scattered geographically and limited by weather, climbing season, and required permits, I realized I couldn't climb them all this year, at least not in the desired style. Either I needed to skip some highpoints or eliminate most sightseeing, instead traveling quickly between mountains. But touring the nation, visiting historical sites and geological wonders, meeting people and experiencing the cultures of our great land had been important—and pleasurable. And they remained more important than trying to jam each mountain into an already crowded schedule.

Two options remained: 1) Skip Denali (20,320 feet), Alaska's highest peak and the most difficult and time-consuming state highpoint, attempting instead to summit all the remaining highpoints, or 2) attempt Denali but forgo any chance during my sabbatical of completing even the "contiguous 48" state summits.

Officially named Mt. McKinley by the U.S. government, it is called Denali (an Athabascan word meaning the "Great One") by native peoples, the Alaskan government, and most mountaineers. By either name it is North America's tallest mountain, requiring a rugged three to four week climb up snow and ice.

However, due to its northerly location and extreme weather, the climbing season lasts barely two months—early May to mid-July.

In 1994 after summiting Aconcagua (22,861 feet), the continental summit of South America, I seriously considered a Denali climb. These two mountains share many characteristics—long approaches, multiple camps, and multi-week expeditions. Both are big, cold mountains—Denali glaciated, buffeted by Arctic winds and frequent storms; Aconcagua a high, cold, exposed desert with much less snow but raked by equally strong and frigid Antarctic winds. Mentally and physically demanding, it takes weeks, even months, to recover from the altitude and exertion after climbing either of these giants.

I did not attempt Denali then, and reluctantly decided I wouldn't this year either. I believed I had the ability and stamina to some day summit Denali. However, this year was to be fun, not an exhausting race between peaks.

Instead I now hoped to complete the "contiguous 48," a less ambitious but still daunting challenge. Earlier I had summited Mauna Kea (13,796 feet), Hawaii's highest point and a state summit included in my total. Thus, seventeen highpoints remained to accomplish my revised goal. Scattered from Maine to California, Texas to Montana, the only geographically compact group remaining was in the central and southern Plains.

Wildflowers bloomed across the Chihuahuan Desert as I drove east from El Paso toward the Guadalupe Mountains and Guadalupe Peak (8,749 feet), the highest point of Texas. These mountains are part of an uplifted, fossilized coral reef, formed in a shallow tropical sea during the Permian Period, 250 million years ago. Named the Capitan Formation, this thick bed of limestone forms a broadly curving arc 400 miles across west Texas and southeastern New Mexico. Much of the formation remains underground, but three short mountain ranges—the Apache, Glass, and the most northerly, the Guadalupes, are exposed remnants of this reef.

El Capitan, the peak for which the reef is named, is the southern terminus of the Guadalupes. Jutting into the desert like a ship's prow, its steep rock walls presented a dramatic vista as I rounded a low hill and turned north, just three miles from its base. Huge sloping piles of talus, here named *bajadas* (Spanish for lower regions), surround the cliffs, sloping from the mountain and appearing as a giant rocky wave, pushed before a ship's bow. Although sharing the same name with Yosemite's legendary granite wall, this El Capitan is of eroding, easily dislodged limestone, making rock climbing impractical and dangerous.

This area's rugged terrain was home to the Nde, a group of Native Americans more commonly known as the Mescalero Apache. A semi-nomadic people, the Nde ranged widely, from west Texas to central Arizona, the Mogollon Rim to northern Mexico. They fiercely resisted intrusion—Spanish and American.

Following the Mexican War, the U.S. Army in 1849 attempted to drive them from west Texas. Led by great chiefs including Geronimo, the Nde effectively used the Guadalupes and nearby mountains as strongholds, launching raids on military outposts, stagecoaches, and settlements. It took the U.S. Army thirty-one years to drive the Nde from these mountains and seven more to capture the elusive Geronimo.

Today this area is part of the Guadalupe Mountains National Park, a preserve created in 1972 to protect one of our nation's most rugged and least accessible landscapes. There are no paved roads in the park. It remains a wild rugged area, a refuge for hikers and backpackers. It is also one of the most isolated. The closest gas station is thirty-five miles away, the nearest motel forty.

Arriving midafternoon, I briefly toured the visitor center, then located the nearby trailhead for the 4.4-mile hike up Guadalupe Peak. As I studied the terrain, dark clouds gathered over the mountain and neighboring El Capitan.

Desert thunderstorms often develop quickly with an intense, violent ferocity. A cool, refreshing wind rushed down the mountain's flanks bringing relief from the searing heat. Then big, fat raindrops, harbingers of the downpour to follow, splatted onto the dry vegetation and dusty ground. Lightning danced along the mountaintops; thunder shook the desert floor.

I retreated to the car, thankful for motel reservations, even if forty miles away. These storms, triggered by a spring cold front, continued well past midnight.

The next morning was delightfully crisp and cool. Soft golden light illuminated the trail up Guadalupe Peak and glistened off rain-soaked vegetation. The deluge had cleared dust and haze from the air, allowing spectacular views. Underfoot the trail had drained quickly and, aided by low humidity, was soft and damp, not muddy.

There are good hikes. Sometimes there are great hikes. Occasionally everything comes together, creating a fantastic hike. This was such a hike.

The well-maintained trail climbs nearly 3,000 feet, a challenging but not overwhelming ascent. Starting just above the desert floor, I walked steadily uphill, passing first through a coniferous forest, fragrant in the damp morning air. Ponderosa and white pine, Douglas fir and aspen, species typical of more northerly latitudes and remnants of an extensive forest that covered west Texas at the end of the last Ice Age, survive here because of the environment created by the Guadalupes—a cooler, moist, high altitude oasis jutting above the Texas desert.

I ascended through the forest then traversed beneath a series of sheer, white limestone cliffs. Often a cauldron of reflected midday heat, this morning these rocks were still cool, damp, and partially shaded. Each bend in the trail brought wonderful sights—a yucca in full bloom, its creamy white flowers covering a stalk extending fully a yard above its dense whorl of needle-shaped leaves; a fir, like a natural bonsai, twisted and stunted by decades of wind and storms; delicate ground flowers, their tiny leaves and brilliant petals seeking shade, protection, and moisture between jagged shards of limestone; and swallows, aerial acrobats twisting and swooping low, plucking insects on the wing.

Above the forest and cliffs, the trail crossed an exposed, brushy slope. I looked to my left, down across the great prow of El Capitan presiding over the tawny landscape that extended south into Mexico. Ahead, up a final gentle slope was a triangular pyramid, gleaming beneath the west Texas sun.

I took the final steps to the summit and gazed down. El Capitan dominated the view south. To the west, surrounded by low hills were large flat saltpans, brilliant white remnants of seasonal lakebeds that provided salt to pioneers and early settlers. To the north was the Bowl, a large, rugged high mountain valley forested with fir and pine.

A six-foot-tall pyramid tops Guadalupe Peak. Erected in 1958, and claimed to be non-commercial, this monument has three sides which commemorate advancements in transportation and communication: the Butterfield Stage, The United States Post Office, and American Airlines.

Other hikers were already on the summit, having camped high on the mountain the previous night. As I waited to photograph the summit pyramid, I overheard them describing yesterday's thunderstorms. Several had experienced buzzing and tingling from electrical static; one may have been struck by lightning but was uninjured. All had been frightened.

One burly young man, speaking loudly via cell phone with his wife, recounted his travails. His wife must have been unimpressed. He elaborated. His voice became louder, the story more dramatic, his situation more desperate with each recounting.

I sought refuge and solitude at the far end of the summit ridge overlooking the steep western wall of El Cap, the saltpans, and desert. Leaning against the warming rocks, I rested, ate, and rehydrated while watching the swallows perform their continuing acrobatics. When I eventually returned to the summit pyramid, the phone call thankfully had ended.

Other hikers topped out, some exhausted and panting, others appearing still strong. But all were elated at having reached their goal. One retiree had journeyed 700 miles from Houston. This was his eleventh, and thus far highest, state summit. A well-conditioned couple in their mid-twenties arrived. They appeared to be strong hikers and related how they had sought a scenic, challenging trail. They had not previously realized this was the highpoint of Texas and listened intently as others shared highpointing totals and tales.

The morning sun slowly became uncomfortably hot beneath the cloudless sky. An hour and a half after reaching the top, I began descending. The morning-long trickle of ascending hikers had swelled to a steady stream. Conditioned individuals adorned in expensive outdoor fashions were interspersed with teenage boys wearing baggy pants, their ball caps turned backwards. The teens' dates followed, wearing shorts, tank tops, and sandals. The girls appeared fatigued and frustrated, asking where they could find water. Heated discussions followed after the young girls learned the nearest water was back at the visitor's center.

Guadalupe Peak, Texas

This pyramidal marker honors three transportation pioneers—the
Butterfield Stage, U.S. Post Office, and American Airlines—the only such
salute to commerce atop a state summit.

A long line of thirsty, unhappy hikers trudging uphill replaced the joyful solitude of my early morning ascent. I quickly descended to the parking lot, now filled to capacity with vehicles baking under a hot afternoon sun.

Escaping the crowds I took a short walk to the Pinery, ruins of a Butterfield Overland Stage station. One of the transportation systems commemorated on the pyramid atop Guadalupe Peak, the Butterfield was a remarkable enterprise. Founded in 1858, its 2,800-mile route extended from St. Louis to San Francisco, arcing like an inverted bow south of the Rocky Mountains. Predating the Pony Express by two years, it was our nation's first overland transcontinental mail and transportation system.

Two hundred stations similar to the Pinery were constructed along the Butterfield's route to provide fresh horses and drivers for the twice-weekly stages. The entire trip took twenty-five days and cost $150 per passenger and ten cents for each piece of mail. Coaches ran day and night. Stops were brief; passengers ate and slept as they traveled.

The service lasted 2½ years but was ended in 1861 by the Civil War. The Butterfield never turned a profit. During this short period, fifty company employees were killed, hundreds of animals stolen and dozens of stations looted or burned, mostly by Indian attacks. However, every stage, east and westbound, completed its journey within the 25-day contracted time.

The following morning I drove north into New Mexico visiting another part of the Capitan Reef—Carlsbad Caverns. Here the fossilized reef remains underground. Slightly acidic water has percolated through cracks in the limestone, slowly dissolving the rock, and creating huge underground caverns filled with graceful, richly colored formations.

Although a national park, the cave has been extensively developed with metal stairs, paved walkways, electric lights and elevator—even an underground restaurant 700 feet beneath the surface. The cave's 56-degree temperature, constant year-round, was a welcomed respite from the 99-degree surface heat.

After viewing the mandatory "cave-etiquette" film, I was allowed to enter the caverns. Cave swallows, brightly colored insectivores, darted briskly into and out of the cave's mouth. Mexican short-tailed bats also roost here. Each summer evening as dusk deepens, millions of these winged mammals stream from this entrance, like a whirling column of smoke dispersing across the desert. During the night they hunt insects and feed on nectar, serving as valuable pollinators of desert plants. Just before dawn they return to the cave to roost and sleep during the day.

I spent half the day underground, marveling at the colorful stalactites and stalagmites, flowstones, ribbons, and curtains that fill the massive chambers and hallways. I traversed the Devil's Den, the Boneyard, and the Hall of Giants, and passed Iceberg Rock, Mirror Lake, and the Bottomless Pit, names reminiscent of climbing routes. Indeed spelunking, as caving is called, shares many of the same skills and equipment as climbing; however, few people regularly do both.

Leaving the peaks and caves of the Capitan Reef behind, I journeyed north, paralleling the Pecos River in eastern New Mexico. In Roswell I passed a UFO museum. Housed in a converted downtown theater, it hoped to draw earthly visitors with tales of extraterrestrial visits. I did not stop.

Instead I continued north to Fort Sumner, an 1862 resettlement camp for Navajo and Apache Native Americans. At Guadalupe National Park I had learned details of the Apache resistance; in another week I would be working with the Apache through the Indian Health Service on their reservation in south-central New Mexico. Here I would learn more of their history.

In 1863, 11,000 men, women, and children were forcibly marched across 400 miles of the Chihuahuan Desert. At Fort Sumner, a 21-acre reservation along the banks of the Pecos River, they were to be taught farming and mechanical skills.

The results were disastrous. Comanche raids, crop failures, chronic food shortages, and disease killed more than 3,000 natives. In 1868 the plan was deemed a failure, the fort decommissioned and sold. The surviving Navajo and Apache were again marched across the desert, back to their homelands, resulting in further loss of life.

Today only foundation ruins remain. Cottonwoods again line the banks of the Pecos and a small visitor center details the tragedy.

Fort Sumner is more widely known for a later event. Here in 1881, William H. Bonney, a.k.a. Billy the Kid, died in a shootout with Sheriff Pat Garrett. A petty thief and cattle rustler accused of killing a dozen men, The Kid was only twenty-one. He is buried at Fort Sumner, his grave and headstone enclosed in a welded steel cage necessary to deter souvenir collectors.

I drove north to Tucumcari, a "Route 66" town in northeastern New Mexico, for the night. Today Interstate 40 bypasses Tucumcari, traveling just south of the city. Modern franchises cluster around the three superhighway exits.

Route 66 is now the business loop, a four-lane city street lined by a collection of aging motels, drive-in restaurants, converted gas stations, and boarded-up buildings. After sundown the old road was nearly empty. Bright neon lights advertising cheap food and clean lodging illuminated the wide thoroughfare, their multiple hues occasionally reflecting off shiny metallic flanks of passing eighteen-wheelers. But automobiles, which brought throngs of tourists to these small towns along the old highway, were rarely seen.

I awoke early and left before dawn, turning north from Route 66 and driving across the sparsely populated ranchland of northeastern New Mexico. Aging windmills atop wooden infrastructures greeted the cool, clear morning. Ranch houses were few; other motorists absent.

An hour later a thin line of clouds appeared along the northern horizon. A chill north wind freshened. The cloudbank grew, expanding into a voluminous, blue-gray mass. The wind intensified. The temperature plunged, heralding the approach of a "blue-norther," a rapidly moving cold front sweeping across the Great Plains. By the time I crossed the Oklahoma state line, three-quarters of an hour after the clouds first appeared, the sky was completely overcast, the temperature had plunged into the mid-30s, and a stiff wind blew steadily from the north.

Black Mesa (4,973 feet), Oklahoma's highest point, rose directly ahead. The largest in a series of flat-topped mesas in this rugged region, 40-mile-long Black Mesa is named for the thick layer of erosion-resistant black volcanic rock that caps this plateau's entire length.

Owned by the Nature Conservancy, the mesa and surrounding area are home to deer and antelope, black bear, mountain lion, and rattlesnakes. Little wildlife was active, however, when I stepped from the car into the cold wind. A few brave sparrows flitted amongst the tall grass and brush that bordered the parking lot. A lone Chihuahuan Raven, a large strong bird, struggled as it flew against the wind beneath thick gray clouds.

I donned jacket, hat, and gloves. Yesterday I had roasted in

99-degree heat; today I needed winter clothing.

The 4.2-mile trail to the high point followed a primitive dirt road two miles along the valley floor to the mesa's base. In the past a difficult scramble up this steep, rocky, rattlesnake-infested slope had been required to reach the plateau above. However, a jeep trail has been bulldozed up the mesa's 500-foot-high flank, creating a safer, more straightforward, though less aesthetic path to the top. I ascended, passing layers of freshly exposed sandstone, shale, and coarse conglomerate before traversing the black volcanic cap.

A cold wind blew unimpeded across the treeless plateau. A few grasses survived atop the mesa, but cacti and other hardy vegetation flourished despite the thin soil. I walked briskly the final two miles across the plateau to the summit.

A nine-foot-high granite obelisk juts from the flat terrain, marking the point determined by a 1954 survey to be Oklahoma's highest point. It seemed little higher than the rest of the flat expanse. Each side of the obelisk gave the distance to a neighboring state: "Colorado—4.7 miles due north;" "New Mexico—1299 feet due west;" "Texas—31 miles due south;" and "Kansas—53 miles ENE." Cimarron County, where Black Mesa is located, touches each of these states, the only county in the nation touching four neighboring states.

From the summit I walked to the southern edge of the plateau and looked across the rugged terrain. A few large ranches filled the valley, one appearing to extend nearly the width of the valley floor. Mesas and buttes dotted the landscape into Texas and New Mexico. To the southwest beyond the buttes rose scattered, symmetrically shaped conical mountains—spatter cones— that are remnants of the area's recent volcanic activity.

As I returned to the summit obelisk, two older men approached along the main trail.

"Mighty strong wind," Jim said, after introducing himself and his climbing companion, Robert. Then, he added nonchalantly, "it always blows like this across west Texas."

"Really?" I stammered, trying to keep my teeth from chattering.

"Yes, this is flat, windy country. Few trees, nothing to stop the wind," Jim added.

These two men, both World War II veterans in their seventies, were still active regional highpointers. This morning they had driven from their homes near Amarillo, Texas, for this, their eighth annual hike up Black Mesa.

"Last year I climbed Mt. Elbert in Colorado," Robert drawled, unable to conceal his pride, "my tallest peak yet. This year Jim and I are going to try Humphreys Peak in Arizona. You been there yet?"

"Yes," I answered, "climbed it last fall."

We talked of climbing and highpointing. Robert had summited seventeen highpoints, Jim twelve. When asked about my climbs, I told of climbing in Latin America and trekking in Asia, only briefly mentioning my hope of reaching all forty-eight contiguous highpoints.

The clouds lowered further; the wind strengthened. It was time to descend. I bid these hardy veterans goodbye, wishing them safety and success on Humphreys Peak, then began retracing my route to the car.

When I reached the parking lot an hour later, clouds touched the ridge tops. I did not linger. Instead I drove the winding five-mile route to "The Merc" in Kenton, Oklahoma, hoping to meet Allan Griggs.

An increasing number of highpoints have unofficial volunteer caretakers—Allan Griggs admirably fills the role for Black Mesa. A retired engineer, Allan owns and operates "The Merc," a combination general store, grocery, gas station, and meeting place in Kenton. On this cold day he was running the store by himself; however, I was the only customer. As I rehydrated and warmed up, he related tales of past highpointers, their idiosyncrasies, successes, and failures.

With obvious pride and excitement he told of a late night phone call received three days earlier, informing him that Kenton had been selected for the Highpointers Club annual convention. "This," he said emphatically, "would be the biggest event ever held in Kenton."

"How many highpoints have you done?" I asked.

"I have met many completers and would-be completers," he slowly answered. Then, cheerfully revealing his highpointing total, he proudly stated, "one, the best one."

A light drizzle and temperatures in the mid-thirties accompanied me as I crossed the Colorado-Kansas border, heading to

Mt. Sunflower (4,039 feet), the highest point in Kansas. Turning onto a gravel road, eleven miles from the state summit, I surprised a badger who froze and stared from roadside vegetation only ten feet away.

I stopped. Our eyes met. A beautiful animal with elongated face and white midline facial stripe bordered in black, he looked at me through unblinking eyes. Uncertain whether to flee or remain motionless, he warily studied both car and me a full thirty seconds before abruptly turning and quickly slinking away.

Continuing north, the road deteriorated. In low areas it was little more then a mud wallow. Fountains of mud spurted from behind the tires, leaving half-foot deep tracks as I revved the engine, slipping and sliding through the muck.

I could only glance briefly across the countryside. Beneath dull gray clouds, with long-range views obscured by drizzle, each gently sloping hill seemed remarkably similar.

I recalled my high school math teacher, an accomplished mountain climber and early highpointer, laughing as he described his difficulty finding the "highest hill" in Kansas. "I climbed many hills that day," he told me. "On each one I searched for the marker proving it to be the highpoint. I must have climbed four, five… maybe six long hills before I found the right one. It took me all afternoon!"

The year was 1970, his story my introduction to highpointing.

I thought back over those thirty years. In high school I had been a hard-working student, received good grades, but lacked athletic prowess. Reading accounts of explorers and adventurers—Peary and Hillary, Byrd and Herzog—I never dreamed such exotic adventures would become possible for ordinary people.

But they had. During the past decade and a half, I had traveled on the Amazon, climbed in the Andes, kayaked in the Arctic, and trekked in Asia. And now I was pursuing The Dream, certainly my longest and most challenging adventure yet.

My recollections abruptly ended when I saw a sign pointing left: "Mt. Sunflower—1 mile." A narrow muddy road led to a field with a barely perceptible rise.

Three decades have brought major changes to Mt. Sunflower. Today it is easy to find, its summit crowned by a 12-foot-tall sunflower sculpture of welded, painted railroad ties. A small memorial, commemorating the area's pioneering families, surrounds the metallic sunflower; a covered picnic table is located conveniently nearby.

I chose to walk the final fifty yards across the grassy field to the summit. The final approach to any summit is exciting and full of anticipation. Mt. Sunflower, surprisingly, was no exception. I wanted to feel the wind, smell the damp springtime prairie air, hear the muffled sounds, and enjoy the limited vista allowed by the clouds and rain.

I touched the monument, highpoint number thirty-five. The undulating terrain gently dropped away in all directions; only a single farmhouse, a half-mile distant, rose above the grassland.

A century ago homesteaders filled this area, each claiming 160 acres and dreaming of a better life. Even then, however, 160 of these often-arid acres—a quarter square mile—could barely support a family. The farm economy declined. Droughts and grasshoppers ravaged the area. Most homesteaders sold out and moved on.

Today farms and ranches are measured in square miles, not acres. But farmers and ranchers still struggle. Consolidation continues. The rural Great Plains have lost so much population that large portions of a half dozen states again meet the federal government's definition of frontier—less than two permanent residents per square mile.

Atop Kansas, surrounded by clouds, space, and wind, I took the summit register from its box. Attached to its cover was a one-page description of the area's geography, history, and residents. Eighty people had signed this notebook during the previous month. Some wrote of the "grand, sweeping views," while others complained of "nothing worth seeing." These vast grasslands evoke varied, often extreme emotions; visitors either love or hate them.

One couple must certainly have loved them. Two months earlier they had married atop Mt. Sunflower. The register records thirty-two guests in attendance.

No crowds joined me on the summit. Alone with my thoughts, I wondered how many highpoints my math teacher had achieved (he had reached thirty plus in 1970 but is not listed as either a "48" or "50 completer" by the Highpointers Club), how life had treated him, and how many other lives he and the other teachers at Denver Lutheran High School had impacted as deeply and positively as mine.

I signed the register then gazed across the Kansas prairie one final time. Unfortunately the weather was forecast to worsen. Snow was possible. Reluctantly, I felt it necessary to hurry north to Nebraska.

Gray skies and mist continued to Sidney, Nebraska, there replaced by dense fog. Thirty miles west in Kimball, three inches of snow covered the ground although roadways remained clear.

The forecast was not encouraging. One hundred miles further west, a blizzard had already closed Interstate 80. More snow was predicted here in the Nebraska panhandle. But schools had been in session, and the motel clerk in Kimball assured me that the roads to Panorama Point (5,424 feet), Nebraska's highest location, should still be passable, although she strongly recommended a different route than that described in the guidebook.

With the storm approaching, I wanted to reach the highpoint, twenty-six miles away, as soon as possible. After reserving a room, I set off, following the locally recommended directions, a better route, I was told, under these conditions. I took water bottle, guidebook, camera, and warm clothes. It was 4:30 p.m.

The road's pavement soon gave way to a gravel surface which was quickly replaced by dirt, or more accurately, mud. My rented Toyota Corolla slid perilously through the soft mud. For the second time that day, columns of brown liquid spewed from beneath the tires. Sometimes deep ruts remained after I passed; in other places, water and liquid earth immediately obscured my tracks.

I had driven six miles since leaving the gravel road; 14 miles of this muck lay ahead. I knew the car couldn't make it. Either I would get stuck or slide off the road into even softer and deeper mud.

But there was no place to turn around.

Worry about road conditions gave way to fear as I was forced to drive on. Resigned to not reaching the highpoint, I now hoped only for a place to turn back before getting stuck along this isolated road.

Then in my rear-view mirror I saw headlights piercing the fog. Reaching a firmer portion of the road I stopped, allowing Vernon, a retired local farmer, to pull alongside.

"What's the road ahead like," I asked, yelling between the cars, "to Panorama Point?"

"It gets a lot worse," he answered, "Here it's pretty good."

Good? Uh-oh.

"Any chance of making it in this car? Or do I need a four-wheel-drive?" I already knew the answer.

"Well," he paused, "the road gets a lot worse. I wouldn't try it in my car." I looked at his mud-covered vehicle, a large late-model Buick sedan.

"Where are you from?" he asked.

"North Carolina," I responded. "Here for a couple of days, traveling throughout the country, attempting to reach the highest geographical point of each state."

Vernon obviously had met other highpointers because he wasn't taken aback by a North Carolinian, 2,000 miles from home, sliding along muddy rural Nebraska roads late on a foggy afternoon, looking for a small hill topped by a granite marker.

"I would take you there if I had a four-wheel-drive," he said, "but I don't."

"Well," this time I paused. "Do you know anyone around here who does and would be willing to take me to the highpoint? I am willing to pay them."

"Well," this time the pause seemed interminable. My chance of completing the contiguous highpoints this year might well be determined by the next sentence uttered. "Why don't you follow me to the house. Your car should be able to make it that far. I will try to find somebody to take you from there."

A slippery mile later, I pulled into Vernon's driveway, the firmest ground I had driven over during the past half-hour. Vernon insisted I come inside. I didn't want to impose more than I already had but acquiesced, thankful to escape the cold damp fog.

He phoned Glen Klawonn, owner of the High Point Bison Ranch, who rented the acreage that included Panorama Point. Glen, I could tell from the conversation, was also familiar with highpointers and wasn't shocked by my quest—or my predicament. Vernon handed me the phone. Glen and I quickly negotiated a fee, a remarkably reasonable price given the weather conditions and time of day.

While I waited for Glen to arrive, Vernon, his wife Lucy, and I discussed highpointing, farming, and the regional economy.

They listened intently as I described my travels and climbing, sabbatical and The Dream. Nine months after leaving the emergency department, with two-thirds of the nation's highpoints completed, I was feeling more comfortable discussing my plans and explaining why I was not regularly employed at age forty-six. We talked of farming: Christmas trees and tobacco in North Carolina and irrigated agriculture in the Plains.

Vernon and Lucy own 400 acres of fertile cropland in the Nebraska panhandle atop the Ogallala Aquifer, a large pool of water that underlies much of western Nebraska. The soil is fertile and the aquifer's fossil water ideal for irrigation. However, they no longer farm, instead renting their land to neighboring farmers. Their two children, both college educated, have moved away.

"Neither of your children want to farm?" I asked.

"Can't raise a family on 400 acres anymore," Vernon replied. "Can't even break even without government price supports." He cited a litany of reasons: low crop prices, high fuel and fertilizer costs, trade policies, expensive equipment. "No, few people can afford to farm anymore," he added, his voice tinged with regret. "Most do it just as a sideline."

Life seemed hard in this region. I had driven past abandoned farmhouses south of Kimball, and seen many dwellings vacant throughout Kansas and northeastern Colorado. No, 400 acres would not support a family; 4,000 might, but few young people were willing to take that chance or able to make the huge investment required to buy the land and machinery. Vernon and Lucy seemed to embody the idealized image of the family farmer—friendly, knowledgeable, helpful people living in a neat well-maintained home on fertile land.

The low rumble of a large flatbed farm truck heralded Glen's arrival. I thanked my hosts for their help and hospitality then climbed into the truck's cab with Glen. As twilight deepened we drove toward Panorama Point. Vernon was right—my rented car would never have made it. Slipping and sliding despite four-wheel-drive, it took forty-five minutes to drive a dozen muddy miles before we turned off the road into a snow-covered field. Here at a slightly higher elevation, the snow lay six inches deep.

Glen drove along a muddy path between two seven-foot chain link fences. "Buffalo fences," he explained. The heavy truck labored through the mud and snow, leaving foot-deep ruts in its wake. Glen shifted into low for maximal traction.

We drove past "No Hiking" signs. "Buffalo risks," he said, pointing to the signs. "The animals are unpredictable and hikers don't realize how dangerous they can be. I can't take the risk of anyone getting injured."

We continued another half-mile across the prairie then drove up a final snow-covered knoll. Through the fog, I saw a polished five-foot high stone monument surrounded by vertical metal pipes—Nebraska's highest point.

It was 7:30 and nearly dark. "It's a real pretty view out there on a clear day," Glen said, pointing into the fog. "You can see both Colorado and Wyoming. It's strange," he continued, "people either really like the expansive views and wide open spaces or they say there's nothing there and are disappointed once they get here." I had read nearly identical comments hours earlier in Mt. Sunflower's register, but now any view, even a fog-shrouded one, seemed beautiful. I stood atop Nebraska.

Flash was required for summit photos, and Glen photographed me standing beside the summit marker before I photographed him beside the truck so ignobly required to reach this state highpoint. Able to see little due to fog and increasing darkness, we left Panorama Point after a few minutes and retraced the slippery route to Vernon's house and my car.

En route Glen spoke of buffalo and the challenges facing today's farmer. He was one of the few farmers in the area still trying to support and raise a young family solely by farming. Managing more than five square miles of land, he raised and bred buffalo, selling both calves and meat. He also permitted "buffalo hunts." For a fee one could "harvest" a pre-selected animal, obtaining meat, hide, and trophy head. Although shooting a buffalo in a fenced pasture didn't sound like sport to me, I admired Glen's ingenuity and business savvy.

"Farming," he explained, "is dependent on governmental subsidies, a two-edged sword." Referring to the land bank, crop subsidies, and myriad programs today's farmer must be knowledgeable of, he said, "I hate being on the public dole, but that is the only way one can stay in this business." Most of the vacant farmhouses, he continued, had been abandoned in the mid-twentieth century, but a few had been occupied as recently as the late 80s. "Farmers retire, move to town, go bankrupt, or simply give up," he said matter-of-factly, "while few young people can afford to enter the business because of expensive equipment, massive debt, and the thousands of acres required to support a family."

At Vernon's we all gathered and talked briefly. Number thirty-six had been a far greater challenge than anticipated, but with the help of these three people I had succeeded. They had befriended a traveler, been inconvenienced and delayed supper, even opened their home to a stranger. My dream of reaching the contiguous highpoints this year remained alive. They wished me good luck with safe climbing and travels on my quest, and after thanking everyone for their help and friendship, I drove off, slipping and sliding through the darkness toward Kimball.

Winter storm warnings were posted for the central Plains the following morning. I decided to head south, relieved to have at least "bagged" the highpoints of Kansas and Nebraska, yet disappointed at being unable to visit nearby geological and historical sites. Someday I hope to return and see these attractions—and the "panorama" from Panorama Point. I hurried south through Colorado, through Brush and Last Chance, Punkin Center and Rocky Ford. The snow finally caught me as I stayed overnight in Raton, New Mexico. The next day, May 6, a beautiful winter scene with wet valley snow and mountaintop rime ice greeted me as I hiked up Capulin Volcano National Monument, within sight of Black Mesa Oklahoma, where five days earlier I had encountered the "blue-norther," the first in a series of spring storms that battered the Great Plains.

I had now touched the highpoints of all the Plains states. The weather had been a challenge, forcing me to alter plans and omit sites I had hoped to visit. Instead my fondest memories were of the people. The friendliness of the Sterlers in Iowa had piqued my interest in highpointing; access permitted by private landowners in Kansas, Nebraska, Iowa, and North Dakota made completion possible; and the help, advice, and kindness of many made this journey more enjoyable.

CHAPTER 16

RETREAT

Mt. Hood

Mt. Hood can be a "gentleman's mountain." Fifty miles east of Portland, its ready access, moderate routes, and luxurious accommodations have made it a perennial climbing favorite. A straightforward yet technical one-day ascent, it is the most frequently climbed major mountain in the United States and, except for Japan's Mt. Fuji, the most summited in the world.

Named Wy'East by Native Americans, Mt. Hood (11,239 feet), Oregon's highest point, is part of the Cascade Range, a chain of snow-capped volcanoes extending from British Columbia to northern California. However, this active volcano's recorded eruptions, the last in 1907, have been relatively minor. Today no smoke, steam, or molten lava is visible from its base, but climbers regularly encounter sulfurous fumes while traversing the crater rim. Composed of layered ash and pumice interspersed with thin lava flows, the mountain's crumbling flanks present high rockfall risk. Consequently Hood is most safely climbed in late spring after winter storms have abated, but while sufficient snow and ice remain to cover and stabilize the rock.

More than 10,000 people attempt the climb each year, most via the standard southern route. About half will succeed. Novices can rent needed gear—helmet, harness, ice ax, crampons, and plastic mountaineering boots—and after completing a required day-long "snow school," attempt an early morning guided climb to Oregon's highest point. En route they will pass the Devil's Kitchen, traverse the Hogsback, skirt the bergschrund (a deep crevasse at the glacier's head), and pass through the Pearly Gates, all colorfully named landmarks that enliven post-climb tales. For some this introduction leads to a life-long passion; indeed many experienced mountaineers first roped up, wore crampons, or used an ice ax on this peak.

Hood's popularity, however, is not a recent fad. The first recorded climb of the mountain took place in 1845, although it is likely native peoples summited many times before. In 1915 Frank Pearce married Blanche Pechette atop Oregon's highest point and in 1936, 411 people, the largest group ever, stood atop the mountain.

But Mt. Hood can be a killer. More than 130 people have died attempting the climb. Its easy accessibility and moderate routes regularly tempt untrained, poorly conditioned, or ill-equipped climbers to attempt the mountain, often with tragic and widely publicized results. Crowding presents additional risks: avalanches are triggered; equipment is dropped; and rocks are accidentally knocked loose, falling onto climbers below. Roped falls can trigger deadly chain reactions as a falling group of climbers may tangle ropes with a lower team, sending both hurtling down the mountain. In May 2002, nine climbers from three groups were swept into a crevasse during such an accident. Three died. Television cameras filmed rescue attempts—and the tumbling crash of an Air Force rescue helicopter.

One month after being driven to the snowy summit of Nebraska, I flew to Portland, Oregon, hoping to ascend Mt. Hood via a technically challenging line west of the heavily trafficked standard route. However, I again faced inclement weather.

For two weeks a high-pressure system had brought clear skies, light breezes, and little precipitation to the Pacific Northwest. But on the day I arrived, a strong storm moved ashore. East of Portland I encountered a cold rain that continued to the base of Mt. Hood, but as I drove up the winding two-lane road from Government Camp to Timberline Lodge, the precipitation changed to snow.

The scene was beautiful—to anyone but a climber. Fir and spruce trees, some 150 feet tall with trunks a dozen feet in circumference, were decorated with rounded clumps of fresh wet snow. At lower elevations the ground remained clear, but as I continued higher the snowfall intensified, first blanketing the earth then sticking to the pavement. At Timberline Lodge, 6,000 feet above sea level, two inches of snow had accumulated; the parking lot was icy and the snow continued unabated.

Built in 1937 by the Works Progress Administration, Timberline Lodge is the finest "base camp" I have ever experienced. After a dinner of shrimp curry, I walked through the luxurious wooden hotel, one of the grand lodges built in our most visited national parks during the first half of the twentieth century. Constructed mostly by hand, with local craftsmen using regional materials, the building features intricate wrought iron decoration, hand-hewn beams, and an 80-foot-tall hexagonal stone fireplace. Sixty guest rooms, two restaurants, and a half-dozen shops line hallways extending from the spacious lobby. Most of the building's woodwork and furnishings are original while upholstery, drapes, and bedspreads are carefully executed reproductions of original designs.

Fires were crackling in all three of the lobby's fireplaces when I returned. But instead of watching the flames, I sat on a large sofa facing Mt. Hood and watched it snow...and snow...and snow, each soft flake increasing avalanche risk and decreasing my chance of summiting.

Avalanches, the biggest threat faced by springtime climbers on Mt. Hood, are most likely after fresh snow has fallen onto ice or previously hardened snow pack. Adhering poorly to the smooth underlying surface, the new snow can be dislodged easily, sliding down the mountainside in gigantic slabs, some larger than a football field. Repeated thawing and re-freezing, a process called consolidation that takes from three to seven days, is needed to solidify the fresh snow and tightly join it with the lower layers. Six inches of new snow present little risk, but twelve can be deadly.

Overnight the storm ended. But the next morning, as I prepared for the one-day climbing school, ten inches of heavy wet snow covered the earth. At 8,500 feet, twenty-four inches were reported; above that, no one had ventured.

Justin, an experienced climber and skier in his late twenties, would be my guide on Hood. Employed through Timberline Mountain Guides, he knew the mountain well, had climbed most of its routes, and understood the risks and terrain better than any guidebook could describe. After reviewing basic skills, we refined crevasse rescue techniques, practiced anchor construction, and discussed route selection. He described the routes on Hood and how each would be affected by the recent snowfall and subsequent avalanche risk. Most, he said, were too dangerous to attempt under these conditions. The only chance to summit, he believed, was via the standard route but even there, success would be doubtful.

That evening, again seated in the hotel lobby, I watched the sun set, casting a golden glow across Mt. Hood's snow-shrouded slopes. Before a big climb, if time and conditions permit, I sit before the mountain, studying it and mentally preparing for the ascent. Each mountain looks so very big—in Hood's case towering a full mile above the Lodge. And during this introspective time I feel very small. Scaling such a massive white hill seems a foolish impossibility. But as with all the great mountains I have been privileged to visit, I viewed Hood with respect and awe, for climbers never "conquer" mountains. Today's straightforward climb may be tomorrow's death trap. Climbers instead summit mountains—but only when conditions permit.

At 12:30 a.m. the alarm rang. Another alpine start. An hour and a half later, Justin and I were ascending with two other groups in a Sno-Cat, an enclosed vehicle that would take us to 8,500 feet above sea level. Gusting winds stripped snow from the mountain's surface and hurled it against the unheated vehicle's windows. At the top of the ski area, in the lee of a 20-foot-high snowdrift, we got out. With frigid fingers covered by bulky gloves, we struggled to tighten crampons and tie into the climbing rope, moving quickly, anxious to begin walking if only to warm up.

Then guide and client ascended the steep drift into the gale's full fury. Ice crystals pelted my face, while my jacket flapped loudly with each gust. But the wind brought more than discomfort; it was rearranging the upper few inches of snow and hardening its surface, further increasing avalanche danger. At times one intuitively senses that a summit attempt is futile. Guides try to remain optimistic with a "let's see what's ahead" attitude. But while studying Hood's topography, I had noted steeper—and riskier slopes above. Yet we pushed on.

At 4:00 a.m. we paused and, joined by guides from the two other teams, assessed risks and discussed strategy. Ahead just below the Hogsback lay a snow-laden 40-degree slope, the route's riskiest portion.

In addition to snow depth and consolidation, slope angle is a critical determinant of avalanche risk. On slopes angled less than twenty-five degrees, like those we had ascended thus far, snow seldom slides because the angle is not steep enough. Very steep slopes, especially those greater than sixty degrees, rarely accumulate enough snow to be dangerous. But on treeless slopes between thirty and forty-five degrees, massive amounts of snow can pile up, then slide without warning.

Using an ice ax, Justin cut a narrow trough into the snow, isolating a 2½-foot-square block. Below the thinly crusted surface, the loose snow had a clean, uniform appearance until ice was encountered thirty inches down. Then to test cohesiveness, he toppled the nearly one-half cubic yard block from its base with a ski pole, using less force than required to knock over a cup of coffee.

We would not summit Mt. Hood today. The risk of a slab avalanche, the largest and deadliest of snowslides, was too great. A small force, perhaps a climber traversing this treeless expanse, or even a tiny crack in the snow's wind-hardened surface, could release a slab thirty inches thick and a hundred yards wide that would sweep us to our deaths. It was time to turn around.

We were back in the Lodge in time for the gourmet breakfast buffet. But afterwards with dismal weather predicted, I retreated from Mt. Hood and the Cascades, driving east to central Oregon's high desert to tour and wait. My itinerary could not accommodate a second journey west during Hood's climbing season, so I had scheduled four extra days this trip for sightseeing—or a second attempt to reach the highest point.

As I watched Native Americans use nets and traditional methods to fish for salmon from platforms along the Deschutes River, I could see thick dark clouds hovering over the Cascades. As I toured Warm Springs Indian Reservation—home of the Wasco, Warm Springs, and Northern Paiute tribes—and visited their museum and cultural center, a chill northwest wind swept down from the mountains. And as I hiked the three units of the John Day Fossil Beds National Monument then ascended the cinder cones and explored the ice caves of the Newberry National Volcanic Monument, puffy white clouds dotted the azure desert sky. But each night the report from Justin was the same: no one had summited and more inclement weather was predicted.

Six days passed without anyone reaching the top. As I prepared to call the final time, one day before returning to North Carolina for a job interview, it again appeared that unseasonable weather would end this year's quest to complete the contiguous highpoints. The report was little changed. Although snow conditions had improved slightly, and although the pack was stabilizing, Justin said another storm was predicted within twelve to eighteen hours. Chances of success appeared minimal.

Steve, one of the company owners, then joined the conversation, offering a new idea. Three men were scheduled for a guided climb in the morning and I was welcome to join them. The storm, he explained, was expected to arrive near daybreak. If it came early, it would force another quick retreat; if it arrived later, summiting might be possible. Yet with the limited chance of success—estimated by him at twenty percent—and with my previous unsuccessful attempt, he offered this climb at no additional charge. I quickly seized the opportunity.

At 2:00 a.m., following a 2½-hour drive from the Oregon desert, I met my teammates. Long-time friends, all in their forties, these men had planned this adventure to celebrate a friend's fiftieth birthday. But a business problem had forced this man to cancel at the last moment. Fees already paid, the others would climb without him.

Of the three, only Paul, a businessman from Silicon Valley, had previous climbing or high-altitude experience. The tallest and strongest of the friends, he had summited Mt. Rainier and trekked in Nepal. Neither David, a San Diego attorney, nor Rob, a banker from Portland, had prior backcountry experience, but both were recreational runners and avid cyclists, and in outstanding physical condition. Pete, one of Timberline Mountain's senior guides, would lead. Yesterday he had taught the others climbing basics; today he would try to help us reach Hood's summit.

Mild temperatures and light breezes prevailed as we stepped from the Sno-Cat at 8,500 feet. The sky was mostly clear; stars shone brightly and a crescent moon hung low in the nighttime sky. Needing only thin gloves to cover our hands, we quickly tightened harnesses and crampons then easily tied into the rope. We moved out quickly, Pete at the head of the rope and me, the second most experienced climber, anchoring the far end.

Above the large drift, where four days earlier I had first

experienced the storm's full fury, we could now see Portland's lights, fifty miles away. But a cloud cap, always a worrisome sign of unsettled weather, enveloped Hood's summit. Hoping to beat the storm, our team maintained a steady pace, soon passing the point where Justin had toppled the large snow block that prompted my earlier retreat. During these four days the snow had changed and become more compact. Now it was firm; crampons held securely and footprints remained, making the ascent more like walking up stairs than scrambling up a snowy mountainside.

The slope steepened, slowing our pace. From vents in the Devil's Kitchen, a portion of Hood's mountainside crater, sulfurous fumes blew across the snow-packed path. We pushed on, crossing the Hogsback then ascending toward the Pearly Gates.

Orange light colored the predawn sky as we ascended through the Gates up a steep icy gully between hundred-foot-tall rock pillars. Rime ice, formed by wind-blown fog freezing onto exposed rock, decorated each pillar with delicate crystals and ice spurs that extended horizontally up to three inches.

Above the pillars, we entered a cloudbank, but there the route's angle lessened, allowing our pace to quicken. Minutes later, Pete stopped and motioned us forward, telling us to unclip as he coiled the rope on the snowy surface. From here, he said, it was a short stroll to the top.

Two of the friends moved on, but Rob lagged behind, head bowed and breathing rapidly. The pace had been too fast, and the altitude was taking its toll. Pete and I stopped while Rob rested, my thoughts alternating between this struggling climber, the gathering storm, and our need to reach the summit soon.

Gradually, Rob's breathing slowed. He took his hands off his knees and straightened his torso. "Let's go", he said, smiling faintly, "but slowly."

Side by side, the three of us moved up the snowy incline. The angle was mild and the altitude moderate only by mountaineering standards as we walked up a 20-degree slope 11,000 feet above sea level.

Paul and David met us on a fog-shrouded snowdrift; half a dozen climbers rested nearby. Stepping above the group, I followed the packed snow to a corniced edge. There the terrain dropped away in all directions, and I could go no further.

Above the Pearly Gates
Five climbers roped together ascend the final snowfield toward Mt. Hood's summit.

Surrounded by mist and cloud, I triumphantly raised my ice ax. I was atop Oregon.

Joy and thankfulness mixed with relief as I stared into the fog, thrilled at having beaten the storm—and the odds—to stand on Hood's summit. Pete and Rob joined me atop the drift; Paul and David followed as we congratulated one another. Feeling better after the slower pace, Rob reached into his pack and removed an acetate-covered sheet of paper: "Mt. Hood—11,239 feet," it read. Together we stood for summit photos, Rob proudly holding the sign detailing our accomplishments.

More climbers came up the mountain. Even though storms were expected, Hood's summit was a busy place early this weekday morning. A light breeze stirred, the clouds thinned, and the morning sun's hazy light cast weak shadows across the snow. A stronger breeze followed, clearing the sky and revealing the rugged terrain below. Though the Dalles and Columbia River Gorge remained mostly hidden beneath valley fog, snow-capped Mt. Jefferson and the hilly landscape to the south was clearly seen. As curling wisps of cloud clung to Hood's flanks, I snapped a few photos. The clear respite lasted just minutes; as suddenly as the view had been revealed, it closed, followed by a colder and stronger wind in advance of the approaching front. It was time to descend.

While Pete steadied the rope from above, the position most able to arrest a fall, I led the group down the snowy slope and through the Pearly Gates, their icy spicules softening and falling as intermittent hazy sunshine warmed the rocky pillars. We descended the Hogsback, skirted the Devil's Kitchen, and continued down to the top of the ski area where, six hours earlier, we had exited the Sno-Cat to begin our climb. There we unroped and individually walked the final 2,500 feet to Timberline Lodge.

I again thanked Pete and the three friends for allowing me to join them and, echoing words told me atop my first major summit, wished for each that Hood would "be one of many safe summits."

"By the way," Rob asked as we neared the Lodge, "how many state highpoints have you done?"

"Thirty-seven," I answered, no longer afraid of discussing my quest or state count.

His eyes widened. "Good luck," he said, extending his hand and bidding me goodbye before hurrying to join his friends for the Lodge's gourmet breakfast buffet.

I glanced back toward Mt. Hood. The cloud cap had thickened, now obscuring much of the mountain's flanks. "Yes," I thought, as I walked toward the car, preparing to return to Portland for an afternoon flight home, "Good luck has been our companion today."

CHAPTER 17

THE EDGE

New England

R hode Island's Jerimoth Hill, 812 feet tall, is the nation's most difficult highpoint—to access, that is. Two hundred yards from State Highway 101 and fewer than a dozen feet higher, this summit is on land owned by Brown University but must be reached by crossing the Richardson property.

Therein lies the challenge. For decades, the late Henry Richardson, a retired music professor, forbade access to the protruding boulder that is Rhode Island's loftiest point. "No Trespassing" signs lined his property along the south side of Highway 101 as did advisories stating, "Violators Will Be Prosecuted." But no other legal or practical route through the dense tick-infested brush surrounding the summit was ever established. So despite the signs, and warnings such as Paul Zumwalt's guidebook reference to a "hostile property owner," highpointers regularly attempted to beg, plead, cajole, or if all else failed, sneak to the highpoint. Highpointing articles frequently featured this issue, and even the *Wall Street Journal* published a lighthearted look at the problem.

Eventually the Highpointers Club decreed that the roadside highway marker would suffice as a surrogate summit, the only such alternative designation among the fifty states. However, after years of negotiations and shortly before Mr. Richardson's death, an agreement was reached: Five public access days would be allowed annually, generally on holiday weekends. Club members would monitor the highpoint during these times, protecting the owner's property and privacy. In return, through signs, newsletters, and websites, the club would actively discourage unauthorized access. Either location, the summit boulder or highway sign, would continue to count as Rhode Island's highest point.

But the sign, although it may be reached any day of the year, is not the loftiest point. Thus far, I had reached the highest apparent elevation in each state completed, crossing the crater high on Mt. Rainier to Washington's true summit, balancing atop a small rock on Wyoming's Gannett Peak, and traveling to Louisiana twice, eventually reaching the apex of the correct hill. I did not wish to settle for less in Rhode Island.

Thus my second northeastern highpointing trip was scheduled around July 1, a public access day. This would be a challenging trip. Four northeastern state summits remained: New York's Mt. Marcy, the longest highpointing trail east of the Rockies; Maine's Mt. Katahdin, the east's most strenuous ascent; New Hampshire's Mt. Washington, renowned for inclement weather; and Jerimoth Hill. Three challenging hikes were planned around a 200-yard stroll up a Rhode Island driveway.

Sheryl would again join me. She steadfastly supported my quest, but when told that three difficult peaks—and her summer vacation—were planned to allow a five-minute walk up a paved path, she was stunned. However, she shared my dream and understood my desire to reach each state's true summit; after the shock wore off, she agreed to the itinerary.

In the heart of the Adirondack Mountains near Lake Placid, New York, Mt. Marcy rises 5,344 feet above sea level. Known also by its Native American name Tahawus, or "cloud-splitter," the Empire State's highest peak is summited via a 7½-mile-long trail traversing forests and heath-filled meadows, gaining more than 3,000 feet.

Geologically distinct from the Appalachian Mountains to the south and east, the Adirondacks are wholly contained within the state of New York, the billion-year-old range extending northward from the Mohawk River to Quebec and eastward from the St. Lawrence to Lake Champlain. Forty-six of these peaks rise above 4,000 feet, but all were buried beneath glaciers during the last Ice Age. As a result, only a thin soil layer covers the underlying granite and basalt, while shallow lakes and marshes fill rounded valleys.

Most of this region is part of Adirondack State Park, a preserve created in 1892 that today encompasses more than six million acres, much of it privately owned. Within a half-day's drive of most northeastern cities, this area is frequented by outdoor enthusiasts and supports a thriving recreation industry. It is also home to a group of dedicated hikers—the 46ers—named for their desire to ascend each of the Adirondack peaks higher than 4,000 feet, a feat accomplished by more than 5,000 people.

But Sheryl and I had come to scale only one of these mountains. A stormy weather pattern abated hours before we arrived, but inclement weather was predicted again within twenty-four hours. So the next morning, an hour before sunrise, we began the long hike up Mt. Marcy.

The sky was clear and the weather cool, dominated by a Canadian high-pressure system. We reached Marcy Dam, an aging mass of wood and concrete two miles up the trail, as the sun rose. A picturesque lake, created by the dam, filled the broad valley. Vegetation sported the varying greens of early spring growth. Surrounding mountains, lit by the sun's earliest rays, reflected from the water's still-dark surface.

Beyond the lake the trail narrowed then deteriorated to a boulder-strewn gully up a steep ravine. I glanced ahead. A dead pine, supported by lifeless limbs entangled with those of its dying neighbors, hung directly over our path. The lowest ten feet had been cut away, but the remaining trunk, eighteen inches in diameter and seventy feet high, remained suspended over the walkway. We stopped short, but finding no alternative, scurried beneath this wooden Sword of Damocles.

Above the gully the forest thinned, replaced with laurel, blueberries, and hardy shrubs. Across wide valleys, surrounding mountains, some only a few feet lower than Mt. Marcy, were scarred with vertical white slashes through forested flanks. However these scars were not from human activity. Instead thin waterlogged soils—with grass, shrubs, and trees—had slid down these hillsides, leaving smooth bedrock that would remain exposed for centuries.

Five-and-a-half hours after leaving the car, we reached the glacier-scoured rocks surrounding Mt. Marcy's summit then scrambled up a rocky face to stand atop New York's highest point. Cumulus clouds cast purple shadows onto distant peaks,

Sheryl Atop Mt. Marcy

while a brisk wind kept insects at bay. Algonquin Peak, New York's second loftiest mountain, rose to the northwest; Lake Tear-of-the-Clouds, source of the Hudson River, nestled below Marcy's southwestern flank. Lake Champlain extended along the eastern horizon, and a faint silhouette of Mt. Mansfield, Vermont's highest peak, was seen through haze hovering above the water. Except for the town of Lake Placid and its surrounding Olympic facilities, little human development was seen.

I had not expected such splendid isolation. I had thought of New York as a state of congested traffic and cities populated by millions. But a rugged, beautiful—and undeveloped—landscape lay before us. Forested mountains extended in all directions, while atop Mt. Marcy, tiny alpine plants clung tenaciously to life, seeking moisture and protection in rocky crevices.

Yet strong personalities and major events have touched this region. In 1855, John Brown moved his family to a 244-acre farm at Mt. Marcy's base—for protection it is claimed—while the abolitionist fought a series of bloody pre-Civil War battles in eastern Kansas. After hacking five pro-slavery settlers to death, the emboldened Brown formed a group that seized the federal weapons arsenal at Harper's Ferry, Virginia (later West Virginia), hoping to ignite a slave revolt. But the plan failed. The leader was captured, then tried and executed for treason. His remains, and those of his two sons and ten followers killed in the raid, are interred near the family's Adirondack home.

Four decades later, as Vice-President Theodore Roosevelt descended from New York's highest summit on September 6, 1901, news arrived that President William McKinley had been shot. The Vice-President hurried to Washington; eight days later when McKinley died, Roosevelt became our nation's twenty-sixth chief executive.

Joyous events have occurred here, too. Twice—in 1932 and 1980—Lake Placid hosted the Winter Olympics. "Do you believe in miracles?" asked announcer Al Michaels as the final seconds ticked from the clock in 1980. Cheering and celebration gave the answer as the game, now known as the Miracle on Ice, ended and a group of little-known American collegiate ice hockey players defeated the vaunted Soviet Red Army team in one of sports' greatest upsets.

But atop New York, as clouds thickened and the cold north-westerly wind intensified, our climb was only half complete. Seven-and-a-half miles and 3,200 vertical feet separated us from the trailhead parking lot. On many mountains, the climb up is more enjoyable, even easier, than the hike down. One is stronger and more rested, scenery and environments are new, and the excitement builds as the summit nears.

Descents, however, generally retrace previously traversed terrain. The weather is hotter, the thunderstorm risk greater. Hunger, thirst, and fatigue worsen. Backpacks, now filled with bulky clothes needed only in morning's chill, raise the hiker's center of gravity, making balance less steady and exacerbating stumbles. And descents are especially hard on the legs: Knees are jarred; toes jam forward; and muscles must simultaneously lengthen and tighten, a process called concentric contraction that is less familiar and more difficult than the muscular shortening used walking uphill.

After a final look from atop Mt. Marcy's summit, we started back, downclimbing bare rocks and crossing heather-covered slopes. But shortly after entering the steep gully, my foot slipped, my backpack lurched upward, and I fell forward, twisting my leg between rocks and hyperextending my thumb. It was a hard, dangerous, and embarrassing fall. No bones were broken, but as I cleaned my bleeding thumb and tested both knee and ankle, I knew our confidence had been shaken.

Sheryl had never seen me fall. Afterwards, her pace slowed; each deliberate foot placement—and fear—sapped her energy. She tired, but all I could offer was a steadying hand because throughout the hike I had carried the backpack and all food, water, and gear.

Nearing the bottom of the ravine, I thought of guided climbers I had met on other peaks. Most clients carry their own gear, but some hire two and even three guides to transport everything. Then they walk slowly, sans backpack, often at the limits of their physical conditioning. Some, including stroke and cancer survivors, have inspirational stories—and all possess great desire to reach the summit. Yet there is little safety margin. If storms threaten or clients tire, guides have few options short of physically carrying their charges from danger.

Meanwhile high clouds streaked the afternoon sky over Mt. Marcy. The weather remained benign, and mid-June daylight would be long. Legs trembled and shoulders ached when we reached the car six hours after leaving the summit. Though tired, hungry, and thirsty, we had made it—and New York's highest mountain had lived up to its reputation as one of the nation's most challenging state summits.

Low clouds and intermittent rain returned by morning. From a covered porch, I gazed across a protected cove of Lake Placid, one of 200 Adirondack lakes of at least one square mile surface area. True to its name the lake's waters were calm, muted light reflecting from the mirror-like surface. Conifers lined the shore, the jagged green line disappearing into distant mist. A family of ducks created short wakes as they swam, the only disturbance on the water's shiny surface.

But the weather didn't matter. We were stiff and sore. My thumb hurt and my knee ached. I felt each of yesterday's fifteen miles; for Sheryl it was the longest and hardest hike she had ever completed.

Lake Placid, an eponymous town along the lake's southern shore, is a bustling village catering to tourists and is the home of the U.S. Olympic Training Center, the nation's premier facility for aspiring Olympians. As the drizzle continued, we opted to tour this sports complex. We were shown the athlete's housing and the cafeteria. But as I began to fear that this would be an hour-long walk through empty spaces, we entered the sports physiology lab. While EKGs, oxygen uptake, exhalation velocity, and lung capacity were measured, athletes exercised on bicycle ergometers and treadmills, one of the latter ten feet across for use by cross-country skiers. Cameras recorded movements, the high-speed images later analyzed by computer and coach for muscular efficiency.

But none of these devices, many differing little except in size from those in hospitals, prepared me for the training innovations we would see next. Stepping outdoors, we watched summertime ski jumpers hurtle down moistened plastic then soar into the mist off the 120-meter ski jump, leaning over outstretched skis before landing onto cushioned Astroturf. Bobsledders drove wheeled sleds down a now-bare fiberglass and metal course, speeding through sharply banked turns backed with refrigeration lines, conduits needed even in winter to maintain a frozen surface. Mogul skiers, Winter Olympic acrobats, slid down a ramp of metal rollers then—wearing life preservers—leapt high, executing a series of twists and turns before plunging into a landing pool.

After practices ended, we ascended to the ski jump's highest level. To the south, near the concrete tower's base, lay John Brown's grave; to the north, a few steps led to the ramp that plummeted more than the length of a football field to a distant landing zone. The scale was awesome; thoughts of hurtling down this chute at ninety miles per hour terrifying.

But as we descended—by elevator—I began thinking about our next climbing goal, Mt. Washington. The regional forecast called for improving weather; on New England's highest peak, we would need the best possible conditions. Rising 6,288 feet in northern New Hampshire, the mountain is claimed to be "home of the world's worst weather." The average annual temperature is 26.5 degrees; twenty feet of snow falls during a typical year; and the summit, frequently shrouded by storms or fog, is visible just seventy-five days annually.

Mt. Washington, however, is most infamous for its wind: the average annual speed exceeds thirty-five miles per hour; hurricane-force gales rake the mountain more than 100 days each year; and in 1934 a 231-mile-per-hour gust—the highest wind velocity ever recorded on the planet's surface—raced over the mountain.

It is also North America's deadliest mountain. Nearly 200 people have died here, most from hypothermia during sudden snowstorms that can strike any month of the year. Others have perished in avalanches and climbing accidents, from heart attacks or motor vehicle mishaps, and a train wreck that claimed eight lives in 1967.

Sheryl asked about our options up this popular but dangerous peak. When I began highpointing, I had hoped to ascend Mt. Washington during the winter, a demanding climb with conditions often rivaling those of the Himalayas or Alaska's Denali. However, I had been unable to arrange an attempt. Now, near the summer solstice, I showed her a map filled with legendary names—Huntington Ravine, Tuckerman Ravine, the Lion Head—and challenging routes, each gaining two-thirds of a mile in elevation.

But there are easier ways to reach New Hampshire's summit. A carriage route—claimed to be the nation's first man-made tourist attraction—was cut into the mountain in 1861. Rising at a 12 percent grade, the route has been widened for automobiles; 45,000 vehicles annually complete the 16-mile round-trip on the Mt. Washington Auto Road. The summit can also be reached by train, the only state highpoint touched by a rail line. Steam-powered cog locomotives have ascended this 3.1-mile route since 1869, today traveling on tracks atop 1,100 wooden trestles, some extending thirty feet above the rocky mountainside.

Remembering the smoking brakes after driving down Vermont's highest mountain, I did not want to drive up—and down—an even higher peak. But as I described possible hiking routes, Sheryl interrupted.

"How hard are these routes?" she asked.

"Each gain between 3,000 and 4,000 feet," was my technically correct but evasive reply. Sheryl is not an avid climber and does not think, as mountaineers do, of total altitude ascended. But she is very practical.

"And, how many feet was Mt. Marcy?" she asked.

"About 3,200," I said. Two days after our nearly 12-hour hike she still hurt, her muscles stiff and joints sore. With little discussion, we settled on the remaining option: hearing the metallic click of a locomotive cog all the way to Mt. Washington's summit.

The next morning we joined dozens of tourists at the mountain's fog-shrouded base. Camcorders scanned the train

and crowd as the engine was filled with coal and water. Tourists in shorts and sandals chatted excitedly about their upcoming "mountaineering adventure."

The train's steam whistle sounded an ear-piercing shriek. Babies cried and parents yelled for children as the conductor shouted "All aboard." Then the engine lurched forward, its smokestack belching smoke and cinders as the steady staccato of the 19-tooth cog gear meshing with the chain-like middle rail began.

Seventy thousand people ride this privately-owned railway each year. For safety reasons, each of the company's seven engines—their boilers angled at twenty-five degrees to match the route's average grade—push trains up the mountain; if brakes fail, the engine's cog will keep the passenger coaches from plummeting down the hillside.

Within a half mile the train climbed above the cloud layer shrouding the mountain's lower flanks, revealing blue skies and clear views of surrounding peaks. A ten-mile-per-hour wind, gentle by Mt. Washington's standards, pushed the engine's dark gray smoke into an improbable arc over and in front of the train as it chugged steadily uphill at three miles per hour. At Jacob's Ladder, the route's steepest portion, gravity pushed us into our seats as the train climbed at a 37.41 percent grade, each coach's front end fourteen feet higher than its back.

After one refueling stop, and after burning a ton of coal to convert 1,000 gallons of water to steam, the train crossed a final exposed slope and reached the mountaintop platform. Weather research stations, maintenance facilities, and a sprawling visitor complex with cafeteria and observation deck ringed the summit. Stepping into the cool sunshine, we joined hundreds atop New Hampshire and stood in line, waiting to ascend a mound of dark gray boulders to Mt. Washington's true summit.

Minutes later we scrambled to the highest rock then, jostled by tourists, took a single photo of each other with a weather radar unit as backdrop. After a brief tour of the crowded visitor center and a short look from the open observation deck, we descended from the mayhem to a sunny nook overlooking Tuckerman Ravine.

Only lichens, scattered grasses, and a few ground-hugging plants survive in this rocky windswept environment. Thousands of feet above timberline, an ecological demarcation

The Little Engine That Does
Coal-fired steam engines have pushed passengers to Mt. Washington's summit since 1869.

that decreases in altitude as latitude increases, we were near the limit of plant life itself. Small birds searched for morsels among bare rocks, finding more snack crumbs than insects or seeds, while vultures rode thermals up ravines and soared overhead.

Trains came and left, each arrival bringing throngs of tourists to scramble over the summit and crowd the gift shop, and each departure signaling a temporary lull in human activity. During one lull, we returned to the summit, again clambered up the rockpile, and this time stood by ourselves atop New Hampshire.

Once I had wished to ascend this mountain during the winter; on this trip I had hoped to complete a demanding hike. But as we together raised our arms in celebration, standing atop New England with Sheryl was more important and satisfying than any climbing achievement. She had encouraged me to follow The Dream, had provided emotional support when voices of doubt—external and internal—threatened its fulfillment, had endured months apart and lived with the uncertainty of safe return known only by climbers' loved ones.

And she never wavered.

Atop Mt. Washington—state highpoint number thirty-nine for me—I thanked her for her love and support as we scanned the Presidential Range. Then a train whistle blew and two commercial tourist vans arrived. It was time to descend.

The mercury topped ninety degrees when we stepped from the car in Millinocket, Maine. Haze hung in the air; oppressive humidity made it feel as though we were visiting a southeastern swamp. Thirty miles from Mt. Katahdin (5,267 feet), Maine's highest point, this aging mill town was decked out in red, white, and blue, in anticipation of Independence Day and the town's centennial celebration.

But Millinocket was showing its age. Factories were shuttered; the central business district dying; and frame houses, many with more bare wood than paint, sported for sale signs with price tags below $30,000. Industry had left for sunnier climes, and although this town of 8,500 serves as gateway and outfitting center for Baxter State Park and Mt. Katahdin, it seems to reap little financial gain from tourism.

Yet the park is one of New England's most popular outdoor destinations. Created in 1931 with a gift of 5,960 acres from then-Governor Percival Baxter, the preserve has been expanded to more than 200,000 acres. To avoid overcrowding and maintain a sense of wildness, daily parking limits are tightly enforced. Lines of cars await the park's 6:00 a.m. opening; on busy summer days the daily quota may be reached within an hour.

Eighteen peaks within this state park exceed 3,000 feet in height. Of these, Mt. Katahdin is the loftiest and most well-known—the northern terminus of the Appalachian Trail and the corporate logo of outdoor retailer L.L. Bean. From the south, the mountain appears as a giant monolith, rising two-thirds of a mile above surrounding rivers and lakes. But from the east, its high ridges and multiple peaks around a glacial-carved cirque give Katahdin a deeply sculpted appearance.

Four hiking paths lead to the summit. None are easy. One requires an overnight stay, allowing this strenuous peak to be climbed in two less demanding days. But most hikers want single-day ascents. Two such routes begin at the mountain's western base: the Abol Trail and the Appalachian Trail. The latter, the park's most popular and developed route, is marked with white rectangular blazes and equipped with metal hand-holds glued into drilled rock. The remaining option is a lightly-used route up the mountain's eastern flank that crosses a subsidiary peak and follows a long exposed ridgeline—appropriately named the Knife Edge—past walls that plunge thousands of feet to the cirque below.

Sheryl, not yet recovered from Mt. Marcy, did not wish to attempt Katahdin. The ranger at the visitor center did not add to her confidence. The Abol Trail was summarily dismissed as a steep unpleasant scramble over loose scree. Even the AT, this official said, was a hard climb—gaining nearly 4,000 feet—and would be hot and crowded. Then she paused, apparently finished.

"And what of the Knife Edge?" I asked.

A frown furrowed the woman's face. "One of New England's hardest climbs," she answered curtly. "No one without extensive climbing experience should attempt it." With that, the ranger turned away. When I looked at Sheryl, I knew that she had already sensed my thoughts, for her concern was apparent. I had read of the Knife Edge, considered one of New England's most beautiful hikes, but had dismissed it as too exposed and risky for her. But alone…the thought was intriguing.

At the visitors center we studied topographic maps and peered at a dusty three-dimensional model of Katahdin. The ridgeline was indeed exposed, but its walls were sharply angled hillsides, not vertical escarpments. Outside we spoke with others. One hiker had attempted the route years earlier. Turned back by high wind, he never tried again. When asked why, he shrugged his shoulders. Then a passing ranger interrupted, stating that if one had doubts, the hike shouldn't be attempted.

But others were less discouraging. A veteran park volunteer told me that, for an experienced outdoorsman, the hike was little more than a straightforward walk. And nearly everyone I spoke with knew of this route, many discussing the legendary path in near-reverential tones.

That night, after driving past Millinocket's Knife Edge Café and perusing gift shops featuring Knife Edge memorabilia, I shared my plan with Sheryl, who insisted that I attempt Katahdin even if she couldn't. Hoping to traverse the peak, I would start from the east; cross the Knife Edge; touch Baxter Peak, Mt. Katahdin's true summit; and descend along the Appalachian Trail. Sheryl would drop me off at the eastern trailhead then pick me up at the mountain's western base. It was a bold and risky plan. If I tired or turned back, lost my way or was forced off the mountain by storm or wind, little time remained for a second attempt at Maine's isolated highpoint. Still, I was drawn to the challenge.

As the sun's first rays touched Katahdin's summit, and a strong breeze rippled a nearby pond's surface, we waited for the park to open. Minutes after reaching the trailhead, a 25-minute drive from the entrance, I was standing in front of a darkened ranger station. Anxious to begin walking, and hoping to be up and over the mountain before afternoon thunderstorms might develop, I signed the register beside the locked door, uncertain if the trail was passable or even open in this wind. Although I knew that later I might have to ask park authorities for forgiveness, I believed the early start more important than waiting for permission.

Sheryl, however, did wait. Half an hour after my departure, a ranger arrived. "Is the Knife Edge passable?" she inquired.

"I wouldn't try it in these winds," the young ranger answered.

"Well, someone left about thirty minutes ago," Sheryl said, growing concerned.

"Don't worry," he responded. "They'll be back soon."

As I scrambled up the steep trail, over granite boulders and across smooth rock faces, Sheryl knew better than to expect my retreat. After watching a family of moose graze at a nearby pond, she returned to Millinocket to rest and relax.

The trail rose quickly, and before mosquitoes and biting flies stirred, I had climbed above the forest and into a stiff breeze that would keep these insects away. The air was cool, the hiking wonderful. Central Maine's topography, a flat patchwork of water and forested land interrupted by scattered hills and mountains, lay below. The morning sun shimmered off the water: lakes with names like Arnhajejus, Pemadumcook, and Debscneag; and meandering rivers—the Wassatoquoik and Seboeis, Penobscot and Allagash.

Here, as in northern Minnesota, water challenges the land for dominance. But as if to compensate for the flatness below, Maine's vertical relief was concentrated directly above me. The trail rose steeply, requiring scrambling up long cracks between boulders and using friction techniques—balance and shoe traction only—over bare rock.

However, steep trails gain altitude quickly, and three hours after passing the darkened ranger station, I stood atop Pamola Peak, the first of Katahdin's ridgeline summits. A roar like that of a waterfall rose from the cirque below. As pack straps slapped against canvas and I steadied myself against the gale, I stepped to the precipice. Yet there was no cataract, just the steady scream of wind rushing to Katahdin's ridgeline.

I met others atop Pamola Peak. A family of four planned to turn back; the parents, an athletic-appearing middle-aged couple had traversed the Knife Edge before but today, with two children in tow, decided to retreat rather than face the wind. Two fraternity brothers, Steve and Matt, were there, too. Fit backpackers, but lacking climbing experience, they had already looked at the vertical downclimb required to reach the Knife Edge trail itself, finding more adventure than they had anticipated. Yet, with youthful enthusiasm, they wanted to go on.

They walked with me to the edge. A 20-foot vertical wall—a fourth class scramble under good conditions but more challenging in the wind—lay at my feet. Beyond, the trail passed behind a rocky outcrop then followed the curving ridgeline to Katahdin's true summit. The young men said nothing as I scanned the distant route through binoculars then studied the difficulties at my feet. I thought of the trail just ascended, a path full of smooth rounded boulders over which I didn't want to return.

Technical downclimbing is more challenging and feared than ascending. While moving up a rock face, holds are near eye level and balance is easier. Descending, however, requires leaning out, searching the wall, and feeling with boots to find toe holds. Equipment and the climber's body often block a clear view, making depth perception and route-finding difficult.

I studied the descent then decided to climb down and investigate the trail's hidden portion. Each man would then decide whether to go on or if all needed to stay together for safety.

After cinching the pack tightly to minimize wind resistance, and having Matt tie the strap ends together to stop the incessant slapping, I turned and faced the rock and started down. The holds were firm and solid. Most moves were short, but six feet above the ledge—a long way to fall—I searched in vain for a foothold.

In my late thirties I began rock-climbing. Fearful of falling, I climbed conservatively and retreated often, searching for better lines and safer holds. But this style gave me confidence. When I began leading, I climbed at nearly the same level as when previously protected by a rope from above. Now, clinging to a cliff and searching for a foothold, the training, skills, and experience merged with focused intensity. Unaware of the wind, its noise or the scenery, my foot searched the wall as arms and legs fatigued.

Finding a tiny irregularity in the rock, I tested it with my boot. Wearing rock-climbing shoes, this nubbin would have been a "bomber" placement—safe and reliable—but with rigid-soled hiking boots, this angled bulge was too risky to attempt, especially in an isolated setting.

Then, extending my six-foot-three-inch frame lower still, my foot brushed against a larger protuberance. It felt firm and solid. Putting weight onto the inch-wide ledge, my boot held tightly to the rock. I moved my hands quickly, one at a time down the wall, improving my balance and reaching a safer stance. From there, the final three moves were easy; seconds later, I stood on a wide ledge beneath the rocky face.

This short descent, I would discover, was the route's "crux," its most difficult portion. After finding the path through the nearby outcrop to be straightforward, I returned to the wall's base. Over the wind I shouted the news to the others. They too, would try. As each man descended, I spotted from below and with cupped hands created an artificial foothold at the long step that had bedeviled me.

On the ledge, the fraternity brothers rested. There we decided that it was safe to separate but agreed to maintain visual contact. For the next hour-and-a-half, I followed the Knife Edge's rocky spine, working across jumbled rocks and traversing angled ledges seldom more than a foot wide. On dark rock beneath an intense late morning sun, the steady wind was refreshing. To my left, south of Katahdin, lay the watery vastness of central Maine; to my right, the mountain's great cirque. The route was a perfect combination of challenge, beauty, and solitude. The time passed quickly, and after scrambling over a final group of boulders, I walked the final steps up a scree-covered slope and touched an eight-foot-tall stone cairn. I was atop Maine.

Dozens of people, all having ascended the Appalachian Trail, rested near the summit, chatting about the view, the AT, and highpoints. "How many have you done?" two hikers were asked.

"Twenty-seven," replied a slightly built man, his sandy-colored hair covered with a sweaty bandana.

"Thirty-three," replied his partner.

Another man told of reaching the top of all the southern Appalachian peaks higher than 6,000 feet. But he had not ascended via roads or trails, instead bushwhacking through briars and rhododendron thickets, crossing rocks and fording streams. "I wouldn't recommend this to others," he added. His wife, seated nearby, chuckled, nodding in agreement.

Others talked of the AT, one man relating having "walked 869.3 miles" of the Trail. But many had come to Katahdin, not as part of a larger goal, but simply for the challenge and beauty of ascending a great mountain. Yet, atop Maine, all shared stories.

I enjoyed the expansive views and friendly banter while intermittently checking on Matt and Steve's progress along the ridgeline. Nearby, a young man leaned against sun-drenched rocks. Chad, today's summit monitor, had spent the night near the summit and clad in jacket, hat, and gloves despite the intense sun, was enjoying the midday warmth. "How many states have you done?" he asked, upon learning I was a highpointer.

"Forty," I replied softly.

Heads turned; conversation paused. "Which ones remain?" several hikers asked, nearly in unison.

For the first time on a summit, I talked about my goal of reaching all forty-eight contiguous state highpoints. Having already summited Hawaii and including this in my total, nine highpoints—five easy walks east of the Mississippi and four challenging western climbs—remained.

"How about Denali?" Chad asked, noting its conspicuous absence from my calculation.

"Some day, perhaps," I replied. "Some day."

He had seen me cross the Knife Edge. "You know you should do it," he said. "You'll never be satisfied with one left."

As I neared completion of my revised goal, this was the first of many times that the question of Alaska's "Big One" would be asked. But today I gave it no further thought; the discussion changed and I chatted with others as Matt and Steve scrambled past the last boulders and up the slope toward the stone cairn. There we congratulated each other—the only three to traverse the Knife Edge this day—and took summit photos beside the rocky pyramid. But an hour had already passed since I first stood atop Maine, and although the weather was stable, I needed to start down.

Wishing the fraternity brothers well and bidding good-bye to the others, I passed a sign denoting the Appalachian Trail's northern terminus then followed the route across a windswept plateau. Thousands of hiker's boots had etched a series of braided paths through the alpine vegetation exposing bare rock. A hundred yards later the trail steepened; the descent became strenuous but remained well-marked.

The ranger had been right: The AT was hot and crowded. Temperature and humidity intensified as altitude was lost; in the forest even the cooling breeze was blocked. And the lower I went, the more people I encountered. Lines formed where hikers waited to cross bare rock, using metal hand and footholds that had been drilled into the granite for protection.

In midafternoon, carrying three empty water bottles, I walked through a busy campground and into a grassy clearing. Sheryl was there to meet me. We rested as I told her of the Knife Edge and summit, of the wind and AT, feeling contented having traversed a challenging mountain along a beautiful route and returning safely.

The next days were spent touring and resting. No more 4:00 a.m. alarms, 12-hour hikes, or 3,000-foot elevation gains. We kayaked and watched moose, took short walks, and enjoyed fine restaurant meals. Mt. Katahdin and Wyoming's Gannett Peak, I would later conclude, were my favorite state summit climbs. But for now, highpointing was on hold—until "Rhode Island Day."

"No Trespassing" signs lined the south side of Highway 101 near the crest of Jerimoth Hill. A small pennant and two strips of plastic surveying tape hung limply from trees near the Richardson driveway. No cars were parked along the road and no one was present. I had planned our entire trip around this moment, but save for the pennant, the site seemed deserted.

Parking near the sign proclaiming Jerimoth Hill as Rhode Island's highest point, I scanned the fence line noting warning signs and boards plastered with official-looking documents. I was worried. Had the date been changed? Had the access agreement been nullified following the recent death of Mr. Richardson? Two weeks had passed since leaving home and checking the Club's website. But it was July 1 and the gate was open.

Sheryl and I discussed our options. Then we walked quickly past the warnings and up the drive, looking neither left nor right, hoping to reach the summit before being stopped. The pavement curved, but from guidebook descriptions I knew that the route continued straight along a dirt path.

Then I looked up. Thirty yards ahead, a neatly dressed man stood calmly, clipboard in hand, near a large gray rock protruding above the sandy soil. "Welcome to Rhode Island's summit," Chris Butler said as we approached, motioning toward the rock and extending his hand in greeting. As we each stepped upon the stone's surface—two of fifty-nine people from a dozen states and two countries that would do so that day—he recorded our names onto a yellow legal pad.

Dense brush surrounded the summit. But the land appeared to drop away, almost imperceptibly, in all directions. We were atop Rhode Island.

Recalling the proximity of Lyme, Connecticut, namesake of the tick-borne disease, I didn't wander far from the rock and small clearing in which Chris stood as we chatted about the Club and highpointing. He and his brother, Henri, are both active members—Henri a 50 completer, Chris having thus far touched forty state summits. And like many discussions between members, conversation centered on still-to-be-climbed state summits and their challenges. Then I thanked him for both his and the Club's efforts allowing public access to the top of Jerimoth Hill.[8]

It was time to return home. Other than a brief detour to hike up Backbone Mountain (3,360 feet), Maryland's highest point and my forty-second state summit, we drove straight back. En route I thought of our trips to New England: the quaint villages, church steeples, and stone fences typically associated with the

---

[8] In June 2005, Jeff and Debbie Mosley purchased the Richardson property. In cooperation with the Highpointers Club, a trail has been established parallel to the driveway, and access to Jerimoth Hill's summit is now permitted each Saturday and Sunday from 8:00 a.m. to 3:00 p.m. The last club-sponsored public access day was October 9, 2005; the six-year agreement with the former owners allowed 2,852 people to reach Rhode Island's true summit.

region; and the large coastal cities, filled with traffic, noise, and congestion. But I most fondly recalled the wildness and ruggedness of the land—the moose, the swamps, the rivers, and especially the mountains, their windswept summits extending far above timberline, fragile yet protected alpine environments where solitude and quiet can still be found. Less than half a day's drive from our nation's largest urban centers, I discovered, wildness remains.

CHAPTER 18

GOING HOME
The Midwest

O hio is one of three states I have called home. I attended college and worked as a paramedic near Dayton, testing my career choice and discovering a love of emergency medicine. In Columbus, the state capital and central Ohio's largest city, I attended medical school but left the Buckeye State upon graduation, completing my internship and residency at the North Carolina hospital in which I was born. Following my father's retirement and parents' subsequent relocation, I had not returned to west-central Ohio. Now, as we planned to ascend Campbell Hill (1,549 feet), the state's highest point, and Indiana's summit, Hoosier High Point, seventy miles away, I wanted to revisit areas of my youth and show them to Sheryl.

Much of our time would be spent in the "other" Ohio, a rural environment far from the sprawling industrial centers along Lake Erie and the Ohio River. It is a land of rich soil and rolling hills, of corn and soybean acreage, and a landscape dotted with small towns reflecting simpler times.

A Canadian high-pressure system brought a welcomed respite from the Midwest's often-muggy late July weather as we drove from Columbus toward the highpoint. Five miles from the state summit, we paused briefly in Bellefontaine, county seat of Logan County. Downtown streets were lined with a nostalgic mix of variety stores and locally owned retailers, while a large Victorian courthouse, a block square, dominated the town's center.

Barricades, however, partially blocked a street beside the

205

America's First Concrete Street
This 1991 statue celebrates the centennial of the nation's first concrete street, a block-long avenue four miles from Ohio's state summit.

ornate structure. A statue, flanked by plaques and interpretative signs, filled one end of the open space. We passed well-maintained shops and walked beside the courthouse's manicured lawn to the memorial, a tribute to America's first concrete road, a surface poured in 1891.

The figure was of George Bartholomew; the sculpture—of concrete—stood upon a pedestal made from the original road surface, while a nearby inscription praised the businessman's efforts "in the paving of concrete streets in Bellefontaine." This memorial, the dedication concluded, was "presented by the Concrete Industries of Ohio and the United States...to the citizens of Logan County." Although this site was noted on Ohio's state map, I had expected a small plaque or single interpretative sign marking this little-known achievement. Instead, I found a shrine. Yet as we strolled down this street, past coffee shops and antique stores decorated with patriotic bunting, I did not feel history's heavy hand. We posed for lighthearted photographs beside Mr. Bartholomew's statue then drove to Campbell Hill along a wide ribbon of asphalt.

In addition to celebrating its historic road, this region prides itself as home to Ohio's highest point. But Ohioans use a different spelling. We passed the Hi Point Motel and Hi Point Beauty Salon en route to the Hi Point Joint Vocational School, once part of the Bellefontaine Air Force Station, a former military base.

A winding route led through the campus toward a flag-topped hill. Fifty feet from the parking area, we stepped onto a concrete plaza at the pole's base. We were atop Ohio.

Campbell Hill dropped away in all directions, most notably to the north, where a steep slope led to a large grassy field. The surrounding region was hilly; Ohio's only ski area, an angled knoll with modest elevation change, lay nearby. We were in no rush. Enjoying the mild temperatures and low humidity brought by the Canadian high, we snacked and chatted then strolled through the campus overlooking Ohio.

From Ohio's neatly maintained highpoint we drove west, and for the second time, I summited two state highpoints in one day. But this time, there was no drama.

A mile west of the Ohio state line, and a dozen miles north of Richmond, Indiana's state summit is a small forested hill, 1,257 feet above sea level. A short walk through a mosquito-infested cornfield brought us to this wooded rise. We touched the state summit, but hungry insects allowed little time for rest or reflection within the shaded clearing. After a few photos, we hurried back to the car.

Forty-four high points had now been checked off. Of the twenty-seven state summits east of the Mississippi River, only Delaware remained to be reached.

We returned to Ohio and Butler County, home to the three campuses of Miami University, my alma mater. Named for Benjamin Butler, Civil War general and Reconstruction-era political firebrand, it is a mostly rural county, but two mid-sized industrial cities, Middletown and Hamilton, contain most of its population. It was in Middletown—then priding itself as home of basketball star Jerry Lucas and industrial giant Armco Steel—that I attended most of my classes.

Thirty years ago, it was already a city of contrast. The university's campus was a small but modern facility near the northern suburbs, while aging steel mills sprawled along the south side. But economics linked the two worlds. Armco was a major benefactor of the university; here many of its employees studied for management opportunities or for other careers. And for young college students, the mill, with high union wages, was always a temptation—or, if grades faltered, a safety net.

A steep drive descended to the campus, located in a large wooded valley. Traffic patterns and parking had changed; new buildings had been added. Nothing seemed familiar. We walked toward the administration building, a brick and glass structure surrounded by tall shrubbery and shaded by mature trees then entered into a darkened hallway, leading past locked classrooms toward a brightly lit lobby.

As I entered the large room, the memories returned. A floor-to-ceiling mosaic depicting Middletown's steel industry spanned the back wall, showing muscular men working fiery furnaces as molten metal pours from giant buckets. Reminiscent of Depression-era portrayals of American industry, its heroic style was already dated when I arrived as a nervous freshman in 1972. Three decades later, its boldly colored tiles still bright, this 1960s mosaic is an anachronism.

The university has prospered and grown; new buildings have been added and new degrees offered. But the nation's steel industry has fallen on hard times. Today in Pittsburgh, a city once synonymous with the industry, not a single ton of steel is produced. Bethlehem Steel, a corporation formerly a member of the Dow Jones Industrial Average, has shut its doors forever. Middletown has fared only slightly better. Although Armco (renamed AK Steel) has remained open, both production and employment have declined dramatically.

I stared at the mosaic and its images frozen in time. Memories of professors and friends, anxieties and hopes, uncertainties and ambitions flooded back. And I remembered as a student viewing this mural as both a threat and a promise: a threat that failure might be followed by decades of monotonous factory toil, and a promise—since proven false—that such a job would guarantee lifelong employment at high wages.

Leaving the administration building, we strolled through the campus, past abstract sculptures that were avant-garde in 1972 but passé today. Sharing recollections with Sheryl, I marveled at the clarity of detail recalled and at the rapid passage of a quarter century since last driving from this valley.

The next morning dawned dreary; light mist dampened the air as we drove toward the steel mill, a two-mile-long complex of aging gray buildings. Thirty years ago, a potholed two-lane road passed a half-mile from these structures. By day, a smoky pall hung over the complex; by night, orange slabs of hot metal could be seen moving through the mills. Trains and trucks brought raw materials and transported rolled steel to factories in Dayton, Cincinnati, and Detroit, there to be formed into refrigerators and washing machines, auto bodies and truck chassis.

But today, driving along a four-lane thoroughfare bordered with concrete sidewalks, there were few trucks. Smooth railroad crossings had replaced busy axle-jarring intersections. Yet there were no trains. And looking at the sprawling complex this morning, neither thick smoke nor orange slabs of freshly made steel were seen.

A lone guard stood beside the only open gate, an entrance that led to an empty parking lot. Although it was the weekend, I hoped to tour the facility, for thirty years ago this factory never closed. Slowing as I neared the guardhouse, an elderly man wearing a neatly pressed uniform sauntered toward the car.

"Good morning," I said, introducing myself. "We're visiting from North Carolina and would like to see the mill."

"No tours," he answered flatly.

"Could we drive around?" I queried, noting the lack of activity.

"No," he responded curtly. Then he paused. "Where you from?" he asked, as if not believing my previous statement.

"North Carolina," I repeated. "Twenty-five years ago I attended college here, at Miami University's Middletown campus. This is my first trip back, seeing how things have changed."

"Hmm," he muttered.

"Has the factory closed?" I continued.

The words had barely left my lips. "No," he quickly retorted, before rattling off a list of continuing operations. His response seemed well-scripted.

As we settled into a superficial banter, I stared through the windshield at the empty buildings, recalling the smog and noise and bustle that enveloped this sprawling facility three decades earlier. And I thought of my career, a choice that led me down gleaming hospital corridors, through brightly lit offices, and into busy emergency departments.

"I can't let you in," the guard said, jolting me from my recollections, "but south of here is the best view of the factory, at least what's left of it."

We thanked him then followed directions to a hilltop neighborhood and a vista of Middletown I had never seen. Furnaces and rolling mills extended into the mist, smokestacks pierced the clouds, and angled conveyor belts, now motionless, reached toward piles of coal and coke.

I stood with Sheryl, silently staring at these remnants lining the "road not taken," a path once exemplified by the brightly colored mural in the university's lobby. The rain intensified, dampening our windbreakers then chilling exposed skin and, as we turned to leave, slowly obscuring the factory.

From Middletown we drove north eleven miles and found the prosperity that had escaped rural America—and fled from our nation's inner cities. For more than a decade, my parents lived in Centerville, a small but prosperous village south of Dayton. During college, I worked here as a paramedic in a fire department serving both the town and surrounding region, a rural area with expansive cornfields and narrow two-lane roads. High velocity motor vehicle accidents were common, the distance to hospitals was great, but our equipment and training were among the best in the state.

However, four- and six-lane avenues now replaced those narrow roads; professional offices, upscale retailers, and luxury automobile dealerships covered land once tilled for corn. And although mid-range suburban homes—including ours—remained, most recently constructed dwellings were "McMansions," huge two and three story houses on half-acre lots, costing up to a million dollars each.

I found the little county park, a half-mile from our home, where my father and I had played tennis for years. But the three concrete courts of my youth were gone, replaced by a dozen red and green composite surfaces. The surrounding woodlands were gone too, cleared for six fenced ball fields, shiny metal bleachers extending along each foul line. The park's rutted dirt road had been paved; modern concession stands bordered the large blacktopped parking lot.

In town, I looked for the fire station, a three-bay brick garage that had housed our ambulance. In its stead, a grand colonial-style building had been constructed, five bays wide, a combination fire, rescue, and administrative facility. Nearby, stately homes had been converted to boutiques, while pricey retailers and purveyors of fine antiques lined the town's main streets. There were no boarded-up structures here, no second-hand stores nor pawnshops. And no starving artist's galleries either.

Twenty-five years ago, as I contemplated rural medicine, my father urged me to return to Ohio. "Work here ten years," he advised, "then you will be able to retire."

In Centerville, for one of the few times in my life, I looked back and second-guessed myself, pondering his words, asking myself "what if?"

CHAPTER 19

FROZE-TO-DEATH

Montana

F orests and grasslands again burned throughout the west. Last year, six million acres had been scorched— twice the annual average—the most destructive season in nearly a century. But this summer's blazes were on pace to equal or exceed those damages. A year earlier fire and snow had kept me from summiting three peaks in the northern Rockies; now fire again threatened access to each of these mountains.

Granite Peak (12,799 feet), Montana's tallest mountain, is the only state highpoint requiring technical rock climbing ability. It is the nation's least climbed state summit and, except for Alaska's Denali, the most difficult. Access to the peak is challenging, with a climbing season—just six to eight weeks—among the nation's shortest. The approach is strenuous and hazardous; climbers camp two to four nights on the Froze-to-Death Plateau, a lightning-prone expanse far above timberline. Snow makes the final rocky ascent nearly impossible, but summertime rains do likewise, dampening the cliffs and eliminating the friction required to grip the nearly vertical mountainside.

Tom Torkelson of Jackson Hole Mountain Guides would join me on Granite. One year and twenty highpoints earlier, we had together ascended Wyoming's Gannett Peak near the beginning of my sabbatical. Now as this period of time wound down, I had begun interviewing, planning to return to fulltime employment. This trip would be my last chance to climb Montana's highest point—and Idaho's and Utah's. Following two interviews, I had two job offers, both with respected well-established groups and both requesting that I start work as soon as possible. As

I considered these offers, it seemed that the sabbatical had not affected my career.

In a dusty trailhead parking lot, 8,200 feet below Granite's summit, I met Tom. We chatted briefly but, to avoid the midday heat, soon began organizing gear, hoping for an early start. It would be a long, strenuous day, hiking a series of switchbacks while carrying fully loaded packs, gaining more than a mile of elevation before reaching the first possible campsite on the plateau's lower edge.

We laid everything onto a plastic tarp and checked off each item as we loaded our packs: harness and rope; helmet and headlamp; capilene and fleece; hat, jacket, and gloves; food, stove, fuel...the list went on. As we began walking toward Mystic Lake, we each carried a densely packed load with provisions for five days.

Granite Peak is located deep in the Beartooth Mountains, a deeply-sculpted range extending along the Montana-Wyoming border. Composed of Precambrian rocks, the Beartooths contain large deposits of nickel and palladium, and the nation's largest reserves of platinum and chrome. In addition to jagged peaks, this landscape consists of high, angled plateaus separated by deep valleys. Glaciers and water carved these valleys from the uplifted land leaving massive plateaus, eleven of which range from ten to fifty square miles each in surface area. High above timberline, these rocky expanses are raked by wind and storm with neither escape nor refuge from tempest or lightning.

A gently sloping path leads two miles from the trailhead to Mystic Lake, a ribbon-like body of water squeezed between steep valley walls. But this scenic lake is not the result of natural forces, created instead by damming West Rosebud Creek in 1926. Like similar dams throughout the west, this structure was built for flood control and power generation, converting the energy of falling water into electricity. Excellent fishing is found in many of these lakes; indeed, I have fond childhood memories of fishing such impoundments in Colorado.

However, nearly every western creek and river has now been dammed. Surrounded by some of the nation's most isolated and rugged terrain, I stared at penstock and turbines, power lines and a curving mass of concrete extending the canyon's width. We crossed the dam and descended to the water's edge. There, as we snacked along the shoreline, I looked at the steep walls and dozens of switchbacks that loomed above, and wondered where man's imprint ended and wildness began.

Created to minimize erosion and ascend steep terrain more easily, switchbacks are generally disliked by hikers and climbers. A series of turns rising one above another, these necessary but monotonous trail features require great effort to ascend but do not provide different views or new perspectives. Today, hours would be spent criss-crossing the hillside above Mystic Lake, wending our way to the Froze-to-Death Plateau.

We chatted as we walked, carrying fully loaded packs up the steep incline and updating each other about our lives. Each faced decisions: Tom pondered leaving guiding and returning to law school, an idea shelved a decade earlier, while I related plans to return to office practice and weighed competing offers. We listened carefully, but neither yet offered advice. Talk turned to nature and mountaineering as we left the intensifying valley heat and ascended into cooler mountain air, with Tom describing Granite Peak, a mountain I wouldn't see for another twenty-four hours.

By midafternoon, we had reached the plateau yet walked another hour searching for a campsite, finding a grassy depression bordering a small rivulet, one of the few water sources on this high barren expanse. Threading tent poles through fabric sleeves, I glanced up. We had visitors.

Mountain goats, some the size of a large dog, others little bigger than a house cat, peered from behind nearby rocks. They called to each other, bleating softly. Then a large animal stepped forward; the others, sensing little danger, followed. A dozen left their rocky refuges and approached within twenty feet. They gazed upon our tent, our gear, and us, staying half an hour, grazing the vegetation beside the water then following its course to the plateau's edge. There, before dropping out of view, the bold male who led the group stepped upon a prominent rock, his profile outlined against the late afternoon sky as he surveyed this wild region.

A golden glow spread over the Beartooths as the sun neared the horizon. An early chill followed. After pitching the tent and organizing gear, I, too, walked the grassy path to the plateau's edge. Melting remnants of last winter's snow fed the small stream that flowed in a series of braided trickles. Flowers, nestled between stones or protected by tall grasses, provided

High Country Visitors
Mountain goats near our camp on the Froze-to-Death Plateau.

splashes of late summer color. Thick mosses gave a soft, springy feel underfoot. As darkness settled, I looked across the deep valley surrounding Mystic Lake toward Fishtail Plateau and the distant mountains. Here, high in the Beartooths, was the solitude I sought, the serenity I loved, and the wildness I desired.

In early afternoon, after walking nearly the length of the Froze-to-Death Plateau, we had our first full view of Granite Peak. Dark clouds hovered near the massive rocky pyramid; shaded light lent an eerie appearance. Granite is feared by high-pointers and considered technically more difficult than Denali. Looking at the storm-shrouded mountain, I understood why. The steep cliffs appeared a jumble of angulated rocks; there was no obvious line up its walls, and the mountainside dropped precipitously, in places plunging 2,000 feet.

However we could not stop and study the mountain's routes or savor its moods, for the clouds were expanding and the wind freshening. Blasts of cold air raced down Granite's flanks and across the plateau. We sped to a trot, packs bouncing and metal gear jangling, reaching a campsite as large raindrops splatted onto the stony ground. We quickly pitched the tent and anchored stay ropes around large rocks as thunder shook the land.

A torrential downpour followed as we tossed loaded packs into the tent then sought shelter within its nylon walls. Cracks of lightning were immediately followed by deafening thunder-claps. We squatted on our packs to insulate and protect ourselves from the potentially charged ground as lightning repeatedly struck the exposed landscape.

The storm's full fury abated within minutes, but we would later quip, the Froze-to-Death Plateau was, at least for a short while, the Scared-to-Death Plateau. Although the lightning stopped and the wind slackened, the rain continued for two hours. The land was drenched; summiting might be impossible, but at least we felt safer as the storm moved away.

Wispy clouds clung to Granite's sides when we emerged from the tent to scout the trail. A cold, damp stillness filled the air as we walked toward a deep valley that separated us from the peak. In the morning, if weather permitted, we would descend a short distance here then skirt a nearby mountain—appropri-ately named Tempest—to reach Granite's base. From there, 1,500 feet of scrambling and climbing would remain to the summit.

At 4:00 a.m. we peered from the tent. Stars filled the sky. "How do you feel?" Tom asked. "Are you ready to try it?" Though the air was cold, the wind was calm. Clear skies and the morning sun would dry the rocks before afternoon thun-derstorms might again develop.

I felt great. "O.K.," I said, "Let's do it."

With nearly ideal climbing conditions, I at last had my chance to summit this isolated and challenging mountain. Early in my climbing career, I had difficulty sleeping before a big climb, anticipating the challenge. With experience and age, I now slept soundly, but the intense morning excitement remained. Tom brewed coffee and cocoa as we began packing. In the morning chill, we would wear all the clothes we carried; only cameras, climbing gear, food and water were placed into otherwise empty backpacks.

Unroped, we followed a footpath beaten into the rocky ground then scrambled across a boulder field, our way lighted by headlamp. Granite could not be seen save for a wedge of blackness jutting into an otherwise star-filled sky.

An hour-and-a-half later, as the sun's first rays touched

Granite's summit, we roped up at the mountain's base, shivering in deep shadow. Here, the technical climbing begins, first crossing a snow bridge, a year-round vertical wedge of snow and ice that is the route's most-feared feature. It is a short walk over this thin drift—less than a hundred yards—but its sides plunge more than a thousand feet down a narrow gully. It is the most exposed terrain that many highpointers will ever encounter.

This summer, like the previous two, had been warm and dry. The bridge was shorter, less than a rope length across, with well-formed steps kicked along its ridge. Still we approached it carefully, Tom crossing first, protected by my belay, as I firmly braced myself, anchored to the surrounding rock.

Safely across, he attached himself to the far wall then yelled "on belay" across the chasm. As he maintained rope tension, I removed the protection anchoring me to the rock. Then I began across. The footing was firm, the snow crunching loudly beneath my crampons. Halfway across, I reached down and removed a picket, a 30-inch-long aluminum spike Tom had driven into the firm snow.

A fall now could be deadly. A rope can prevent a long downhill slide, but during a traverse, cannot protect a falling climber from swinging like a pendulum below the belayer, a mishap that can propel the climber with deadly force against rocky outcrops. The picket had protected me during the traverse's first half; only sure-footedness could do so during these final yards.

I glanced down a quarter-mile-long chute to a rocky plateau, then looked ahead at the steep walls lining the channel. Concentrating on each step, I followed the snowy ridge to the dirt and rock near Tom. We were safely across.

Rock climbing is rated by a decimal system ranging from 5.0 to 5.14, higher numbers representing greater difficulty. Routes on Granite require basic to intermediate skill and are classified between 5.4 and 5.8. But these rankings are determined by comparable moves in a controlled environment while wearing specially designed shoes and firmly anchored by a rope from above. Here we would be climbing on a cold morning, wearing hiking boots and carrying backpacks. An injury in this isolated wilderness could have serious consequences with prolonged evacuation times.

Although the mountain's sides appeared vertical as we gazed at them from high camp, we now saw they consisted of steeply angled blocks of granite. There were no long cracks to follow as when I had climbed in Yosemite or smooth rocks to scramble over as in Maine. Thin-soled rock shoes would be of little value during this ascent for the technical rock moves were interspersed with yards of walking and scrambling.

There was no obvious line up this steep wall. Experience and intuition guided Tom as he searched for a route. I followed, roped up and yards behind, seeking hand and footholds along the same path.

We climbed above the largest wilderness in the contiguous United States. Alpine meadows, glaciers, and windswept peaks extended west toward the Tetons, today obscured by a fire near their base. From there this protected ecosystem—home to grizzlies and wolves, bald eagles and bighorn sheep—continued past Yellowstone and into Idaho. Save for the smoke along the western horizon, the air was clear and, except for the metallic clicks of climbing gear as we ascended, silence prevailed.

A lone raven soared past as we stepped onto a ledge, halfway up the steep wall. A yard wide and twenty feet long, this rocky platform would be the largest flat area encountered during the ascent. Here we paused, enjoying both views and solitude, resting and preparing for the final push.

Above the ledge, the route remained steep; hearts raced and lungs strained as we moved higher in ever-thinning air. Our pace slowed but we pushed on, stepping onto inch-wide ledges and holding onto rock irregularities a fingerbreadth across. Then the angle lessened, and for the first time in two hours, I saw the hint of a trail. Skirting a rocky prominence, we scrambled up a steep incline and stepped onto a large flat rock above which we could climb no higher. We were atop Montana.

Wilderness spread below in a complete arc. The midmorning sun warmed the mountaintop while the sky remained clear and the winds calm. We congratulated each other, took celebratory photos, and thanked one another for the friendship that had developed during the climbs of Gannett and Granite Peaks. I felt fortunate to have ascended both of these challenging summits with someone whose companionship I enjoyed, whose advice I trusted, and whose leadership and guiding skills were superb.

We remained atop Montana nearly an hour, much of the time enjoying the views while sitting on a foot-thick slab of stone lying horizontally at the apex of this steep peak. A dozen feet long and a third as wide, this rock is one of the largest flat surfaces on the mountain. Although it weighs many tons, its placement nevertheless looks artificial, as if supernatural forces laid this boulder here as a platform on which climbers could pose for summit photos.

Forty-five minutes after reaching the top, four more climbers ascended the final incline. James Moffatt of Texarkana, Texas, with his son and daughter-in-law, followed their guide onto the horizontal slab. James, too, was seeking to touch each of the contiguous state summits, while his son and daughter-in-law, both expedition climbers, joined their father only on the most difficult peaks. Age sixty-three, this retired football coach and school administrator had already touched forty-four state highpoints, most in the company of his wife, an avid hiker. But James' record was better than mine: Thus far he had ascended each peak on the first attempt, a streak he would maintain, becoming the only person to reach each of the forty-eight contiguous summits on the first try.

We congratulated each of them as they joined us atop Montana then chatted briefly, sharing highpointing tales and exchanging information about state summits each of us needed to climb. It was soon time for Tom and me to start down. I surveyed the scene from Granite's apex one more time, thankful not only to have reached this summit but, as on Gannett, to have done so via a challenging aesthetic route, acquiring new skills and meeting new challenges while surrounded by a magnificent natural area.

The descent was uneventful; afternoon thunderstorms missed both Granite Peak and our camp high on the Froze-to-Death Plateau. The next morning, however, we awoke to low clouds and light rain. Montana's highest mountain remained shrouded as we packed and, in conditions reminiscent of those on Gannett Peak a year earlier, began a wet descent.

The precipitation eased as we left the plateau and before completing the switchbacks had ended altogether. While descending, the discussion about hopes, concerns, and plans for the future resumed. We joked, as climbers often do, about "real jobs" and "fitting in."

Generally, however, the banter is superficial, for personal changes are seldom imminent. Yet within weeks, we each faced major career choices. I doubted that Tom, after years of leadership, freedom, and challenge in the mountains could again submit to being a student. In the mountains there are no excuses, no negotiations with nature—and often no second chances. Here humans must adjust in order to survive. Nature is neither benevolent nor hostile. It simply is.

Tom listened carefully, acknowledging some points and disputing none.

However, I was surprised by his comments when the discussion turned to my future. At times I had felt uneasy about returning to the private practice of medicine, with doubts I had not consciously addressed nor shared with anyone—even Sheryl. I had no doubts that I could again submit to the pressures of tight schedules and the rigor of hard work. But it had been eight years since I closed my private practice and thirteen months since leaving the emergency department.

I had changed—and grown. Perhaps Tom sensed this for he did not reassure me, didn't encourage me to work long hours and earn huge amounts of money to spend consuming, living the so-called American Dream. Memories of work on the Indian reservations flashed through my mind as I recalled how I had enjoyed the work, looked forward to my times there, and even now, wished I could return. Doubts nagged me; Tom's lack of reassurance troubled me. Yet I pushed these concerns from my mind as we passed the dam and neared the cars, reflecting instead on our climbs and talking of upcoming adventures.

In the dusty parking lot we said good-bye, Tom returning to Wyoming to lead a Teton climb, while I followed the Yellowstone River Valley westward across southern Montana. Today the nation's longest undammed waterway, this river was William Clark's route while returning from the Pacific in 1806. The land of the Shoshone and Crow, this valley was bloodied by warfare as these tribes resisted first the westward expansion of the Sioux and later that of the Europeans.

But before white men brought the horse to the Americas, life on the northern plains was more difficult and certainly more tenuous. Instead of mounted warriors chasing buffalo on horseback, the shaggy animals were hunted by men on foot armed with spears and bows and arrows. These hunters could not risk a direct confrontation with an adult bison, an animal weighing a ton and capable of running thirty miles-an-hour. Tact and cunning were needed; smaller, weaker animals were taken and occasionally large groups of bison stampeded over cliffs. Some of these slaughter sites were used for centuries resulting in bone accumulations dozens of feet deep.

West of Bozeman, I visited one of these locations, the Madison Buffalo Jump, today a minimally developed state park. A short trail led past teepee rings—stone circles 12-25 feet across—to the base of eroding cliffs where thousands of animals had plunged to their deaths.

I walked up the debris-covered slope, past bone fragments and coarsely chipped scrapers that littered the exposed ground. The 40-foot-high walls of crumbling sandstone were pockmarked with irregularities; a pack rat's den filled one crevice while a hawk's aerie perched on an inaccessible ledge. I scrambled up a gully that cut diagonally across the rocky wall, struggling to reach the plateau.

Undulating grasslands spread before me as I stepped from the steep chute atop the escarpment. From the parking lot, the plateau had appeared short and narrow, but now I could see it extended eastward for miles and although it narrowed above the cliff, remained hundreds of yards wide. Traces of driving lanes, paths along which buffalo were stampeded, remained faintly visible. Yet these physical features provided little protection for the hunters.

Mass killings, however, were neither random nor fortuitous events but carefully planned activities involving hundreds of people whose survival—individually and collectively—depended on a successful hunt. Following prayers, dances, and purification ceremonies, young men, some disguised as baby bison to lure animals forward, others dressed as wolves or coyotes to frighten them onward, tried to move the herd nearer the cliff. The process took days, sometimes weeks.

When conditions were right—and both people and animals properly positioned—a few hunters attempted to frighten the herd. As the bison fled toward the cliff, men and boys stepped from behind trees, brush piles, and rocky cairns that lined the drive lanes, shouting and waving blankets, panicking the animals yet trying to keep them in a narrow column. When the first animals reached the precipice, they tried to stop, but the stampeding column surged on, pushing the leaders forward

221

and sending the group over the cliff. Most bison died from the fall, but if any survived, hunters stationed at the wall's base quickly dispatched the injured.

A successful hunt was followed by days of feasting and weeks of activity. Meat was cut and dried, hides tanned, and preparations made for the approaching winter.

But this was more than a killing field or meat-processing location. North of the high cliff, atop a lower plateau, I found densely scattered teepee rings—an encampment serving as a village during the hunt and a place where scattered nomadic bands could gather, trade, share news, and meet others. A short distance away, three stony ovals, each little larger than a man's body, lined the edge of the rocky slope, each brush-filled mound decorated with offerings of shiny coins, fading prayer bundles, and small tobacco pouches. Men once crawled into these now-collapsed structures and, after brush had been heaped over them and a dead rabbit placed atop the pile, lay in wait for an eagle to swoop down. As the raptor reached to seize the prey, the hidden warrior attempted to capture the bird by grabbing its extended legs. If successful, the eagle would be plucked, its feathers—one of the most revered Native American symbols—used in religious rites, for battle ornamentation, or as part of ceremonial regalia.

Alone in the park, I rested, overlooking this vast landscape. A steady wind stirred the prairie grass but brought little relief from the midday heat. Despite the warmth, I lingered, scanning the savannah where millions of bison once grazed, looking toward the cliffs where thousands had been driven to their deaths, and staring down at the teepee rings and eagle pits, relics of nomadic peoples that once roamed these expansive plains. Beneath Montana's big sky I thought of the Native Americans I had worked with—the Sioux and Apache, proud descendents of once-nomadic tribes—and recalled the natural beauty I had seen during this year. My sabbatical was ending and now I frequently thought of the people, places, and events seen, trying to synthesize these experiences into a coherent view of our nation.

From the buffalo jump I continued westward, past the headwaters of the Missouri where three rivers—the Gallatin, Madison, and Jefferson—join to form our nation's second-longest waterway. I visited Virginia City and Alder Gulch, site of

Montana's greatest gold rush, then followed the Beaverhead Valley to Dillon and Interstate 15 south to Idaho.

Nearing the state line and surrounded by natural beauty, a wave of apprehension suddenly flooded my mind. My skin tingled and throat tightened as I wondered when, or if, I would again gaze upon Montana's landscape. I had thought I was ready to return to work—to 60-hour workweeks, after-hours call, and limited travel opportunity—but now wondered if these thirteen months of freedom, instead of sating my desire for adventure, had only intensified it.

Montana quickly disappeared behind rugged mountains after I entered Idaho, still struggling with uncomfortable emotions. These feelings, like those experienced while descending Granite Peak, had troubled and surprised me.

This time, however, they had been stronger—and taken longer to suppress.

CHAPTER 20

WHERE THERE'S SMOKE...
The Northern Rockies

Arco had changed little since my last visit. This Idaho town still proudly proclaimed its distinction as the nation's first community lighted by nuclear energy, while Pickle's Restaurant continued to advertise itself as "Home of the Atomic Burger." There was no new construction, and existing businesses appeared to be struggling. Returning to the motel in which I had previously stayed, I found that the "No Vacancy" sign had been turned off and a "New Management" pronouncement hung beside the office door.

There was no need to scout the trailhead or route up the Lost River Valley. Images of the valley and trail, of Borah's rocky profile looming a mile above the parking lot, and of last year's early season snowstorm which had forced me off the mountain and out of the northern Rockies filled my mind. Uncertainty returned too, as did unanswered questions: What lay above timberline, the point where I had turned back; could the mountain be climbed solo; and how difficult was Chicken Out Ridge, the rocky traverse that made this ascent so challenging?

Borah Peak (12,662 feet), Idaho's tallest mountain, was now the most difficult of my four remaining contiguous state summits. Driving north from Arco early the next morning, I recalled the cold rain that had dampened the windshield last year and the crowded parking lot that Labor Day weekend. Today that lot was empty; stars filled the sky as I laced up my boots. At 4:30 a.m. I was walking, carrying three liters of water, snacks, rain gear, compass, map, and camera up the narrow path.

By daybreak I had reached tree line, there startling a pair of campers sipping coffee and trying to awaken while fending off the morning chill. I chatted briefly then followed a well-worn trail up a long ridgeline. The terrain was stark, the mountainside barren. To my left, the land dropped precipitously into a glacially carved valley while elsewhere, raked by wind and covered by snow most of the year, Borah's slopes supported little plant life.

Here was a wild rugged mountain. Chicken Out Ridge dominated the skyline, while the summit rose far to the left. I now saw how dangerous—and futile—a summit attempt would have been the previous year. But today, instead of dozens of weekend climbers crowding the trail, I walked alone up the steep hillside. Other great peaks rose nearby—Leatherman and Donaldson, Elkhorn and Breitenbach, all sharply angled mountains ranked among Idaho's tallest.

Near the rocky wall that swept around the head of the deep valley, the trail ended abruptly, the route blocked by a mass of tan rock ten stories high crossed by ledges no wider than a boot width. No stone cairns or rectangular white blazes marked the path; at the base of Chicken Out Ridge, I knew that both rock-climbing and route-finding skills would be tested.

Route-finding—traversing unmarked wilderness terrain—is an underappreciated but vital mountaineering skill. Without trails, cairns, or chalk marks to follow, one must plan not only the next move, but a series of moves along a potential path. If any of these steps prove impossible, then the route "won't go"—and the climber must retreat, seeking another line, wasting both time and energy. I have seen parties founder across moderate terrain, not because they lacked necessary climbing skills, but because of poor route selection. Guided groups led by an experienced local climber often move faster, for perhaps the greatest asset such a person brings is knowledge of the mountain and its topography.

On Borah, however, no one was ahead to show the way, and no one trailed to whom I could turn for advice. I stepped onto the light-colored rock and followed a narrowing shelf, facing the wall and using an eye-level crack for handholds and balance. The solid ledge angled inward, but although the traverse was straightforward, its exposure was frightening. A rocky platform lay forty feet below, but from there Borah's slopes continued down another thousand feet.

I took shuffling steps, moving my feet side-to-side and never crossing one behind the other. A hundred feet later the shelf ran out onto a rocky slope that continued upward. A faint path led across the loose rocks, crossed the ridgeline then traversed above the deep valley I had skirted since timberline. Although steep, the trail was straightforward, and I wondered if perhaps the tan wall had been the route's "crux"—its most difficult portion.

Minutes later, however, the footpath again ended, blocked by a higher and longer promontory. This rock was different—black and crumbly—with no apparent route along its sides or over the top. Climbers prefer to follow ridgelines whenever possible, for they are typically the widest and safest paths with the least risk of rockfall. But these crumbling walls were steep and reaching the ridgeline would be risky—and I saw no apparent exit down the promontory's far end.

Below the outcrop, however, a series of ledges—some fifteen feet long, others fifty—traversed the hillside. These surfaces were narrow, all less than a foot wide; none spanned the entire distance and all were covered with loose rocks and scattered stones. Yet with short scrambles the horizontal paths might connect to provide a line bypassing the ridge.

I looked back. No one else was ascending the mountain. Alone above timberline, I stepped onto the dark rock and followed a narrow route along the steeply angled mountainside. Working across this exposed terrain, I sought to move up, trying always to reach higher ledges, hoping to crest the ridgeline just past the promontory. But the further I traversed, the more difficult it was to ascend. Above me, the ledges narrowed then disappeared, buried beneath crumbling rock. The ridgeline continued higher while my path gained little elevation.

Half an hour later the shelves ended, cut off by a scree-covered chute that plunged the full distance—here nearly half a mile—down the mountainside. Further progress was impossible; attempting to cross this unstable mass of rock and stone would be suicidal. I looked at the ridgeline forty feet above and scanned the debris-covered slope alongside the chute, knowing I must either ascend these eroding ledges or retreat.

Twelve thousand feet above sea level, despair crept into my mind as I struggled in the thin air to concentrate, weighing options and evaluating risks. Throughout the traverse I had searched for a better route but found none. Now directly below the promontory's far end, I still failed to see a ridge top trail or even a practical line down the outcrop's 15-foot vertical face. Without alternative plans, retreat would accomplish nothing except to end my summit bid.

Unable to sit or rest because of loose rocks underfoot, I stood and scanned the slope above, weighing the consequences of each move I considered. Ten minutes later, I had plotted a path halfway up the slope, each step protected by a solid handhold or located above a small platform that could arrest a sliding fall. Beyond that, however, the angle precluded a detailed assessment; if the line couldn't be completed, retreat would still be possible.

Gripping the rock bands and stepping upon stones along the chute's edge, I moved up. My heart raced from both fear and exertion as I struggled higher, each strenuous move made more difficult by the rarefied air. Fifteen feet below the crest, I came to a vertical ledge. Scrambling up would be easy, but climbing back down could be treacherous. Crossing this band, I realized, would cut my line of retreat and commit me to reaching the ridgeline.

I looked above. The line seemed straightforward until just below the crest where a deep layer of gravel blocked the route. I thought briefly then went for it, clambering over the ledge and advancing quickly to the loose scree.

Climbing is taught as a smooth, graceful skill, relying on balance and leg motion instead of pure strength. Many of today's most accomplished rock climbers are women who move with ballet-like grace up vertical walls. But there are times when sheer strength matters. As I looked at the gravel in front of me, I drew rapid breaths to extract more oxygen, hoping to refresh fatiguing muscles. Stepping onto the pebbles, I took quick steps as the pile slid beneath me, running as if on a treadmill, trying to ascend two vertical yards. But each step gained little elevation, while the rubble carried me downward.

Three steps, six, ten. Legs burned as I thrashed across this rock pile, stones tumbling wildly down the steep chute as each footstep left gaping depressions but resulted in little uphill progress.

More steps. I reached ahead, extending full length yet failing to reach a rocky protuberance. My lungs strained as I tried to move uphill faster than the rocks carried me down.

Four more steps. Again I reached up. As gravel slid from

beneath my feet, fingers grasped the rocky outcrop, and then hand-over-hand, I pulled myself higher until my feet touched solid ground. Physically exhausted and emotionally drained, I dropped to the level terrain atop the crest, too tired to enjoy the scenery or celebrate having passed Chicken Out Ridge.

Yet I recovered quickly. Within minutes I chuckled thinking about the ungainly technique used to reach the ridgeline; a quarter hour later, fueled by snacks and refreshed with water, I again began ascending, scrambling over boulders up a physically demanding but straightforward route. At 10:00 a.m., I stood atop Idaho.

A land of quiet beauty, of tall mountains and deeply sculpted valleys lay before me. Leatherman Peak, its summit 400 feet below Borah's, pierced the southern horizon, giving the illusion of an equally tall mountain. Irrigated crops in the Lost River Valley contrasted with the surrounding desert scrub. Save for two climbing teams ascending toward Chicken Out Ridge, nothing moved on Borah or the surrounding peaks. No human sounds drifted to the summit, and except for the highway and farmland below, no evidence of development was seen. Surrounded by wildness and wilderness, I sat against a warm rock beneath the late-morning sun, savoring the moment and letting my mind wander.

Under a cloudless sky, there was no need to hurry back. Alone atop this great peak, I watched a pair of ravens ascend on thermals then soar over the summit before slowly gliding down into the valley. I enjoyed the solitude, gentle breezes, and warm sun as I rested and snacked. Unable to locate a summit register, I documented my visit by photographing my backpack beside the mountaintop USGS marker, then took two photos of myself, the first a hand-held self-portrait and the second, a full-length shot as the camera rested on a nearby rock.

An hour passed. The weather remained tranquil, but I knew it was time to descend—and again face Chicken Out Ridge. Following a final glance across Idaho, I started down, working my way through the boulder field and watching as the two groups below, five climbers in all, sought a route past the ridge. Yet neither found a better line, and both struggled as I had across the crumbling rock.

Just above the ridge, I met the first party, two men in their early 30s. Each walked slowly, exertion and altitude taking a toll.

View From Borah Peak's Summit
Chicken Out Ridge is left-center.

"How many times have you done this peak?" the first climber asked as he stopped and bent forward, gasping for air. With hands on bent knees and panting rapidly, he opened the conversation with neither salutation nor introduction.

"First time," I responded, breathing deeply, trying to refresh tiring leg muscles.

"You must be from around here, man," he continued, his voice rising in pitch and volume.

"No, North Carolina," I said, removing my pack and retrieving my water bottle.

"You mean," he stammered between rapid breaths as he raised his head to stare at me, "you did this alone on your first attempt?"

"I've climbed some big peaks," I explained, "but here there was no one to climb with, so I had to go alone."

As the second group, a three-man team, approached, the discussion turned to the route. Though they welcomed the news of a straightforward yet demanding ascent, they offered little advice and no encouragement about the crumbling black promontory I again prepared to cross, Chicken Out Ridge. All were experienced climbers and all hailed from western states, but no one had found a clear path past the ridge and each man worried aloud about recrossing the rubble.

We wished each other the best then continued on. My descent beneath the black walls was no more elegant—and only slightly less difficult—than the climb up. After stepping from the last ledge onto the well-worn trail leading towards timberline, my stride lengthened, my pack felt lighter, and the tense fatigue that had gripped my legs eased.

Borah Peak, and especially Chicken Out Ridge, had challenged my abilities and tested my resolve. But as I neared the conifers, I calmly looked back toward the skyline ridge and smiled, knowing that today I had met the mountain's challenges and was returning safely.

That is what mountaineering is all about.

The next morning I left Arco and drove south, this year skirting the Snake River Plain's eastern border. Warm sun and dry winds dominated as I crossed the arid landscape into southwestern Wyoming. The exceptionally dry summer had created extreme fire danger throughout this region and into northern Utah.

Forty miles southeast of Evanston, Wyoming, lies Kings Peak (13,528 feet), Utah's tallest mountain, and a state summit generally requiring a two to four day backpacking excursion. This was the only highpoint I planned as an overnight solo hike, and I believed that pack weight would be my greatest challenge.

For weeks I had considered how to reduce this weight, checking and rechecking the gear list. Yet the essentials remained: tent and sleeping bag; stove, food, and fuel; sleeping pad and bear repellant; headlamp and warm clothes for high altitude nights; maps, compass, iodine, and of course, toilet paper. And each item needed to be carried nearly thirty miles, gaining a full mile of elevation.

I had pondered alternatives. I could leave the tent behind, sleeping under a lightweight tarp or in the open, a fine option in drier climates. But here if it rained, my sleeping bag's down insulation would become useless, the damp feathers offering no protection from the cold. Perhaps the stove, fuel, and cooking pot might be eliminated, reducing both weight and bulk. But like Napoleon said of his armies, hikers march on their bellies too. A warm, tasty meal is often the highlight after a difficult hike, and the physical and psychological benefits of warm drinks are numerous.

Lastly I had thought of attempting Kings Peak as a day hike. Although long, it is possible; a handful of fit individuals complete the feat each year. But even a 4:00 a.m. start would place me above timberline and exposed to lightning storms throughout the afternoon.

Named in honor of Clarence King, chief surveyor of the Union Pacific Railroad and the first director of the U.S. Geological Survey, Kings Peak is located in the Uinta Mountains, a short east-west range in northeastern Utah. Composed of Precambrian quartzite, sandstone, and shale, this chain is just 150 miles long and 35 wide but contains over a thousand natural lakes and 400 miles of streams. It is a beautiful area; indeed many highpointers consider this mountain the most scenic state summit.

In Evanston, I opted for a rest day to recover from the rigors of Borah, prepare for the hike, and tour these mountains. However, at the entrance to the Mirror Lake Scenic Byway, a 42-mile drive through the western Uintas, the rangers had troubling news. High wind, single-digit humidity, and dry lightning strikes were predicted each of the next four afternoons. I stood by as park officials discussed closing all of Utah's High Uinta Wilderness backcountry—including Kings Peak—a decision tabled for reconsideration in twenty-four hours. But as I drove the byway, one of our nation's most scenic driving routes, and walked beside clear mountain lakes, I glanced at the ridgelines, scanning for smoke and fearing that fire might again keep me from attempting a state summit.

I fretted about that risk as I returned to Evanston to sort gear and reconsider plans. Again I thought of the day-hike option but quickly eliminated it due to the predicted storms. Likewise, the open-air sleeping idea was again discarded; although the thunderstorms might not bring rain to the valleys, precipitation was likely at higher altitudes. But as the pack bulged and its weight neared sixty pounds, I decided that the stove, fuel, and utensils—along with hot meals and warm drinks—had to be left behind.

It was a difficult decision. Novice backpackers believe they can survive a week on trail mix, water, and energy bars. Many have. But the monotonous fare takes its toll, and few hikers choose this subsistence diet again. Yet if needed—and with careful planning—a cold but nutritious and varied menu can be achieved. Tom Torkelson had described a climb in Montana during which, due to extreme fire risk, stoves had been banned. Instead of snacks and energy bars, however, he had packed cheeses and meats, pouches of tuna, and dehydrated fruit, and although ready for a hot meal after descending five days later, both guide and client did fine.

That evening at a nearby Evanston supermarket, I purchased a selection of cheese and deli meats, bagels and rolls for sandwiches, cereal and powdered milk for breakfast, instant coffee for a morning caffeine fix, and powdered Tang as an energy drink. Supplemented with snacks of fruit, nuts, and candy, I would be well nourished, even without a hot meal.

Early the next day I left the motel, driving two hours to the Henrys Fork trailhead just south of the state line. But a pre-dawn start was not necessary. This would be an approach day, hiking nine miles to Dollar Lake, there camping beside the water before attempting Kings' summit the following morning.

At the trailhead, the air was crisp and cool. Dragonflies buzzed loudly above the rippling waters of Henrys Fork, a small stream I would follow most of the way. Jays sounded shrill alarms as I ascended the well-maintained trail, while finches and warblers darted nervously into creekside brush upon my approach. For two miles I walked alone, enjoying the late summer flowers and soothing rhythm of the tumbling water, feeling at one with my surroundings and moving ahead easily despite the heavy pack.

But the tranquility was shattered as two women rounded a curve and rushed downhill, eyes wide with fear.

"Don't go up there," they blurted, nearly in unison, though still a dozen yards from me.

"There's smoke in the valley," said one, a thin fifty-ish appearing woman wearing khaki shorts and an olive-green T-shirt.

I looked ahead. No plumes of gray marred the perfectly blue sky, and I could smell nothing except the fragrance of the surrounding pines.

"Where's the fire?" I asked.

"No one knows," answered the younger woman whose blonde hair was tied into a ponytail that threaded through the back of her ball cap. "But there's smoke by Dollar Lake and everyone is leaving."

Before I could respond or ask further questions, the older hiker added anxiously, "We're getting out of here," and the pair rushed on in a frightened frenzy.

Fire can race across mountainsides and up dry canyons with deadly speed. But this morning there was no wind and I saw no smoke. Yet the risk was extreme and I was out of my element, knowing little about such blazes.

My pace slowed as I considered my options, now oblivious to nature's sounds. I thought of turning back, of following the women down and escaping while I could. But with no smoke visible and no known fire location, retreat might be unnecessary, resulting only in delay. Yet if I continued upward for hours and then was forced to retreat rapidly, the resulting fatigue might postpone a second attempt for days—if the peak remained open.

Minutes later, a middle-aged couple approached. They walked strongly and spoke calmly, relating that when campers awoke, smoke had hovered over Dollar Lake. But no one had seen a fire or knew the smoke's source. Rangers had been dispatched, but this couple, having already summited Kings Peak, opted for an early morning descent. When they left the lakeside, the man told me, dozens of people remained in the valley and, although evacuation was not yet mandatory, nearly everyone was preparing to leave.

The pair continued on, but I paused, removed my pack and sat upon its bulky mass. In the gathering morning heat, I munched snacks yet never truly tasted the food, weighing options before deciding to slowly walk on, knowing that others would be descending and able to relate further information.

A solo hiker came next, reporting that even those who had yet to attempt the peak had decided to descend. However, he added, no blaze had been spotted and the smoke didn't appear to be worsening.

Barely a hundred yards further, two burdened packhorses, led by a uniformed ranger wearing a holstered pistol, walked downhill. Shod hooves struck the trail's rocky surface, each step creating a dull metallic thud. I stepped from the path as the animals neared.

"What's going on by Dollar Lake?" I asked the official as he and the animals paused.

"Smoke was seen in the valley this morning," he said.

"Has a fire been spotted?"

"No. We have choppers searching for it. But they haven't reported anything yet," he said, tapping his fingertips against a two-way radio to indicate his information source.

"Is Kings Peak closed?" I asked, dreading the expected response.

"No, not yet. Not until we know more. We won't close this area until we find a source and determine the danger level. But the smoke near Dollar Lake is already clearing," he added, again tapping his radio.

When asked about continuing upward—and if the Forest Service would inform backpackers of the need to evacuate—he replied matter-of-factly, "Can't guarantee that or even a rescue, but you're a big boy. If the smoke worsens or you see a fire, use common sense. Turn and get out." He wished me good luck as he tugged firmly on the horses' reins, again leading them down.

With conditions improving—and now with tacit permission to continue—I moved ahead strongly. The deep azure sky of the arid west, although now sporting a few cumulus clouds, remained smoke-free, and as the hours passed, I learned from descending hikers that the smoke had cleared, departing as mysteriously as it had arrived.

The route alongside Henrys Fork was indeed a scenic path and one I could again enjoy. Crossing the creek, the trail continued upward and by midafternoon I had reached a large plateau near timberline. Marshy lakes surrounded by reeds and tall grasses lay to the right, while to the left, conifers surrounded Dollar Lake.

The smoke was gone as were the people. I scanned surrounding mountainsides and ridgelines, forests and grasslands searching for evidence of an earlier fire. Yet I found none. The air was crisp and clear. Scores of hikers had camped here the previous night, but now I was alone, walking beside this high altitude lake, choosing from among dozens of excellent campsites.

But my decision was made quickly when the wind freshened and a dark thundercloud blew from Kings Peak over Gunsight Pass toward the lake. Winds gusted and giant raindrops splatted against nylon fabric as I set up my small tent. The storm, however, brought little precipitation and after a few peals of thunder, drifted past.

As the clouds moved away, the sun again emerged, its late afternoon light illuminating the cliffs across the lake, highlighting rocky bands of red and orange and tan. The lake's now-calm surface reflected this image, a scene framed by the trees growing near the water's edge. With the tent securely anchored and no need—or ability—to cook, I strolled to the lakeside, climbing onto a flat boulder to eat while enjoying the changing light.

The water was shallow and clear. Grasses extended to the shoreline, but save for a submerged log, the pond's bottom was free of debris and vegetation. There was no movement; no fish were seen, and even on the land, all was quiet. Berry bushes had long been stripped of their bounty and summer's insects had been killed weeks earlier by August's early frosts. With food sources depleted, songbirds had migrated to lower elevations, and even the ravens, ubiquitous mountain residents, were not active in the early evening chill.

I lingered, watching first the intensifying colors then the deepening shadows as the sun neared Kings Peak. A chill settled over the water after the sun dropped from view, and as the first stars appeared, I retreated to the warmth of my tent.

Before daybreak I began walking beneath a sky filled with thousands of stars, a brilliant display seen only at high altitudes on clear moonless nights. Frost covered the valley; icy crystals coating the trailside vegetation reflected and scattered my headlamp's thin beam of light. I warmed up quickly and, nearing Gunsight Pass half an hour later, began shedding clothing layers.

By sunrise, I had crested the pass, 11,888 feet above sea level and watched the sun's first rays reflect off the lakes in Henrys Fork Basin. Behind me, still shaded by the high pass and tall mountains, lay Painter Basin, an equally picturesque valley filled with marshes and lakes. And here, for the first time, I saw the full size of Kings Peak.

Yet the mountain was disappointing. Instead of the vivid colors and steep cliffs seen elsewhere in the Uintas, this peak was a sharply angled mass of gray rock that rose in stark contrast to the lush valleys below. Boulders lay jumbled upon the sides of this giant pyramid, a mountain on which there was no water and little vegetation.

No established trail led from the pass to Utah's highest point. Instead a sweeping traverse across a grassy boulder field brought me to the mountain's base from where I started up the pyramid following a prominent ridgeline. Although some rock scrambling was required, by 9:30 a.m. I stood atop the state.

To the west, the mountainside dropped precipitously as if part of the pyramid had been cut away, its sides plunging 2,000 feet to the valley floor. A cold wind raked the summit. There would be no resting or contemplating today. Clad in hat, jacket, and gloves, and again wearing every piece of clothing brought from high camp, I removed the summit register from beneath a heavy rock. Tightly clutching the tattered notebook, I retreated to a protected enclave and there inscribed my name and city. Then I paused. Kings Peak was my forty-seventh state highpoint; two of the contiguous state summits remained. I reached toward the paper to write more then changed my mind, replacing the pen into the notebook's wiry spine. I had yet to record my high-pointing total or detail my quest in any summit register, and with one major peak remaining, I didn't want to tempt fate.

After replacing the logbook beneath its stone, I shot a few summit photos, but the wind and chill found every mountain-top nook and cranny. Although alone atop the state, I stayed just fifteen minutes, retreating quickly to escape the frigid gale.

Descending, I boulder-hopped in the mountain's lee, there protected from the wind by the rocky ridgeline. Below, two dozen climbers formed a broken line of humanity extending from Gunsight Pass through the boulder field and partway up the peak. Most were well-clad outdoor enthusiasts, but even in this high wilderness, the T-shirt-and-shorts crowd, shivering in the cold mountain air, was represented.

Worried by reports of lakeside smoke, nearly everyone had camped alongside Henrys Fork below Dollar Lake. Yet there were exceptions. One man, seeking a solitary wilderness experience, had crossed Gunsight Pass, descended into Painter Basin, and there spent three nights before today's summit attempt. Two strong climbers in their early 20s hadn't camped at all, instead departing the trailhead parking lot hours before sunrise, hoping to complete a single-day ascent.

However, I met only two fellow highpointers. A veteran mountaineer hailing from northern Utah, Robert was a strong climber whose weathered face sported several days' growth of gray stubble. He had touched thirty-seven state summits, had led teams up both Granite and Borah Peaks, and today was helping a friend reach Utah's highest point.

"I've made all the western states except Alaska," he said. "Got to 17.2 (referring to the altitude of Denali's highest camp) but got pinned by the weather. Ran out of food before we could go for the summit." As he spoke, it appeared as if that retreat still haunted him.

While his companion rested on a nearby rock—head bowed, breathing rapidly, and seemingly disinterested in the conversation—Robert and I talked of highpointing and the "Great One," and of my quest to reach the contiguous state summits. Although impressed by my climbing accomplishments, he nevertheless looked me in the eye and said, "You gotta do it," referring to Alaska's tallest mountain, "You gotta do it."

Denali looms large—figuratively and literally—in discussions among serious highpointers. Twenty thousand feet above sea level and 300 miles south of the Arctic Circle, it is the highest, coldest, and most strenuous climb most highpointers attempt. Some 48 completers, especially those who started as day hikers and backpackers, are relieved to hang up their crampons after Hood and Rainier and gladly put away climbing harnesses after summiting Gannett and Granite. But most, especially those who began as mountaineers, want to top out on North America's loftiest point.

I listened politely to Robert's words and nodded occasionally but was so focused on completing the contiguous forty-eight that his sentiments seemed idle chatter. After all, I had not only chosen to omit Alaska's state summit during this quest but had earlier ascended South America's Aconcagua, a mountain half a mile higher than Denali, and a peak requiring a similar three-week expedition. Yet as this experienced mountaineer described plans to again attempt the Great One, his admonition, like that of the summit monitor atop Katahdin, lodged in my memory.

We said goodbye as Robert's climbing partner stirred. Descending toward Gunsight Pass and Dollar Lake, thoughts of Denali vanished as I again focused on the trail, topography, and beauty of the Uintas. Torrents of rain poured from a thundercloud minutes after I reached camp, a deluge that lasted a full hour. When the rain abated, the sky cleared quickly, and with six hours of daylight remaining, I shook water from the tent then stuffed the damp nylon into its sack, loaded my pack, and began descending, following the sun-lit trailing edge of the thundercloud down the valley.

Wet leaves, washed clean of dust and dirt, glistened in the afternoon light. The trail, now damp but not slippery, felt soft underfoot.

Halfway down, my thoughts turned to a question and a plan I had considered for weeks: Five days before flying home, should I attempt Mt. Whitney? I had hoped to reach California's state summit via the east face, a technical rock climb considered one of North America's classical mountaineering routes. But no guides were available for a late August climb; ascending this route would require returning to California the week of September 11.

Yet if a permit could be obtained, the mountain could be summited in a single day, a grueling 22-mile walk gaining nearly 7,000 feet in elevation. To reach Whitney, however, would require a two-day drive; to return to the Salt Lake City airport, one-and-a-half more.

This would be peak bagging at its finest, a highpointing style I had sought to avoid. But having climbed in the Sierras and toured the Owens Valley, I weighed a rushed excursion and strenuous hike against the inconvenience, expense, and uncertainty of a September return.

Before reaching the car, my decision was made.

CHAPTER 21

PERMISSION

California

L eaving for Mt. Whitney could only be described as an act of faith. Although respectful of the mountain, I did not fear it. Nor was I scared of the summit hike, a 22-mile walk for which, after two weeks at high altitude, I felt prepared. And although tired, the long drive did not worry me.

But the permitting process did. Since visiting the Lone Pine ranger station en route to Nevada's Boundary Peak a year earlier, I had researched the allocation procedure. Sources—even those published by the Forest Service which oversees the process—differed, listing varying deadlines, different quotas, and conflicting requirements. Phone calls to Lone Pine only added to the confusion, bewilderment temporarily put to rest when I decided to climb the east face, a technical route not limited by permits.

But uncertainty returned after changing plans and opting for a single-day ascent. En route to the Golden State, I called from a northeastern Utah pay phone and was told that although the office opened at 8:00 a.m., I would need to be in line by 6:00 to receive a permit. Within thirty minutes of the headquarters' opening, the ranger said, the allotment would be exhausted and subsequent hikers turned away. "But," she added, "call later for further information when we aren't so busy."

Phoning again from northwestern Utah, I was told by another worker that the coveted passes were available "all day" but that I needed to talk with her supervisor who wouldn't be back until "after lunch."

In Wells, Nevada, I called again, learning that for a fee, a permit could be reserved, a policy of which I had been unaware. A credit card could assure a place on the mountain. It was the best fifteen dollars I ever spent.

The following afternoon, I arrived at Forest Service headquarters in Lone Pine. A small queue of hikers waited as bureaucratically efficient rangers processed applications. Upon reaching the desk, pages of rules and forms in triplicate were thrust at me: permitting policies, liability waivers, bear rules, litter rules, toileting rules. I feigned interest before signing each in turn, a process more akin to a loan application than a wilderness escape. Finally I received the precious document, a folded paper enclosed in a Ziploc bag which, I was told, needed to be displayed outside my backpack "at all times."

A four-hour drive from Los Angeles, Mt. Whitney (14,494 feet) is not only California's highest mountain but also the loftiest peak in the contiguous forty-eight states. Yet this area is an uneasy interface between recreation and wilderness.

En route to Whitney Portal, thirteen miles west of Lone Pine, the road winds through the Alabama Hills, a group of wind-eroded sandstone outcroppings at the base of the Sierras. Here was a quiet, stark landscape. A small tan lizard, startled by my approach, scurried into the safety of a rocky crevice, a crack nearly obscured by drifted sand. In these arid canyons, little vegetation survived; at the base of one boulder, a yellow aster bloomed, nature's only bold color in this otherwise drab panorama.

Nearby, however, the colors that nature didn't supply, a graffiti artist did. A large face—with sharply demarcated features, long eyelashes and bright red lips—had been painted onto a 20-foot-wide boulder. This well-proportioned caricature spanned the rock's entire width, its bright blue eyes staring across the desert.

Yet these hills, seemingly barren and isolated, have been the stage for wild chases and wagon treks, ambushes and gun battles. Since 1920, moviemakers have used this rugged scenery as a backdrop for more than 300 films. Tom Mix and Hopalong Cassidy starred here. So did Gene Autry and Roy Rogers, John Wayne, Humphrey Bogart, and Clint Eastwood.

However, after seven decades—and classics including "Gunga Din," "Tycoon," and "How the West Was Won"—the

Desert Face
A smiling visage in the Alabama Hills.

industry moved on, these Sierra landscapes replaced by back-lot scenery, computer animation, and more distant locales. A dozen years had passed since cameras last rolled here; accommodations that once catered to Hollywood's elite today survive by serving tourists, climbers, and backpackers.

I also moved on, anxious to reach Whitney Portal, there expecting to find a dusty parking lot and rugged trailhead but finding instead a crowded village. Khaki-clad tourists sipped wine at an open-air café while sweaty campers hauled large coolers to nearby campsites. Elegant women dressed in the latest fashions brushed against grimy backpackers in the small convenience store, a venue where Madison Avenue jostled with the backcountry for shelf space as coffee mugs, place mats, and even computer mouse pads were displayed beside mountain stoves, iodine tablets, and sunscreen.

Outside, glass shards lay in scattered piles atop the parking lot's asphalt surface. Bears, possessing both an excellent sense of smell and a sweet tooth, had raided four vehicles. Whitney's wily bruins have learned to recognize food not only by smell but also by shape and packaging, entering locked vehicles by breaking windows or peeling down a door's sheet metal until the glass falls out. Officials have responded with bear-proof containers—and more rules. Foot-square orange citations, issued by authorities for visible food, hung from six vehicles, placards that bears will someday recognize as markers of an easy meal.

I traversed the maze of tourists, searching for the summit trail, then walked a quarter-mile up the path seeking to escape the human chaos. For two-and-a-half weeks I had been alone, or nearly so, in some of North America's most isolated and pristine landscapes. Now at the base of a trophy peak, the highest in the United States prior to Alaska's 1959 statehood, I felt out of place, overwhelmed by the crowds. Radios blared and tourists chattered incessantly, while returning hikers spoke not of Whitney's beauty, its lofty summit nor its wildlife, but of round-trip times as if completing a competition.

I stayed but a few minutes, soon turning and descending, satisfied that in the early morning darkness I could find the correct route among the many footpaths crossing near the Portal.

"Did you make it?" one tourist asked as I neared the parking lot.

"How long did it take?" queried another.

"Tomorrow," I responded. "Tomorrow will be the day."

Yet driving down the steep road toward the Alabama Hills and Lone Pine, I wondered: Did I appear so disheveled and tired that it looked as though I had just climbed a 14,000-foot mountain? Or, after weeks of climbing, did I look so strong that it seemed I could ascend California's tallest peak without sweating?

I hoped it was the latter.

At 3:30 a.m. I returned to Whitney Portal. Gone was yesterday's bedlam, the parking lot now mostly empty save for climbers preparing to ascend California's state summit. Above the lot, a broken line of lights already marked the trail as scores of climbers had begun pre-dawn ascents. More cars arrived as I walked toward the trailhead, today's permit holders heeding Forest Service advice to begin walking before 4:00 a.m.

There was no boisterousness. Twenty-two miles—and nearly 7,000 vertical feet—had to be traversed. It was difficult to conceive of the task's enormity; as I began up the trail, I didn't even try, focusing instead on nature's nocturnal sights and sounds

The Whitney Zone

and smells. Bright stars decorated the sky while small rodents scurried nervously from beside the trail, tiny feet scuffing as the animals fled. The fragrance of damp vegetation filled the still night air.

I fell into a rhythm. Step, step, breath. Step, step, breath. My headlamp was one of nearly a hundred points of light that marked the sinuous path up the hillside, some lights brightening as the trail doubled back, others suddenly disappearing as the trail again turned, always leading higher.

Step, step, breath. It was a hypnotic rhythm as hours and miles passed.

Day broke. Stepping from the trail and exiting the line of hikers ascending Whitney, I placed the headlamp deep into my pack and watched as the sun's first rays touched rocky mountainsides, illuminating previously dark cliffs and turning them a brilliant burnt crimson. Below, a pall of dust and smog—the latter blown north from Los Angeles—hung over the Owens Valley, obscuring the Alabama Hills and blotting out all but the highest peaks of the White Mountains across the valley.

I would reach Whitney's summit. Somehow, with four hours, six miles, and 3,500 vertical feet remaining, I knew I would make the top. There was no anxiety or cockiness, just an inner peace and sense of tranquility, a oneness with nature.

243

Again walking, I slowed slightly, savoring each step as the rich crimson color of Whitney's steep eastern face turned to ochre then faded to a bleached tan as the morning sun intensified.

The trail was excellent. It should be. A century ago this path was dynamited from the mountainside, today ascending a series of ninety-nine switchbacks that rise upon beds of blasted rock, some stacked twenty feet high. Climbing more than a thousand feet, this series of hairpin turns is the route's most difficult portion, ascending steeply through a landscape that can become a cauldron beneath the late-morning sun.

The chain of hikers broke apart as the swiftest walkers moved past Trail Crest and onto the mountain's cooler west side, while others struggled, seeking refuge in the little shade offered by this exposed terrain. A gray-haired man sat beside the trail, leaning against a shaded rock, his legs sprawled across the footpath. "This is how far I made it last year," he said, pulling his legs toward his body as I approached. "Guess I'm not going to make it this year either," he admitted before noting that, although dejected, he had sufficient food, water, and energy to make it back down.

The heat intensified as I continued on, doubling back frequently as the trail zigzagged up the escarpment like a nearly closed accordion. At 13,777 feet above sea level, I made the final turn then stepped over the ridgeline and onto the mountain's western side. Here, as on Whitney's eastern flank, the cliffs dropped steeply, plunging thousands of feet to the valley below. Glimpses of the summit, two miles away, could be seen as I walked below rocky pillars following a route blasted just below the ridgeline.

Step, step, breath yielded to step-breath-step-breath, a slower pace necessitated by the altitude. Other climbers, some having arrived from sea level within the past twenty-four hours, rested frequently as the rarefied air extracted a toll from everyone, slowing progress along the Sierras' rocky spine.

It took more than an hour to traverse the mile-and-a-half-long, 14,000-foot-high ridgeline that gently rose towards Whitney's summit. The trail turned sharply up a rocky slope. No blasting had been necessary here; stone cairns marked the path across flat boulders, a natural route that led toward a prominent knoll.

Tears filled my eyes as I began up this final promontory. With the last strenuous summit of the contiguous forty-eight a quarter mile away, memories of highpointing—and The Dream—flooded my mind: the joy of reaching Iowa's muddy state summit; the beauty of Wyoming's Gannett Peak; the late-season snows that nearly kept me from topping out in Nebraska and Oregon.

And I recalled some of the people who both made this journey possible and more enjoyable. Although nearly three miles above sea level, steps came easily as I thought of Sheryl, whose approval of, and emotional support during, this sabbatical never wavered and whose love through these months apart never waned. I thought of my mother, of her love and worries, as her only child traveled the country traversing wind-swept plateaus, scurrying up icy walls, and clinging to rocky cracks along exposed cliffs.

Then I thought of Dad. A survivor of the Depression, he would not have understood—nor approved of—this career interruption. But he would have been proud of my accomplishments. Throughout this quest, I wished I could have shared my stories and photos with him as I had after previous adventures. But now, walking as near the heavens as one can in the contiguous forty-eight, I prayed that he could see me atop the Sierras and be aware of my thankfulness for his love and guidance.

Nearing a rocky cabin, thoughts turned to the friends, guides, and former strangers who had helped me during this journey. Each memory was cherished as I recalled helpful deeds, practical advice, and words of encouragement. At the cabin, however, a century-old cubicle built to house Smithsonian researchers, these recollections ended.

A stony outcropping, less than fifty yards away, rose above the landscape. Dozens of people rested near this knoll, beyond which only blue sky could be seen. My pulse quickened as I scrambled up massive rocks and walked toward the highest boulder.

A few steps later, I stood atop California.

To the east, the White Mountains, home to Methuselah and the ancient bristlecone pines, rose above the smog-shrouded Owens Valley. Behind me, Whitney's western flank plunged steeply into Kings Canyon and Sequoia National Parks, a region where rainfall wrung by these mountains from moist Pacific winds support the planet's largest trees. And just eighty miles southeast of California's highest point, today hidden by haze although often visible from the summit, lay Death Valley's Badwater, a desiccated lakebed 282 feet below sea level that is North America's lowest elevation.

I had visited these sites and many more while seeking each state's loftiest point. But the thrill of success mixed with unexpected twinges of regret as I realized that this great adventure was nearing its end.

Others approached the summit. I stepped aside then moved to a nearby rock, sitting and facing east, overlooking our country. Since leaving the emergency department, I had logged 25,000 miles by air and had driven a similar amount. And although reminded daily by news reports of our national problems and cultural differences, I had found a strong, unified people sharing similar hopes, ambitions, and dreams. No region, race, or philosophical group held a monopoly on kindness; instead I found it spread across the continent like a nationwide blessing.

Today, with mild temperatures, clear skies, and calm winds, there was no need to hurry down. My mind drifted as I recalled the sights, experiences, and people from this multi-year quest. For weeks, I had anxiously checked off the remaining state summits, planning carefully, hoping to reach them all before resuming my career. Now with only Delaware remaining, I recalled cherished memories yet wondered what goals would form following The Dream, a plan a quarter century in the making.

After many minutes I rose from the rock—and my introspective solitude—joining others nearby, sharing stories and posing for summit photos.

It was a diverse yet amiable group. There was a Boy Scout troop from Colorado and an unacclimatized man from Florida. Arriving the previous day, he hadn't slept since the flight, had hiked all night—eighteen hours in all—and now stared blankly across the landscape. Authorities were aware of his condition, but as rangers sought to determine if his lassitude was due to fatigue or altitude sickness, the climber kept refusing assistance. Several people had climbed Whitney as part of a goal to reach each of California's fifteen summits higher than 14,000 feet; one man was trying to walk the length of the John Muir Trail while others had ascended the mountain simply to test themselves on a challenging high-altitude trek.

But I met no other highpointers nor technical climbers on Whitney. Hikers listened politely as I told of this, my forty-eighth state summit. Yet there were no oohs and ahhs as I described my nationwide travels and climbing achievements.

However, the conversation changed abruptly as I removed my camera from the pack. "Look at that massive camera," a strongly built teen exclaimed, pointing as he spoke loudly to his companion.

"You brought that all the way up here?" questioned another, although the answer was obvious.

Yet at five pounds, this camera with power winder and three interchangeable lenses was the least gear I had taken to any state summit.

I glanced around, surprised by the reaction. Each hiker held a camera. But these small units ranged from lightweight point-and-shoots to single-use plastic models. "You must be a masochist to carry that heavy thing up here," an athletic thirtyish-appearing man said in awe as he watched me adjust the camera's settings. But he graciously obliged when I asked him to take my photo atop the mountain. He then asked me to photograph him—which I did—using his disposable drug store unit.

I stayed atop Whitney nearly an hour, chatting, photographing, savoring memories, and enjoying the brilliant sunshine. When it came time to leave, I walked to the large summit register beside the cabin. "Doug Butler. Crumpler, North Carolina," I inscribed. But this time, there was no pause. "Highpoint # 48," I added, before writing a message of love and appreciation dedicated to my family.

Then I began the descent.

CHAPTER 22

TRAGEDY

Delaware

At 8:46 a.m., September 11, 2001, American Air Flight 11 struck the World Trade Center's north tower. Within 102 minutes, both New York towers had collapsed, the Pentagon had been attacked, and a fourth jet crashed into a Pennsylvania field. Three thousand people lay dead, and our lives—individually and collectively—were forever changed. As volunteers rushed to the affected sites and relief monies pledged, pundits voiced surprise by our nation's solidarity and generosity.

The attacks shocked me, but our nation's response did not. Since leaving the emergency department fourteen months earlier, I had experienced the kindness of our people, a goodness that cut across racial and ethnic differences and transcended political, economic, and religious divides. Though politicians squabbled and special interest groups aired attack ads throughout the 2000 election, and the media portrayed our nation as rent by "culture wars," I had seen a nation of diverse individuals bound by common aspirations. These hopes and dreams far outnumbered the differences contrived by politicians or tested by terrorists.

Neither was I surprised by the quick thinking aboard United Flight 91, when passengers attempted to retake control of the plane, a plan that spared countless lives and nearly succeeded in saving their own. For throughout history we have been a nation of innovative people, responding quickly to change and willing to risk all for religious freedom, economic opportunity, and personal liberty. Throughout my travels I had learned of these struggles, saw results of pioneer endeavors that both developed and exploited the land, and spoke with descendents of European trailblazers—and with Native Americans whose ancestors had been displaced.

Many settlers found riches, but more importantly they established a government that permitted freedom and individual choice. I had benefited from these liberties, traveling wherever I desired, and speaking with whomever I wished, never clearing a military checkpoint nor, with the exception of airports, showing identification. And except for being asked my citizenship by a Border Patrol officer in Texas, I was never questioned by authorities nor banned from taking photos.

Yet, I too, had taken a huge risk, albeit a modern-day one, leaving full-time employment to pursue The Dream. As I planned a triumphal journey to the intersection of Ebright Road and Ramblewood Drive—Delaware's highest point—I also signed a contract to resume full-time medical practice upon my return.

But grand ideas of touring Washington, D.C., and Baltimore en route to the suburban Wilmington location that would complete my highpointing quest vanished with the terror attacks. Delaware's most populous city lies within 150 miles of each attack site, nearly centered in a triangle formed by these locations. The excursion, planned for September 13, was delayed, then instead of the crowning achievement of a continent-wide quest, became a hurried journey into a tense region.

Delaware's state summit, 448 feet above sea level, is the nation's second-lowest—and only metropolitan—highpoint. Located in a residential enclave between Wilmington and Philadelphia, there remains uncertainty where, in the nearly flat terrain, the highest soil particle lies. However the intersection is the officially recognized summit, making this highpoint, named Ebright Azimuth, not only a drive-up but also a drive-over.

The car's alternator light glowed intermittently as Sheryl and I drove north through the Shenandoah Valley into Maryland. Early the next morning, although an alpine start was not necessary and weekend traffic would be light, I was up before dawn, anxious to reach the intersection.

We left Maryland and entered Delaware, drove past shopping malls and convenience stores then, following guidebook directions, turned into a residential neighborhood. The homes lining Ebright Road were aging but well-maintained, the lawns lush, and the third-acre lots tastefully landscaped. Nearing Ramblewood Drive we parked and together walked the final yards.

At 8:30 a.m., September 22, 2001, I stood atop my forty-eighth contiguous state highpoint. Relief, coupled with incredulity at having completed the quest, filled my mind. Sheryl congratulated me then gave me a hand-lettered sign that read "All 48." As I held the painted cardboard placard, she snapped my photo in front of the street sign, considered Delaware's "official" summit.

Crossing the pavement, we took more photos beside the "official" marker describing Ebright Azimuth then touched the "official" USGS disc a dozen yards away. We ambled to the base of a radio tower, strolled through a nearby trailer court, and walked across a mown field—all locations some claim to be the state's highest speck of land.

Cars passed but few motorists slowed, and no one stopped or inquired why I was taking pictures in their neighborhood early this Saturday morning. It was a peaceful stroll as I thought of the journey that had taken me throughout our nation. But none of the strong emotions felt three weeks before on Mt. Whitney were present. And there were no regrets that the journey was ending.

Our world had changed. Two weeks earlier, I would have toured Wilmington, home to one of the east coast's busiest seaports. But the city is also a center of chemical manufacturing, and in the uncertain days after the terror strikes, I didn't wish to linger.

At the intersection we again congratulated each other, and I thanked Sheryl for her love and support throughout my journeys. We stood silently as I scanned the suburban landscape a final time, a last look like many others from atop America's highpoints.

It was time to leave. The quest had ended. These months had been more enriching than I ever thought possible, impacting my beliefs, changing my attitudes, and altering my life. Now I would resume work, returning to daily patient care and intense human interaction—but also to call rotations, insurance rules,

Number Forty-eight
The author atop Delaware, completing his quest to reach each of the
"contiguous 48" state highpoints.

and governmental regulations. Yet I never doubted I would
return to my chosen profession; I had not undertaken this sabbatical to explore alternate careers and, although frustrated by
the current medical system as most physicians are, have always
enjoyed direct patient care.

However, uncertainties remained. Driving home, as the
alternator light continued flickering, I recalled Tom's comments
while descending Granite Peak about "changing too much,"
then remembered the anxiety and dread felt while leaving
Montana.

Had I changed too much? Were my priorities different? Hours
after completion of a long-sought goal, and days before the start
of a new endeavor, it was impossible to judge. Nevertheless it
was easy to push these questions from my mind as we drove
south, savoring the completion of a quest and facing a very different future.

CHAPTER 23

THE GREAT ONE

Mt. McKinley

D ays after touching Delaware's summit, I began work with a long-established medical group. I was warm- ly welcomed by senior partners, office staff, and fellow physician-employees, and again found great pleasure caring for patients and meeting the intellectual challenges of my profession. The adjustment from unstructured freedom to intense workplace demands was surprisingly easy, yet thoughts of the mountains never vanished. During free moments I fondly recalled favorite climbs and cherished memories, and tried to display kindnesses and courtesies similar to those received throughout my travels.

But within weeks, challenges mounted. Since shuttering my office practice eight years earlier, the medical system had changed. In the emergency department—our nation's health safety net—we had been shielded from many of these changes, examining patients irrespective of insurance status and pro- viding emergency care to everyone. However, in the private outpatient setting, I discovered that physicians now needed myriad insurance pre-approvals and to be paid, must meet reimbursement requirements that rivaled the federal tax code in complexity.

And, as this well-respected group's newest member, I became heir to old conflicts. From others I learned of seemingly every wrong committed by our physicians and likewise heard of each injustice visited upon us. Inexorably I was drawn into decades-old power struggles.

But I had undergone profound changes. Although finding

solace caring for patients and being well-received by the local population, when told by a trusted colleague that each physician now in practice had needed to "fight his way in," I knew I was in the wrong setting.

Pressure mounted as hope and reality collided. My desire to again practice medicine had been so strong that, for one of the few times in my life, I had not devised a back-up plan. Now driving to work in pre-dawn darkness and returning home after sundown, I weighed options and considered alternatives as the right side of my brain longed for a better situation and the left calculated its cost.

I thought of the compensation now received—an amount well above the norm for primary care physicians—yet also recalled the joy felt while working on the Indian reservations. There the pay had been small, the assignments temporary, but the rewards great. And during my sabbatical, I had found that a thrifty but quality lifestyle was possible, living fifteen months without a regular paycheck yet not exceeding my budget.

Sheryl listened carefully, yet said little as I related these deliberations. Even before my employment began, she later confided, she believed I was too changed by my nationwide journey to again practice profit-oriented medicine. Yet she had been reluctant to discourage my pursuit of that goal, a desire she knew I had held for years.

Now I carefully crafted another plan, an idea months instead of years in the making: control expenses, maintain my North Carolina home, and work part-time helping an underserved population through the Indian Health Service. In April I announced my resignation, giving the required three-month notice. Then, on another sultry July evening two years after leaving the emergency department, I again stepped into uncharted territory.

Thoughts of climbing Alaska's Mt. McKinley—Denali to most climbers—had never vanished. An ascent omitted due to scheduling conflicts and overlapping climbing seasons, I had never doubted, if given satisfactory conditions, that I could summit the mountain known to Alaska's indigenous people as the "Great One." In 1994 I had scaled Argentina's Cerro Aconcagua,

a similarly difficult peak that is the western hemisphere's loftiest mountain and a summit half a mile higher than Denali's.

However, following completion of the forty-eight contiguous highpoints, I felt as though an asterisk remained behind
my name, a mark signifying a failure to reach Alaska's summit.
The words of Todd, Mt. Katahdin's summit monitor, and Robert,
the experienced alpinist on Kings Peak, were recalled during
my employment as I considered how time might be arranged
for a Denali ascent. But as the job ended, neither excuse nor
obstacle remained, and while planning the upcoming year, I
kept May and June—Alaska's short climbing season—free of
commitments.

Soaring nearly four miles above sea level, Denali (20,320
feet) is our nation's—and North America's—tallest mountain.
Located in the Alaska Range, a short chain of ice-covered mountains between Anchorage and Fairbanks, this peak rises 18,000
feet above the surrounding tundra, giving the "Great One" the
highest relief, base-to-summit, of any mountain in the world. It
is also the planet's most northerly 20,000-foot-high peak, a distinction accompanied by severe storms, high wind, and bitter
cold.

More than 1,000 climbers attempt the mountain each year,
flying by ski plane to its base then spending nearly three weeks
ascending glaciers and enduring storms, trying to reach the top.
About half succeed, while others turn back because of weather,
fatigue, or the stress of isolation and Arctic cold.

It is also a tightly regulated mountain. Following a series
of widely publicized tragedies, the National Park Service now
screens planned climbs in the Alaska Range. Applications listing team members, planned routes, and dates must be submitted
months in advance. A climbing résumé detailing mountaineering experience is required from each individual. So are medical
statements, liability releases, training plans, and fees to defray
rescue and evacuation expenses.

Although these measures have decreased a fatality rate that
once rivaled Everest's, the Alaska Range remains a dangerous
place. Avalanches, crevasse falls, and rock slides all claim lives.
But in this extreme environment, climbers also succumb to
hypothermia and dehydration, fluid accumulation in brain and

lungs from ascending too rapidly, and stroke and blood clots from prolonged altitude exposure. A medical clinic manned by EMTs is located at 14,000 feet, while rescue supplies and emergency oxygen are stashed at 17,000.

In Talkeetna, an upscale tourist destination exuding a frontier image, our team gathered in late May, eight men ranging in age from 33 to 58. The group included a plumber from Wisconsin and a supermarket heir from New York, a California pharmacist, an Oregon computer programmer, and a Minnesotan who regularly piloted a 747 past Denali en route to the Far East. Marty Schmidt, a friend and veteran alpinist who had guided me on Aconcagua a decade earlier, would lead, assisted by Eric Remza, a strong, young climber with extensive backcountry experience.

Since the success of a lengthy and remote climb depends heavily on logistics, nothing was left to chance. Three hundred pounds of food was organized into meals then placed into waterproof sacks and labeled for intended day of use. A high quality white gas—more than a gallon per climber would be needed to cook and melt snow for water—was purchased and the nearly 100 pounds of flammable liquid placed into tightly sealed metal canisters. Ropes were checked and coiled; tents examined carefully; snowshoes, plastic sleds, ice screws, and snow pickets sorted and counted; and both emergency medications and rescue supplies carefully packed.

The guides scrutinized each climber's gear, ascertaining that required items were present and that clothing was of sufficient warmth, and ordering unnecessary items left behind. At Park Service headquarters, we spent an hour viewing a required safety video and listening as a ranger detailed climbing rules and regulations.

But low clouds persisted, grounding all flights to the mountain. At Talkeetna's small landing strip, 300 miles south of the Arctic Circle, supplies and gear were weighed then piled beside the tarmac, while a half dozen climbing teams waited for skies to clear.

Late that afternoon, the overcast thinned then vanished. Plane engines were throttled up; the supercharged motors designed for steep mountain take-offs produced a roar that obliterated conversation. Excitement built as gear and climbers were shuttled deep into the Alaska Range, bypassing forty miles of muskeg and bog. By late evening our turn came; an hour later we began establishing base camp on the Kahiltna Glacier twenty-six miles from, and 13,000 feet below, Denali's summit.

Ascending Alaska's tallest mountain is as much a psychological as a physical challenge. Although roped together when walking across snow and ice, the climb is not technically difficult. But frequent storms and prolonged confinement in cramped tents test every climber's resolve.

For nearly a week we hauled supplies up the Kahiltna Glacier, each climber carrying a fully loaded backpack and pulling an equally weighted sled. Yet with 150 pounds of supplies per individual, two trips between each camp were needed. Upon arrival at an anticipated site, packs and sleds were unloaded; food, fuel, and heavy clothing, all enclosed in plastic bags, were buried in a snow pit and marked with a long wand. Returning to the lower camp for the night, another trip would be made the next day, bringing tents, stoves, and sleeping bags, requiring us to climb each portion of the route twice.

Conditions varied widely. Calm winds, clear skies, and reflected sunshine combined one afternoon to push temperatures to near ninety degrees, turning the glacier's surface to slush. On other days, storms lashed the mountainside, keeping us tent-bound.

Gradually we moved up. Though conditions were often difficult, there were periods of incredible beauty. Under soft Arctic light, mounds of glistening white snow sparkled above dark crevasses, the contrasting light and shadow accentuated by the sun's low angle. To the south, Mt. Hunter, a steep-walled 14,000-foot-high peak, towered above the glacier, while Mt. Foraker, a 17,000-foot-high pyramid, dominated the southwestern skyline. And to the northeast, Denali's summit could occasionally be glimpsed above the dark, rocky walls lining the glacier.

We ascended Motorcycle Hill then passed Windy Corner, an appropriately named traverse where an unrelenting gale sheared tiny particles of ice from the glacier's surface. Cold gusts cut through multiple layers of "wind-proof" clothing, chilling our torsos, while icy crystals stung our only exposed skin, an inch-wide strip between goggles and neoprene facemask.

At 14,000 feet we established our fourth camp as this latest storm intensified, a tempest that would last thirty-six hours and dump two feet of snow. Climbers ventured outside only for bodily functions and to remove accumulating snow from atop domed tents to prevent their collapse. Avalanches of snow and ice crashed down nearby slopes, the thunderous sounds reverberating throughout the valley while cloud and storm hid the slides' proximity.

After the clouds lifted, however, both the size of this camp— known as "advanced base"—and the area's spectacular scenery became apparent. Scores of nylon domes dotted this two-acre campsite, one of the largest flat areas on the mountain. National flags fluttered above the brightly-colored structures, flown by mountaineers from Spain and Switzerland, Australia, Mexico, Russia—and Azerbaijan, displayed by two people who would become their nation's first to summit Denali.

But behind the tents loomed a towering white cliff, the West Buttress's headwall, a 2,000-foot-high obstacle that blocked the path up the mountain. To a photographer, this white rampart set against a deep blue sky was a beautiful sight; to a climber, the steep cliff covered with unconsolidated snow was a cause for worry and fear. For two days, climbers renewed old friendships and made new acquaintances while the steeply angled snow alternately slid and consolidated.

Then, with high cirrus clouds portending the approach of more unsettled weather, more than a hundred alpinists made their move. A line formed at the cliff's base as climbers dug fixed lines from beneath thigh-deep snow then clipped onto ropes. Halfway up the escarpment, a squall struck. Three miles above sea level, the line of humanity slowed as each climber struggled to handle ropes, reposition carabiners, and operate ascenders—all while pummeled by high wind and snow. Hours later we crested the wall but were forced to make camp at 16,000 feet, erecting tents upon an excavated platform of snow and ice then anchoring them to a nearby cliff with climbing gear.

Overnight, the storm eased. On average, such storms rake Denali's upper reaches five of every six days, so to take advantage of this brief lull, we left early for high camp, reaching the 17,200-foot-high site as conditions deteriorated once more. Fog, snow, and ice particles sheared from the mountain's surface combined to lower visibility as the blizzard strengthened. All team members helped erect each tent, more than a dozen heavily gloved hands clutching the nylon to prevent the fabric from ripping or an unexpected gust from carrying the entire structure away.

This camp—Denali's highest—was a forlorn scene. Forty small tents housed more than a hundred mountaineers. Walls of snow and ice surrounded some tents, providing a modicum of protection from the gale. But other structures, their occupants too exhausted to construct such labor-intensive walls or like us, arriving during the storm, lacked protective windbreaks, allowing stretched nylon fabric to flap loudly in the constant wind.

For two days we remained tent-bound, huddled together sleeping bag to sleeping bag. A deck of cards became our group's most cherished possession. A paperback book was taken apart, the individual pages circulated among interested readers. One climber incessantly tapped his watch. I wrote in my journal for hours. Two others did not go outside during the entire storm, unzipping the tent only to receive food and water or empty urine bottles.

As conditions improved, climbers ventured forth. But the news from other teams was not encouraging. No one had summited for days. Several had tried, making last-ditch efforts before food and fuel ran out, forcing their descent. Yet no team had made it beyond Denali Pass, an 18,000-foot-high ridgeline, only a third of the way to the top.

Even as skies cleared, the wind persisted. Plumes of ice, a sign of continuing high-altitude gales, streamed from the mountaintop. Climbers remained physically strong but the stress of confinement, sub-zero temperatures, and unrelenting wind extracted a psychological toll. Two Americans, preparing to descend, told me of their weeklong ordeal at this camp. This was their second journey here; last year they had been here for a similar period. Yet during these fourteen days, weather conditions had not permitted a single summit attempt.

Discouragement was followed by resignation. Groups split as some climbers opted to retreat, teaming with members of other parties for a safer descent. Others stayed, hoping that their food, fuel, and stamina would outlast the inclement conditions. Voting unanimously, our group decided to remain at high camp, waiting for a summit bid. We had two days of food and fuel left, but wind and squalls were forecast to last at least three.

The next night, a period during which twice-daily weather reports had predicted intensifying winds, the tent flapping ceased. At 4:00 a.m. I looked out. No white plume extended from Denali's apex. A cloudless blue sky contrasted with the jagged mountain.

The world's loftiest and most challenging peaks can be summited on only a handful of days each climbing season. These conditions were among the best encountered on Denali, but no one knew how long this unexpected lull would last. As the Arctic sun's weak rays fell across camp, providing light but little warmth, climbers prepared to ascend. Some had already packed for an early morning retreat; they now hurriedly rearranged gear. Excitement spread as the first groups left, breaking trail to Denali Pass, 1,000 feet above.

Today's climb, however, would not be a wilderness experience. Our group's two rope teams joined a long line of climbers and followed a narrow path of packed snow toward the pass. The scenery was spectacular but my energy was focused on the trail and on my next step. I developed a rhythm, sucking in a lungful of frigid oxygen-starved air as I began each step, then forcefully expelling the used breath as I planted my foot, resting before the next effort.

With temperatures hovering near minus twenty degrees Fahrenheit, we crested the pass, and for the first time looked down the Wickersham Wall at the full size of the Peters Glacier. The sky remained clear and the winds calm as the route's angle briefly lessened. Climbers spread out as rope teams traversed exposed rock whose dark, icy surfaces had been scoured clear of loose snow.

We skirted Archdeacons Tower then ascended a steep slope to the Football Field, a 19,500-foot-high plateau. A half-mile later, we neared the headwall, the route up its snowy flanks outlined by fifty climbers zigzagging up the steep slope. Seven hours after leaving camp, our two rope teams started up this obstacle, laboring in the thin air. With the weather holding and with round-the-clock Arctic light, there was no sense of urgency as the steep wall and rarefied oxygen combined to require two and three breaths per step.

Halfway up, I looked back. Sixty climbers trailed behind, a line of humanity extending onto the Football Field below. Our team ascended slowly, carefully stepping over ropes at each switchback to keep the braided lifeline uphill of each member. An hour later we reached a snowy ridgeline; altimeters read 20,110 feet above sea level.

A path, two feet wide, slanted gently uphill. To its left the headwall dropped 600 feet to the plateau below, while to its right the mountainside plunged nearly two miles to the Ruth Glacier. Tested by the slope and thin air, the queue of climbers had broken apart, the teams above moving ahead, while those behind lagged further, leaving us alone and with a sense of remoteness on this lofty crest. Although surrounded by grandeur, I seldom looked around as we ascended, focusing instead on the narrow path and forcing all ten crampon points deeply into the snow and ice, constantly aware of the precipice an arm's length away.

Then the angle diminished and the path widened. I glanced ahead and saw a rounded promontory, a white mound beyond which I could see only blue sky.

Three steps. More sky.

Four more paces. Marty had stopped and was coiling the rope. And still I saw nothing but blue beyond the knoll.

More steps. Marty grinned as I neared. "Congratulations, Doug," he said, extending his hand. "Congratulations on number 50."

Atop Alaska—and North America—we hugged, congratulating and thanking one another. The others came up, each man's arrival prompting a similar exchange of celebration and friendship. Each had been tested physically and emotionally and now, for a few moments at least, each could savor the summit.

From the roof of America I looked across the Alaska Range. Legendary peaks—Hunter, Deborah, Dickey, Foraker—lay below. As I stared at a frozen land of blue and white I thought of home and family, of Sheryl and my mother, both of whom had given so much support and encouragement. And I thought of Dad. Five years had now passed since his death, yet I daily recalled his love and guidance and wisdom.

Then as I looked at the great glaciers, striped rivers of ice that cut through rocky valleys, I thanked God for His guidance and safekeeping—and for enriching my journeys more than I ever imagined possible. As I scanned the distant tundra, a thin line of vegetation that extended to the horizon, the full realization of having reached my 50th state summit slowly sank in.

I had done it.

For many minutes I stood and stared at the magnificent view, neither reminiscing about past climbs nor thinking of the future, but savoring a panorama that, almost certainly, I would never see again. Then as the Arctic sun neared the horizon the

The View From Atop America

already frigid temperature dropped further. Thirty minutes after reaching Denali's summit, it was time to go down. Stormy weather would lash us again before high camp, but save for the descent that would take us home safely, the quest had been completed.

And The Dream? During my travels The Dream had become more than the journey—and both had changed me. My goal of reaching fifty state summits had been realized, but as I descended from America's loftiest point, I knew that The Dream would continue.

BIBLIOGRAPHY / INFORMATION

GUIDEBOOKS

Holmes, Don. *Highpoints of the United States.* 2nd ed. Salt Lake City, Utah: University of Utah Press, 2000.

Winger, Charlie, and Diane Winger. *Highpoint Adventures, The Complete Guide.* Golden, Colorado: Colorado Mountain Club Press, 1999.

Winger, Charlie, and Diane Winger. *Highpoint Adventures, The Pocket Guide.* Golden, Colorado: Colorado Mountain Club Press, 1999.

Zumwalt, Paul. *Fifty State Summits.* Vancouver, Washington: Jack Grauer Publisher, 1988.

ORGANIZATIONS

Highpointers Club
P.O. Box 6364
Sevierville, Tennessee 37864
www.highpointers.org

American Alpine Club
710 Tenth Street, Suite 100
Golden, Colorado 80401
www.americanalpineclub.org

RELATED READING

Ashley, Frank. *Highpoints of the States*. Glendale, California: La Siesta Press, 1970.

Cox, Steven, and Kris Fulsaas, eds. *Mountaineering: The Freedom of the Hills* 7th ed. Seattle, Washington: The Mountaineers Books, 2003.

Huston, Todd, and Kay Rizzo. *More Than Mountains: The Todd Huston Story*. Nampa, Idaho: Pacific Press Publishing Association, 1995.

Marshall, A.H. "Forty Eight State Summits." *Appalachia*. 1936-1937; 21:167-182.

"The Highest Point in Each State." *National Geographic Magazine*. 1909; 20:539-541.

Index